Strictly Professional

Bob had seen Ruth Sinclair progress from a young and vigorous yet astonishingly naive newlywed to a housewife and mother. It would have been untrue to say that sex never entered his mind in all the years he had known her. There had been moments when he could easily project a mental image of her, abundantly endowed, reclining voluptuously nude or locked in the passionate heat of sexual embrace. But these were fleeting moments. Sitting on a stool between her thighs, scrutinizing her cervix via a speculum or palpating her uterus he could be as totally absorbed in his work as a mechanic tinkering with a balky carburetor . . .

Other SIGNET Fiction You'll Enjoy Reading

The Nine Months

Evan McLeod Wylie

A SIGNET BOOK from
NEW AMERICAN LIBRARY
TIMES MIRROR

SIGNET TRADEMARK REG. U.S. PAT. OFF. AND FOREIGN COUNTRIES
REGISTERED TRADEMARK—MARCA REGISTRADA
HECHO EN CHICAGO, U.S.A.

SIGNET, SIGNET CLASSICS, SIGNETTE, MENTOR AND PLUME BOOKS
are published by The New American Library, Inc.,
1301 Avenue of the Americas, New York, New York 10019

FIRST PRINTING, FEBRUARY, 1972

PRINTED IN THE UNITED STATES OF AMERICA

*For my wife Marion, and my sons
David, John, and Joshua*

Acknowledgment

The author is truly grateful to the men and women in medicine who inspired this book and to all those who generously lent their support to the effort to produce an authentic narrative. The medical description and information is intended to be accurate. The people and events in this story are, however, fictitious.

Contents

1

In the Middle of the Night

Mingling with the persistent rattle of sleet against the windows of the farmhouse bedroom there was suddenly the muted ringing of the blue bedside telephone. He rolled over, flicked on a nightlight, illuminating a table clock whose hands told him it was three-ten in the morning, and said softly, "Dr. Henderson speaking . . ." and then, alertly, "Yes, Honey, what's happening?"

The young woman's voice was tense and strained. "The pains are getting stronger . . . "

"Well, good!" he said making his voice wide-awake, warm, and interested. "How often are they coming?"

"They were about ten minutes apart but the last two were only eight minutes. Do you think I'll be all right until morning?"

"I think you'd better have your husband drive you over to the Hospital," he answered. "Tell him not to rush. Keep calm and I'll meet you up on the Maternity Floor."

"Baby coming," he said to his wife after he hung up the phone and swung out of bed. "I've got to get going."

"Why do you always call them Honey?"

"Because I love them all."

11

"Because you can't remember their names—that's why! Listen to that storm. Can you make it all right?"

"Easy."

"Well, don't forget to pick up my new car plates in the morning. It's the last day to get them."

He had finished dressing—sports jacket, slacks, topcoat but no hat—and went out, shutting the front door softly behind him so as not to awaken the children.

Without warning a heavy black mass launched itself out of the darkness and struck him full in the stomach, driving the breath from his body and sending him staggering backwards into the porch furniture.

"Down!" he grunted. "Down, you maniac! Down, damn it all!"

It was Bingo, a stray dog that the children had adopted a few weeks earlier. A young dog, still poorly coordinated, high in spirits and weak in mind. At first they had let him sleep in the house but he was so enthusiastically unhousebroken that he had been banished to the barn to sleep with the pony. Restless and lonely, he managed to escape nearly every night and stationed himself on the porch to assault Henderson with overwhelming affection on nocturnal trips to and from the Hospital. Now here he was lying patiently in wait again, even though the wind howled and the snow drifted. Why didn't he go back to the pony's stall where it was warm and protected? Had the fool wriggled out through some narrow space and couldn't get back in? Or was the pony loose, too? There was no time to investigate.

"You'll have to freeze your ass until morning," Henderson muttered as the dog frisked around him as if they were both in West Palm Beach. "Stand clear, dope! Our of my way!"

The icy wind and sleet stung his face and he ducked quickly into his car. The headlights were nearly lost in heavy gusts of sleet and snow whipping across the frozen Indiana cornfields. Wheels spinning, he skidded out the rutted drive and hit the freshly plowed highway.

His wife might be right about the names, but the cases always came quickly into focus. Now, as he drove, windshield wipers flailing, frosty air from the still-cold heater blasting his ankles, he could run over the details of this one as easily as if he had the file folder in front of him. "Nancy Russell. Age twenty-five. Married two years. This her second pregnancy. Her first terminated in a miscarriage in the third month. Why? Don't know. Never could figure it out. So far this pregnancy completely normal. Her anxieties about losing this baby relieved by tranquilizing drugs, frequent office visits, and lots of phone conversations."

Her due date was three days ago. Her first pains came late yesterday—mild contractions, lasting less than a minute, thirty minutes apart—and he had said she would be better off spending the evening at home instead of in the Hospital, but he hadn't figured on the weather.

His destination, the Valley Community Hospital, loomed up, an L-shaped block of light amidst the swirling snowflakes. Flanked by the blinking red beacons of a television station and a beautiful old red barn, it proclaimed the swift-changing pattern of American life, the problems faced by scores of similar new hospitals striving to serve the needs of the new suburbs exploding across the nation.

Just five years ago the cornfield in which it now stood had been part of the rim of the Western prairie. A citizens' committee, concerned over the medical needs of the rapidly spiraling local population, had sparked a community drive by businessmen, women's organizations, and volunteer youth groups to raise three million dollars, and had proudly erected a handsome, modern, beautifully equipped model hospital. It had been completed two years ago, but so fast had more developments sprung up that already it was swamped with patients. Here, last year, he and a dozen other doctors had delivered 1,600 babies, more than were delivered in the average city hospital.

Even at this hour the second-floor Maternity Wing was as usual lit up like a Christmas party and bustling.

"Good morning, Doctor Henderson," the nurse at the Call Desk greeted him. "We just admitted Mrs. Russell. She's in Labor Room 3."

"Be right with her," he said. He shook hands with the young husband, who was fumbling self-consciously with the white smock they gave to all the waiting-room fathers, stepped quickly into the doctors' locker room to strip down to bare feet and shorts, pulled on a short-sleeved white jumper and white trousers and shoved his bare feet into conductive white operating-room shoes. He emerged transformed from civilian into physician, a huge, youthful-looking doctor, his brown eyes and naturally ruddy color accentuated by the white suit, moving with a rolling, flat-footed gait as he entered Room 3.

A screened bed held a young brunette whose eyes were wide with apprehension. Esther Bates, the Night Delivery-Room Nurse, garbed in white gown and helmet-style white cap, was checking the unborn baby's heartbeat with a headset.

"Good morning," he said cheerfully. "How's my girl doing?"

"Very good, Doctor," Nurse Bates said. "She's having good contractions about five minutes apart. She's about six centimeters dilated."

"And the baby?"

"I've been getting good heart tones. About 144 per minute."

"Sounds real good," he said. He palpated the patient's abdomen with his right hand while his rubber-gloved left hand gently explored the pelvic region. The cervix (the opening of the womb), he noted, was thinning nicely, and he could feel the baby's head, already down low, entering the narrow passage between the spines of the pelvic bones.

"The baby is at Station Zero," he reported to the nurse who was filling in the chart. "The head is in good position. The bag of waters is still intact but ready to go."

"Am I all right, Doctor?" his patient asked, her voice wavering a bit.

"You couldn't be any better," he said. "You see, I told you it wasn't going to be as hard as you thought."

"Not yet anyway."

"And it's not going to be," he said. He sat with her, observing the next contraction, which left her weak and shivering. The nurse was gone and they were alone.

"Listen to me now, Nancy," he said gently but firmly. "Remember all our talks about having this baby. Half of it is not being afraid and you've got nothing to be afraid of. Everything is fine.

"I'm going to give you a sedative to make you more comfortable. When the contractions come, just relax and let the baby take care of itself. Don't try to bear down yet. Just rest. If you feel like dozing off, don't fight it. The nurses will watch you and I'm only going to be right across the hall having a cup of coffee."

She managed a smile for him. "All right, Doctor."

Out in the hall he said to Nurse Bates, "Give her Demerol, fifty milligrams, one-200th grain scopolamine and then a good enema—the best in the house."

He went down the corridor to the little lounge used by the doctors and nurses, snagged a sweet roll from the tray beside the coffee urn, and drew himself a cup of coffee. "Some storm out there," he said to the night-duty anesthesiologist who was yawning over a newspaper. "How many have you had tonight?"

"Three so far," the anesthesiologist said. "Yours will be the fourth. Unless you think she's going to last until morning."

"Nope," he said amiably. "She's not going to do you any favors. You might as well stay awake."

The lounge phone was ringing and he picked it up.

"It's Bill Sinclair, Doctor," a voice said apologetically. "I'm sorry to bother you at the Hospital at this hour but my wife is still vomiting."

"Did you get the prescription from the drugstore?" he asked, taking a bite of bun.

"Yes, but it doesn't seem to be doing her any good. We've been up all night and she thinks she's got cancer or something."

"She hasn't got cancer, Bill," he said. "But she's going to get herself dehydrated. I think you'd better let me admit her to the hospital like we did last time. We'll get her quieted down."

He hung up the phone and sat sipping coffee and reflecting about Mrs. Sinclair. Diagnosis: hyperemesis —a medical term for persistent vomiting. All her tests were negative. Nevertheless, drugs—at home, at least— wouldn't stop it. Ruth Sinclair simply didn't want to be pregnant. An unexpected pregnancy coming on top of three small children had her in a tizzy. She was not faking. She really felt terrible. The vomiting was related to the resentment about the pregnancy and the added burden it would bring to her domestic woes. According to Marvin Laden, the psychiatrist he had sent her to, subconsciously she was trying to vomit up the baby. Put her in a hospital away from the house chores and children and she recovered miraculously in one day. Sent home she soon resumed making life an ordeal for herself and her husband. Yet, so far, despite all his efforts, she couldn't see the connection. Neither could her husband, poor devil.

Will men, he thought, ever really understand how profoundly different women are from men? How long did it take me—nearly ten years of medicine—before I began to get it through my own head?

A female and her emotions are never separated and the pendulum-swinging range of maternal emotions is truly one of the wonders of the universe. Why is it that at a time when women were most apt to feel insecure and in need of support they are also most apt to be impatient, critical, and nervous with their husbands? How many times had he seen a homeward-bound new mother spend an hour prettying herself up for her mate and then throw a screaming tantrum because the poor guy brought the wrong blanket to wrap the baby in!

The Nurse was in the door. "Three minute contractions with Mrs. Russell. She's nearly fully dilated."

He heaved himself out of his chair. "Okay. Roll her in." The stretcher went by while he was still scrubbing at the corridor sink.

By the time he had donned his white cap and mask, Esther Bates' team of night nurses had his patient on the table set in the center of the brilliantly illuminated, green-tiled Delivery Room. The anesthesiologist was perched on his stool beside her head, checking the gauges on his battery of green, blue, and orange gas cylinders. Mrs. Russell lay flat on her back, blue sheet tucked up around her neck, a cap over her curls, draped legs elevated in the stirrups, her shoulders supported by thick sponge-rubber pads, her arms strapped but hands free.

Her voice was fuzzy from the drugs but still insistent. "Where's Doctor Henderson?"

"Right here, Honey," he said reassuringly, thrusting out his bare arms for the sleeves of the white, knee-length sterile gown the circulating nurse was holding and then taking, from a tray, the pair of gauntleted rubber gloves. "I'm right here with you."

When the nurse had cinched the knots on the gown tight, he moved over and gazed down at her. "Nancy," he said, "you're going to have your baby now, and you're going to be all right. Just do what we ask you to."

He stepped around to the foot of the table, positioned the low metal stool with the toe of one foot, dropped down on it and propelled himself forward to a position between the high-stirruped, blue-draped thighs. From the small table that the nurse rolled up he took his umbilical cord clamps, scissors, and tail sponge clamps and snapped them fast to the patient's left thigh drape so that they hung ready for instant use at his elbow.

Bates was getting the baby's heart tones, an eye on

the sweep hand of the wall clock, her forefinger tapping out the pulse beat on the mother's mounded abdomen.

"One hundred and thirty," she said. "Strong."

"Good," he said, his voice slightly muffled by the mask. "Nancy, can you hear me?"

"Yes," she answered hazily.

"You're doing fine and so is the baby. Now when you feel the next contraction coming, take a deep breath, hold it and bear down as hard as you can. Dr. Newcomb will give you enough anesthesia to keep it from hurting too much."

This one, he thought to himself, is going to be no problem. The lower abdominal muscles were joining in the contraction. The perineum, the muscle bed at the base of the pelvis, was distending normally. The vaginal borders were parting nicely.

"Soap, please," he said. And as the circulating nurse cascaded a pitcher of green soap over his gloved hands he gently parted and enlarged the birth canal opening.

From his patient a sudden sharp exclamation: "Oh, here it comes!"

"That's it," he said. "Bear down now, Nancy. Give me a real push."

Under the bright lights her young face, pale, pinched with strain, bore that curious arrested look of intense concentration you saw in labor. Her eyes staring ceilingward, her slender feminine fingers, white knuckled, gripped the gleaming chrome handles at the sides of the delivery table.

The anesthesiologist put her under for the contraction's climax and then adjusted his gauges, increasing the oxygen mixture to bring her back again.

"She's a left occipital posterior, George," he said to the anesthesiologist. "I'm going to do a manual rotation with the next contraction."

His gloved fingers inside the birth canal gently found the infant's tiny head and forehead, feeling for the infant's ear to confirm its position. The contraction came on and her hips rose off the table.

"Oh, my gosh!" she gasped, her back arching sharply.

"No. Not that way," he said. "Keep your fanny on the table. Don't raise up."

She would remember none of this. Later she would say, "Why, the last part was the easiest! They put a mask on me and I went to sleep." The nitrous oxide blotted out all memory of the labor.

So many women worry about what terrible exclamations they will utter while under anesthesia during the climactic pangs of birth. What do they really say? Usually just "Oh gosh!" or "Oh God!" or "Oh, my goodness!" or "Oh, boy!" and mostly "Help me!"

"She's crowning nicely," he reported to the Delivery Team from his vantage point. A patch of black hair, soaking wet, plastered down mussily, was becoming visible in the parting borders of the birth canal. His left hand, pressing upward from below, supported the infant's head, slowing its progress so that it might not emerge too swiftly.

His right hand automatically reached up for the scissors. With a first baby you couldn't expect the perineum to stretch any more than this without tearing. He snipped a two-inch-long cut in the distended muscles at the base of the birth canal. Simultaneously, his left hand guided the patch of wet black hair.

Suddenly there it was: The tiny crumpled human head with the puckered face and eyes screwed tight shut and, with it, a tremendous gasping exhalation of relief from his patient.

"Nancy," he said. "Are you back with us?"

"Yes," she murmured faintly. "Is it all over?"

"Almost," he said. "You're doing fine. Rest now. Wait for the next contraction."

In this brief interval there was time for him to make the routine quick inspection. This infant's head was normal. A finger run quickly inside its mouth revealed there was no cleft palate. The umbilical cord was not entangled around its neck in any way that might cut off its oxygen supply.

"Oh, my gosh!" she cried, getting another contraction.

"That's the girl," he said. "That's a good one."

The tip of the tiny right shoulder was pushing out. His fingers grasped it carefully, assisting it as it rotated naturally beneath the mother's pelvic bone, followed quickly by the rubbery little body, slipping out—trunk, arms, hips, and legs—in one continuous motion, as Nancy Russell bore her first child.

"How can the *whole* baby get out?" people were always asking and the answer was you had to feel the amazing elasticity of its tiny framework, still much more cartilage than finished bone, to understand how it managed to navigate the canal's narrow passage.

"It's all over, Nancy," he said, although he knew she probably couldn't hear him. "You did fine. We've got the baby."

The infant, a boy, pot-bellied, caked chalky-white, soaking wet, lay limp, head downward, in the hollow of his left forearm as he swiftly used a bulbed ear syringe to clear the fluids from its mouth and nasal passages. He discarded the syringe, "milked" the wrinkled, blue-gray umbilical cord toward the infant's body, clamped it three inches apart, severed the section between the clamps with one snip of his scissors, and flipped the cord up to rest on the mother's abdomen.

Now this newborn baby, detached from its mother, had reached the momentous crisis of birth. Its tiny lungs, up to this point collapsed and unused, must be triggered into inflating with oxygen within two minutes.

Twirling left on his stool, he rested the baby gently upside down on the low warming table the nurses had wheeled into position, rubbing its back, flicking the soles of its feet lightly with a finger, pinching it a bit, rudely thrusting a finger tip inside its rectum.

"Come on there, you," he admonished the baby. "Get going! Give him a whiff, Essie."

Bates was ready with the portable tank, spraying the infant's mouth and nose with a hissing stream of oxygen. There was a convulsive heave of the tiny chest and a gurgling gasp which opened the air passages. On its heels followed a steady thin squawling. This little one had successfully managed the enormous sudden transition from an enclosed aquatic creature to an air-breathing animal.

"Keep tickling him, Essie," he said. "Turn him pink for me."

The nurse took the baby. He remained hunched on his stool, sponging and dabbing at the birth-canal entrance, resting a hand lightly on the unconscious mother's abdomen, watching intently.

Now began the third stage of labor with its threat of hemorrhage. In this period immediately following the birth of the baby, the uterus was hard at work, contracting, kneading to rid itself of the placenta. For months this organ, attached to the upper wall of the uterus, had provided the bridge by which nourishment had passed from mother to fetus. Now it was being sheared off and expelled from the body. But until the uterus contracted sufficiently to close off the exposed endings of its huge blood vessels, there was always danger of a serious blood loss.

Suddenly a gush of crimson fluids splashed on his gown. Pressing gently on the abdomen, leading gently with the clamped umbilical cord to which the placenta was still attached, he drew it gently from the body and lowered it into a tray for later inspection.

"Normal separation and delivery of intact placenta," he said to the Delivery Team as he sponged out the birth canal. "No excessive blood loss," ruefully glancing down at his drenched gown and spattered white shoes, "except on me. Give her Ergotrate, two-tenths, Esther."

The nurse's hypodermic pricked the mother's buttock. The drug would aid the uterus in contracting to normal size and lessen the chances of any more bleeding.

"The uterus is intact," he told the chart nurse. "The cervix is intact with no vault lacerations."

"How is she doing, George?" he asked the anesthesiologist.

"Out cold but in good shape. Blood pressure: 110 over 70. Pulse: 80."

"Hold her there while I get in a few sutures." The two-inch cut he had scissored in the perineum had to be sewn up tidily. As he finished, his patient was stirring. The nurses were back with the new baby, washed pink and clean, swathed in blankets, finger-printed, foot-printed, and ankle-banded for identification.

He got up from the stool and joined the nurse. "Nancy," he said. "Look, here's your baby—it's a boy."

The glow was returning to her cheeks. She turned her head to gaze at the infant. "Oh, he's wonderful!" she said. "He's beautiful, isn't he?"

Impulsively her arms shot up and around Henderson's neck in a tight hug. "Thank you! Thank you all!"

The mask concealed his wide grin. "Any time," he said. "I'll go out and congratulate your husband. But first let me get out of this gory gown. Otherwise he'll faint for sure when he sees me."

"Good morning everybody," said the cheery announcer on the transistor radio in the Delivery Floor lounge. "Here's a brand new day and the six A.M. news."

The storm had finally subsided. Back in the doctors' lounge he rested with his feet up and took the call from the switchboard.

"Mrs. Sinclair has just been admitted," the third-floor desk said. "She's in Room 320."

2

Room 320

When Henderson entered Room 320 Bill Sinclair was hovering over his pale and tearful wife.

"Hey!" said Henderson, "You've been having a bad time of it, haven't you?"

She was so weak that her normal full-volume pear-shaped tones were practically reduced to a whisper. "Oh, Doctor, I feel so sick! Something terrible must be wrong with my insides. I'm sure of it."

"Didn't I tell you there's really nothing wrong?" he chided gently. "The tests showed nothing. We're going to get you fixed up."

He completed a swift physical examination and found no danger signs which might necessitate stopping the pregnancy. There was no jaundice. Her pulse was ninety but strong. There was no fever, no evidence of hemorrhages in the retinas, and she was not yet in serious acidosis.

To the nurse he said, "Let's have an IV setup. I want to get her started on dextrose and sedate her with sodium amytal, 200 milligrams. Let me have another needle and Vitamin B_1B_6."

"I had the heaves so terrible tonight," Mrs. Sinclair said, "I could hardly hold out until Bill got home. I was afraid I was passing out . . . dying . . . "

"Just take it easy, Honey," Henderson said.

The nurse handed him the hypodermic needle with

the sodium amytal and he injected it into her left buttock and then the Vitamin B into her right hip. They rolled the IV stand up beside the bed and got her hooked into a bottle of dextrose solution. For the first twenty-four hours he wanted her to have nothing but this and the moderately strong sedation.

"There you are," he said. "Now just rest."

He sat beside the bed for a moment, waiting and watching for the sedative to take effect.

"Sit down and hold her hand, Bill," Henderson said in a low tone to Bill Sinclair. "She'll be sound asleep in another few minutes."

Holding the chart on which he was writing the orders for her medication, Henderson paused at the foot of the bed regarding his patient. After four pregnancies, three deliveries, one miscarriage, and six years of office visits, physical checkups, and countless telephone conversations, he felt as well acquainted with her as a man might be with a close member of his own family.

Ruth Sinclair, thirty-four, was one of the winners of his own "Wonderful World of Women" awards. Amidst the wide range of suburban women in his daily practice she was a standout—a big-boned, long-legged, shapely, auburn beauty.

The husky, sandy-haired man sitting beside the bed holding her hand was her husband, Bill Sinclair, who had risen through the ranks of the fire department down in the city until he was now a captain commanding a hook-and-ladder company that rolled out of one of the busiest firehouses in the city.

The Sinclairs were typical of a new breed of American suburbanites. Both had been born and had grown up in the city. There, too, they met and married when Bill was a young fireman and Ruth a salesgirl in a store.

Later, when the first baby was on its way, they had moved out to Henderson's nearby suburban village to escape the city's growing social chaos, noise, dirt, polluted air, and rising cost of living. For what the city's landlords were charging for apartments, they were able to afford a mortgage on a split-level home with a patch of lawn. Nearby were schools and a shopping center.

Bill Sinclair led a double life, riding sedately to his job in the city on the commuting trains, wearing a business suit and carrying a brief case, and then spending his working hours responding to fire alarms in the front seat of an eighty-five foot hook-and-ladder truck, garbed in fireman's helmet, heavy knee-length turn-out coat, and rubber boots, careening through city traffic to the accompaniment of a bedlam of bells, blasting horns, and shrieking sirens, scaling aerial ladders, dashing into tenement buildings to rescue men, women, and children, bellowing commands to his fire company through clouds of thick billowing smoke and above the thunderous roar of high-pressure hoses. Then, when the fire was out and his tour of duty completed, he donned his business suit and rode back on the train to his suburban home to water the lawn, wash the car, trim the shrubs, and docilely follow his wife around the supermarket with a shopping cart.

You would have to look far, Henderson had often thought, to find a more devoted husband and family man than Bill Sinclair. And Ruth Sinclair was a woman in love, passionately committed to her husband and children. Yet their family life in this portion of the American twentieth century was filled with stress, strife, and anxiety as they coped with the demands of children, money, and daily living.

By far the less articulate of the two, Bill Sinclair often could manage no more than a baffled shake of the head and a comment such as "Ruth, she's some case!"

Ruth Sinclair, on the other hand, proclaimed loudly and frequently that "He's driving me *crazy!*"

Day in and day out, the Sinclair family survived an emotional roller-coaster ride as she swung through her monthly physiological cycles of hormone balance and imbalance, premenstrual tension, headaches, backaches, and sharp reactions to all events whether consequential or of no importance. Her children and home were the core of her life, yet she was constantly complaining that it was all too much for her. Totally in love with her husband, she relied upon him for tempestuous love-making but also subjected him to fits of irritability, nagging, sulks, tears, and temper tantrums.

She had come to Henderson soon after they had moved to the suburban village when she was four months into her first pregnancy. Over the intervening years there had developed between them an excellent professional relationship of physician and patient. There was good communication and mutual respect. He admired her strength, pride in her family, and devotion to her husband and children. On her part, he felt, there was a dependency and gratitude toward him as "her doctor." On his part there had been the rewards of using his professional skill, the challenge to treat her and sustain her through her medical crisis—thus for him the sense of fulfillment in his role as physician.

There were stretches in between her pregnancies when he had not seen her for six months. Then perhaps merely for a minor complaint and the annual physical examination and a cancer-detecting "pap test," which he had convinced her was so important. Occasionally when he had come across her name in the office files he was reminded she was out there somewhere—living, coping, weeping, singing, laughing, nagging, yelling, gabbing. Then suddenly she was again pregnant and for nine months there again grew between them the unique relationship of physician and pregnant woman as they worked together to bring about the birth of a baby. He had seen her progress from a young and vigorous yet astonishingly naive newlywed to a housewife and mother. She had exasperated him, confused him, and made him laugh, as well as gain perception and confidence in himself as he progressed from young doctor to seasoned obstetrician.

It would have been untrue to say that sex never entered his mind in all the years he had known her. There had been moments when he could easily project a mental image of Ruth Sinclair, abundantly endowed, reclining voluptuously nude or locked in the passionate heat of sexual embrace but these were fleeting moments and for the most part he regarded her with a professional detachment that was difficult for a layman to understand, because even more vivid in his mind were her unique combinations, anatomic, physiological, and psychological, that challenged him as a physician. Once she became his patient and medical problem he could be warm but always totally detached and concentrating objectively on her problems. He could be as unyielding as he could be sympathetic. Sitting on a stool between her thighs, scrutinizing her cervix via a speculum or palpating her uterus he could be as totally absorbed in his work as a mechanic tinkering with a balky carburetor.

Waiting for the sedative to take effect, he sat quietly as Mrs. Sinclair rambled on, "I'm a sick woman! I'm practically deranged! I know who's crazy around here. I know who's nuts. You're as _nutty_ as a fruitcake, and that's the proof of the pudding. I was once a sane nice person—brother—what a wreck I am now! I haven't had a night's sleep since that building fell on them. But my hands are tied. Because he calls it 'his career.' Suffer ... suffer ... suffer ... that's all I get out of life! When was the last time we had a good time? But _I'm_ the failure! I'm the lousy person! I'm the schlep! The louse in the house!"

He sat beside the bed listening to Ruth Sinclair go on, feeling quite at home. It was fascinating how the attitudes of certain types of women didn't vary. It was almost like hearing his own wife, variations on a familiar theme.

She tossed, moaning in an exhausted whisper continuing with a summary of her husband's shortcomings. "He's perfect. Mr. Wonderful! That's what everybody thinks. Big Hero! Gets his picture in the paper. But what am I doing? Dying with pains in my chest! Scared to death! Waiting for the next news bulletin to interrupt the late movie on TV. I'm wise to you, Big Boy! Big Hero! You thought you got yourself a dumb broad who wasn't going to ask questions, didn't you? You big bastard!"

The mumbling dwindled to a murmur and then she lay sleeping quietly.

"That's it," Henderson said. "Bill, I think she's going to stay that way at least until tomorrow. We'll just keep up the sedation and intravenous feeding and bring her around to liquid and then solid foods in a day or two but I think she'll come out of it in good shape if I keep her here in the Hospital for the rest of the week. Can you manage at home with the kids?"

"Oh, sure," Bill Sinclair said. "Her sister is with us right now and I've got seventy-two hours off this week."

"You look like you could use it," Henderson said as they walked down the corridor toward the elevator.

Bill Sinclair grinned and fingered a slight stubble of beard. "I just came off duty at midnight," he said. "I caught the late train out from the city and found her on the floor in the bathroom with Betty—her sister—holding her head. So I didn't get to bed yet."

"She's still got that building cave-in on her mind, hasn't she?" Henderson said.

Sinclair shook his head. "She can't seem to shake it. She's driving herself nuts with it."

One morning in the previous autumn, eight firemen had been buried in a building cave-in when fire swept through an aging wooden tenement on the east side of the city. Bill Sinclair had been one of the eight. He had been inside the building on the third floor, getting people out to a window so that they could be carried down aerial ladders when the floors suddenly buckled and most of the firemen in Bill's hook-and-ladder company went all the way to the basement in a roaring, flaming mass of timbers and rubble. Rescuers had reached Bill Sinclair and five of the other firemen but three men from his company had died, along with several women clutching small children.

It had been one of the worst fire disasters in recent history and Ruth Sinclair had seen the whole thing on television. By chance, a TV crew had been roaming the city and reached the scene soon after the first fire companies began arriving. A neighbor had telephoned Ruth Sinclair, who switched on the set in time to see the building collapse and recognize her husband's hook and ladder by its number just before it was eclipsed by a Niagara of falling bricks and clouds of smoke. She fainted flat on the living-room rug, but as soon as she was revived by the neighbors insisted on sitting next to the set for two hours while the rescuers fought to get Bill and the others out.

The visual impact of television had once again left its mark. Wives and relatives saw their fire-fighting husbands, sons, and relatives in all the stunning reality of a big-city fire; a reality that somehow had never been brought home to them by newspaper headlines, news photos, or radio reports. The TV camera put them right on the scene, and it was too much for many of them. From then on many firefighters had been under pressure from their families to get out of fire-department work into some safer line. The distraught Ruth Sinclair was one of the most vocal.

Adding to the emotional conflict and stress were the tremendous changes and civil disorders within the city. In the past, city firemen had enjoyed such admiration and high regard in even the worst ghetto neighborhoods that they left their firehouse doors wide open when they sped out to answer alarms; now it was necessary to post police guards to keep the firehouses from being looted, and fire trucks were pelted with rocks and beer cans from rooftops when they responded to alarms.

Bill Sinclair's old-fashioned red-brick firehouse was situated in the heart of one of the city's largest slum neighborhoods. There, Negroes and Puerto Ricans and West Indians dwelt in ancient buildings owned by absentee "slumlords" who ignored the health and safety of their tenants. They carved up the flats in the old brownstone buildings and sublet them as one and two bedroom "kitchenette" apartments at outrageous prices.

As the buildings became rundown, the fire hazards

increased. For a hook-and-ladder company such as Bill Sinclair's, it meant scaling ladders and smashing windows to climb into thick, black, choking smoke to grope about for human bodies or listen for the muffled cry for help; to find a child huddled beneath a bed or in a closet, wrap its small form inside the heavy fireman's coat and crawl back through heat and smoke and often flames to hand the child out the window and get everyone down the aerial ladders which in the winter were treacherously slippery from the frozen spray of fire hoses.

And thanks to television, firemen's wives such as Ruth Sinclair were privileged to view it all. It was no wonder they tended to become nervous wrecks and nagged their husbands to seek suburban jobs even if it meant foregoing city and union pension plans, salary increases, and other fringe benefits.

For dedicated firemen such as Bill Sinclair it created a bewildering conflict between love for their families and the pride and satisfaction they found in the challenge, action, and drama of big-city firefighting.

"It's always been all in a day or night's work," Bill Sinclair had once told Henderson. "You take the risks but you get a certain feeling out of working at top speed as part of a team, and until you've saved a couple of kids or a mother or father or brought an old party down a ladder with her praying in your ear, you can't appreciate how good you can feel about it. This new stuff we run into with the rocks and the snipers, sure it gets to us. It burns you up and gets you depressed and confused but if the government really cleans up these lousy neighborhoods, it could pass. I keep telling Ruth I'd rather take my chances and sweat it out than find myself driving a bakery truck."

"I know what you mean, Bill," Henderson had said. He felt a kinship with the big fireman. Both of them enjoyed their chosen careers and lived them to the hilt. Both of them had trained themselves to leap out of bed in the middle of the night, to work at top speed with all the discipline and skill they could command—to act swiftly, calmly, and decisively in moments of total stress and crisis—to feel later the deep sense of elation and satisfaction at having saved a human life. Yet both of them were pressured by their wives who resented their being away from home at all hours of the night amidst risks to their life and health. Both had been told innumerable times that they were selfish, egocentric male brutes who were sacrificing their families.

"Do you know what's going to happen to you?" Henderson's wife, Mary, had snapped during one recent domestic altercation. "You're going to drop dead with a coronary before you're fifty! You're going to wind up sick and broke. There won't be enough money to bury you!"

"Do you think they'd leave a corpse around the house?" Henderson had replied, sipping a beer as they sat on the patio. "It's against the law. They'd put me in the ground or up the chimney at the crematorium. And anyway, I've already signed myself up for organ transplants. After that they're supposed to pack me in ice and ship me back to medical school. I'm going to be a cadaver for the first-year anatomy class."

"You? A specimen? Of what? You'd be no use to them unless they wanted to use what remains of you as an object lesson!"

Henderson bade goodby to Bill Sinclair at the elevator and returned to Room 320 to see how the IV bottles the nurses had rigged were working. Mrs. Sinclair seemed to be sleeping soundly. If all went well, the regime of intravenous fluids, vitamins, and sedation would bring her around quickly. By tomorrow she would probably be sitting up with a magazine so gay and chatty it would make you blink to see the difference.

He flicked back her eyelids for one more check for any signs of retinal hemorrhages. There were none. But she startled him by stirring in her sedated slumber.

"Dr. Henderson?"

"I'm right here," he said. "Go back to sleep."

"You won't forget about going to court?" she whispered huskily.

"Court?"

In the dawning light of the new day he sat for a moment trying to force his mind into some sort of free association: court—jail—lawyers—judges—cops? What in the world was she talking about?

"You know," she whispered, still lying flat with her eyes shut. "My case. It's coming up in court next month. You promised you would testify for me. About my miscarriage and that automobile accident."

"Oh, sure," he said. "Of course."

Now he remembered. Mrs. Sinclair's *accident*. For six years she had been getting ready to go to court with a lawsuit about an automobile accident. The case had taken forever to get on the clogged court calendar and then there had been postponement after postponement. Now the case was finally coming up in court. He had promised to appear as a witness and promptly forgotten about it. Of course, his office nurse had put the date on his schedule and he would have been there.

Ruth Sinclair was the plaintiff in two cases relating to the accident. One had been simply for recovery of damages to the Sinclair family automobile. In the other she was contending that the accident had caused her to suffer a miscarriage and she was seeking a financial settlement by the defending insurance company or a sum set by a jury trial.

She had been three months pregnant when a citizen in his seventies had stepped on the accelerator instead of the brake at an intersection and charged into the side of her car. She had been tossed in a heap and wound up in the Hospital Emergency Room with contusions of both knees and a sprained wrist.

Henderson had been summoned from the Maternity Floor, treated her and examined her and admitted her to the Hospital for a possible imminent abortion. Her injuries were minor but the shock to her nervous system had been severe. She was, of course, certain she was going to lose the baby.

During a fortnight's observation in the Hospital nothing developed to indicate a miscarriage was coming. There was no evidence of internal injuries, not the slightest sign of a hemorrhage. Finally he had discharged her. She was home two weeks and then, a month after the accident, suffered a miscarriage. Had the accident precipitated the miscarriage? Who could say positively yes or no? There was no doubt that the elderly driver was at fault in the accident. Even his insurance company had agreed to that and after the usual haggling had paid for the damage to the Sinclair car. But then one of the Sinclairs' neighbors, who happened to be a lawyer, had decided that the accident had caused the miscarriage. How could he know? It was a typical lawyer's assumption: in favor of his client and a contingency-fee settlement.

Henderson had told the lawyer and Bill and Ruth Sinclair that he frankly could not say positively that the accident had brought on the miscarriage. All he could do was offer an opinion and acquaint the jury with what was known about the relationship between a sudden physical shock to the body, nervous tension, and a spontaneous abortion. Miscarriages were often blamed on injuries or shock resulting from some sort of accident. In fact, so popular was this notion that when he had been a resident in obstetrics in the city he had seen an endless parade of unwed pregnant girls from the city ghettos who had deliberately gotten drunk and let their boy friends push them down a flight of stairs to abort the pregnancy.

"I rolled down six flights," one girl who was brought to the Hospital with a broken arm confided to him. "My ass is all bruised and bumped. My arm is busted and I've still got that damn baby inside me!"

It was true. Her pregnancy was totally unimpaired by the stair plunge. Some females might survive even more serious injuries, such as a fractured pelvis, and still have an intact pregnancy, but with others all it seemed to take was tension, fatigue, anxiety, or a sudden nervous shock. Of some of them you could say, "You blow in her ear and she may miscarry."

Which category did Ruth Sinclair fall into? He suspected she was far more vulnerable than many but he wasn't absolutely sure. Certainly she wasn't the placid type. She worried, fussed, fumed, raged, and over-emoted about everything. She also overate and drank beer and smoked cigarettes until he made her cut them out. Yet she had borne three healthy children. The miscarriage after the automobile accident might have been directly related to the crash and the shock even though she didn't abort until a month later, or it might have been caused by some abnormality. The pathology post-mortem report had found the fetus normal and the cause of the miscarriage inconclusive.

Now here she was in the third month of her fifth pregnancy reacting psychosomatically to being pregnant but again with no indication that she was going to miscarry. Not even the slightest irregular staining that would be related to a problem within her uterus. And how typical of her while drifting off into sedated slumber to regain consciousness long enough to remind him that he was due in court! While he had been sitting there beside the bed mulling over her problems, she had slipped into a sound sleep.

"Well, I'm sorry you've been vomiting all night, Mrs. Sinclair," he said to himself, "but before morning rounds begin there is still time for breakfast and I am hungry!"

In the doctor's locker room of the Maternity Floor he took a brief hot shower and selected a fresh set of whites, chuckling appreciatively as he noted that an unseen hand had been slyly tampering with the supply cabinet's shelf labels. Undoubtedly it was his anesthesiologist friend, Dr. Herbert Goodman. To a neatly printed tape reading "Medium Sized Pants" had been added the scrawl: "For Medium Important Doctors" and to "Large Size Pants"—"Awnings and Tents for Gigantic Important Doctors."

Descending to the staff dining room, he got a tray of

bacon and eggs and joined a table of night nurses just going off duty, listening to their banter, tired but relaxed and at ease in this familiar hospital world in white.

How does a boy decide what he shall seek to be in life? He had been lucky; he had found his purpose early. He had grown up in an Illinois suburb on the shores of Lake Michigan north of Chicago. Animals were the joy of his early boyhood. He had a Great Dane named Fritz, a pet raccoon, hordes of white rats, rabbits, and guinea pigs, and a one-eyed, broken-winged seagull he had rescued from the lake after a gale. Before he was twelve years old, this warm, deep feeling for living creatures was being drawn into focus for him by his father.

A college elopement that, in the days when his parents went to school, carried with it automatic expulsion had crushed the senior Henderson's dream of becoming a doctor, but as he went up the ladder in advertising, a big, hearty man with many friends, he had made medicine his hobby. He cultivated the acquaintance of physicians and neurosurgeons and developed a skill in medical photography.

The Henderson home was always strewn with medical journals, anatomy books, and boxes of photographic slides of surgical specimens.

The boy's curiosity, fed by his father's enormous enthusiasm, supported by his mother's gentle tolerance, flared into flame of ambition that, once kindled, never wavered.

"With Bob," his mother was fond of saying, "it was always going to be medicine."

He studied the slides and medical journals, devoured popular medical classics such as *Devils, Drugs and Doctors* until they fell apart. When a stray dog was slain by a car, he dissected it on the back porch before a gaping audience of his fellow twelve-year-olds and, abetted by his father, borrowed his mother's pressure cooker to stew dead cats for their skeletons.

He matured early, growing tall like his father and powerfully built for his age. While he was still only a sophomore in high school, a doctor friend of his father's entrusted him with the task of giving electrocardiogram tests to his patients. At sixteen he became an informal apprentice to a psychiatrist who gave shock treatment, using his strength and bulk to prevent patients from injuring themselves while under therapy, but losing interest in a career in this field when a patient he pursued into a closet dented his skull with a tennis racket.

That same year he obtained what he alone considered a "dream job" for the summer vacation period— working as a diener in a hospital morgue, assisting the pathologists with their postmortem studies, embalming bodies, hanging around the autopsy rooms until all hours.

He would always remember the orthopedic surgeon who had a habit of coming down to the autopsy lab the night before a major operation and performing the entire surgical procedure step-by-step on a cadaver to prepare himself for the next morning. Sitting there quietly watching him, Henderson had begun to sense the dedication medicine demanded of a really good doctor.

The determination had settled deep within him and sustained him from then on, no matter what the obstacles. It had kept him going during the family uproar when he and Mary had gotten married while he was still a premed student, when the pressure of having not enough money was at its greatest. Despite strenuous objections from in-laws, the bellows of his outraged father, the knowledge he probably would be in debt until he was thirty-five, he had known he would *still* be a doctor.

Once medical school started, Henderson's life was a rugged grind of classes, study, and after-hours jobs. Mary often complained that she was spending more of her time with "George" than she was with him.

"George" was a human cadaver that Henderson had contrived to obtain from the medical school anatomy lab and which he kept at home in their only bathtub for midnight dissection studies. "George," Henderson recalled, had bothered the hell out of his mother-in-law whenever she came to call and would have to use the bathroom.

His own mother was less concerned. She had already lived through the experience of having a gas-station attendant nearly die of fright and call the police when he opened the trunk compartment of her car and found it crammed with human arms and legs, which Henderson had forgotten to tell her he had borrowed for study purposes from the medical laboratory.

"George" wasn't as hard for the women to take as "Henry" who came later. While "George" had been long embalmed and therefore was nearly mummified, Henderson had brought home "Henry"—freshly embalmed—in the middle of the night and had refused to tell Mary or anybody else in the family how he happened to get him.

Finances plagued them throughout his medical school and interne-resident years. All Henderson got was $100 a month as an interne. The rest of the budget he had to earn on the side. He worked nights in a local blood bank and in a medical laboratory that used rabbits to test for pregnancies in women. After each rabbit was sacrificed, Henderson always claimed the body and brought it home, neatly skinned, to Mary. He couldn't begin to remember how many of their Saturday night dinner parties had featured rabbit stews and ragouts.

Determination plus the sheer excitement of his learning experiences had carried him through the most tremendous period of his medical career—four years of training as an interne and resident in Obstetrics and Gynecology at Chicago's massive Cook County General Hospital.

Cook—bigger than New York's famed Bellevue Hospital and the largest general hospital in the United States—has been since the beginning of the century an island of hope for relief from sickness and suffering for the successive waves of people, Polish, German, Jewish and Negro surging through Chicago's sprawling South Side, a place where sixty babies were born between each sunrise and residents in Obstetrics delivered as many babies in six months as you might in ten years of general practice.

It had been an incredible ordeal of broken sleep, furious learning, and harried days and nights in delivery rooms and operating rooms. Where for four years most of his waking hours revolved around babies to come, babies that refused to come, babies being born backwards, forwards, and sideways, and all the minor and major ills of the intricate female apparatus that conceived them, nurtured them and, finally, propelled them forth into the outside world.

He worked an eighteen-hour day, often going for weeks at a time without getting much further from the Hospital than "The Greek's"—a noisy, disorderly restaurant just across the street where internes and residents gathered to swig coffee and talk about cases and nurses and complain bitterly about bilious-natured department heads.

But the deeper he got into it, the more he knew he had found what he wanted. Obstetrics was a special kind of heads-up, firehouse medicine that appealed particularly to his nature. It was dramatic. Each case built to its own natural climax with the delivery of the baby. Its crises came fast and furiously and you met the challenge of each one right then and there. Most of the time there was a happy ending. It was not like laboratory or internal medicine. In no other branch of medicine was contact between the doctor and patient so close and intimate. In no other way save surgery was the skill of his own hands and the force of his own personality so important. A medical student soon found that he liked it or wanted little part of it.

Forever in his mind would be the memories, some blurred, some sharp as yesterday, of the cases right out of the textbooks—Eclampsia, Hemorrhages, Breech Deliveries—and learning to battle with them under the critical eyes of the Cook doctors—"Christ bite me, Henderson! You're clamping that patient's bladder!"

Learning the free-wheeling ways of meeting an emergency! A prolapsed umbilical cord putting an unborn baby in imminent danger of death by strangulation— "Henderson, get your hand inside that patient and hold the baby's head and don't let go until we've done a cesarean section."

His bewildered protest, "But how can I walk down the hall with my hand inside . . . ?"

"You don't walk, Son. You ride! Get up on that stretcher with your patient and we'll roll you both to the Operating Room."

For the rest of his life he would vividly remember the tiny Residents' Duty Room on the Delivery-Room Floor with its battered bulletin blackboard, the new internes in their paper "simple simon pieman" hats solemnly manipulating a rubber baby through a plastic pelvis, the radio playing loudly with the resident snoring beside it, the stifling hot Chicago nights when the staff gulped down gallons of the "red glop"—cherry-flavored sugar water that was supposed to be reserved for the patients—the parade of rubber-tired stretchers headed for the delivery rooms and the endless refrain that went on night and day up and down "the line":

"Push! Momma! Push! Come on, now. Bear down!"

"Oh, Jesus! Help me! Somebody help me!"

"We are helping! Momma. Push that baby!"

The upstairs chamber in which the residents gathered to sleep, study, and play poker. The shower never worked. The toilet only half-flushed. But when you were utterly exhausted, it was paradise.

And the moment: "Congratulations, Doctor. As of this instant, at four in the morning, you have completed your training and are Chief Resident in charge of this Department—and you've got ten babies coming on 'the line' right now, so take over!"

3

Office Hours

They had already cleared the night's snowfall from the parking lot outside the building that held his new suite of offices but as yet there were only a few cars there. He vaulted a snowbank and entered through the waiting room, feeling proud as usual of the job his wife had done with purple and beige decor and walnut furnishings. The recorded music playing softly in the background was also her idea.

"Give the girls a place to relax, Bob," she had insisted. "Make it *no* place like home—a spot where they can escape the clatter of TV and kids and washing machines and they won't care how long you have to keep them waiting."

"Hi, there," he said to Gloria, the office nurse on duty this morning. "Are we still in business?"

"For once, you're early," she replied. "You said to remind you about those Pap smears this morning."

"Okay," he said. "Bring me yesterday's batch and a cup of coffee."

He sat down at the desk in his office, slipped his feet out of his shoes and wiggled his toes and sipped hot coffee while he slipped one slide after another into position beneath the gray, twin-barreled microscope, studying the magnified clumps of cell samples he had obtained from his patients during routine pelvic examinations.

The first eight were clearly negative but then there was number nine. He felt a sudden, sharp tingle of excitement as he found himself staring at a smear that was unmistakably "positive"—the grapelike cluster of abnormal cells with dark, heavy-bodied centers stood out among the normal cells. There it was! Early cancer —the kind that could be cured! He had found it with nothing more than a cotton-tipped swab stick in a woman who was otherwise perfectly healthy.

Cancer of the cervix and uterus was the second most common form of cancer in women. An estimated 14,-000 American women died of it annually. Yet the rate of cure could be better than ninety-five percent if the cancer were detected early by a "pap test." No other form of cancer was so readily detectable years before it became dangerous.

Now that he knew that the disease menaced this patient he could go after it and cure it completely with perhaps nothing more than a few radiation treatments or the most minor sort of surgery. Not only would he be able to cure her completely, he would also keep her a fully functioning wife and lover.

"Mrs. Michaels is here," Gloria said. "She didn't have an appointment but she thinks she may be going into labor."

"Set her up in Room A," he said, stacking the rest of the slides. "We'll see how she's doing."

Barbara Michaels, a broad-hipped, sturdily-built, placidly calm brunette. To look at her you'd think she'd have her babies easily; yet, her first two pregnancies had culminated in prolonged labor—sixteen-hour ordeals that had left her exhausted.

"What's happening, Honey?" he asked, leaning over the examining table, taking her pulse with one hand and conducting a pelvic examination with the other.

"I was in the library returning some books when I felt a pain kind of high up toward my back," she answered. "I sat down and waited and had two more about fifteen minutes apart, but then they stopped. I saw your car so I thought I'd stop in anyway."

"Right you were," he said. He had found the cervix thinning and about four centimeters dilated and the baby's head down low. The bag of waters was unruptured. With his stethoscope he got good heart tones from the baby—140 to the minute.

"Barbara, I don't think you're going to have the baby right away but you're definitely going into labor."

"I hope it's not like the last time," she said resignedly.

"So do I," he said. "But this time let's make it easier for you from the very beginning. Drop off your shopping things at home and then go on over to the Hospital. Once you've been admitted I can keep an eye on you and try to make you more comfortable."

"You mean right now?" she protested.

"Sure. Right now. Take those library books with you."

His office nurse as usual stayed one step ahead of him, notifying the Hospital and making all the necessary arrangements. After Barbara Michaels had left, she continued efficiently setting up the patients for examination, standing by to assist him, or retiring discreetly when he wished to talk privately with a patient in his office.

As usual, many of the problems that his patients brought him that morning had nothing to do with pregnancy. Gynecology is a specialty of medicine that deals with *all* the illnesses and health problems of women. This day, as every day, he would be confronted with backaches and headaches, find a fibroid tumor that would call for surgery, and cope with complaints of missed periods, "heavy" periods, painful periods, and "mixed-up" periods.

Some ailments would require prolonged treatment. Others could be diagnosed and dealt with on the spot with local treatment or a scribbled prescription. The itching fury of vaginal infections, so long the bane of the world of women, seemed to be responding remarkably to treatment with new oral drugs. But you had to allow plenty of time for the explanations. At Cook, it had always been "anything you say, Doctor" but out here in the suburbs, all the patients wanted to understand exactly what was wrong and what was being done. Perhaps it was time-consuming, but it was also a boon—a patient who understood her condition was better able to help him treat it properly.

On his desk was the usual stack of telephoned requests from women who wanted him to renew their birth-control pill prescription as well as appointment lists for new patients who wanted to come in with or without their husbands to discuss family birth-control programs.

In a brief span of years The Pill had had an enormous impact on the sex life and family planning of Henderson's suburban patients.

The Pill unquestionably was the most effective contraceptive measure ever devised by man. The current United States version that Henderson relied upon in his practice contained two synthetic chemical compounds. Both closely resembled the natural hormones produced by a woman's body: estrogen and progesterone. Estrogen normally was produced continuously in the human female from adolescence to menopause. Progesterone was manufactured chiefly during pregnancy to suppress ovulation. The Pill halted the release of the ovum while maintaining the uterus in a healthy state. All a woman had to do was to remember to take one pill a day for twenty days. Several days later she should have a normal menstrual period and a week later, resume the daily dose that would prevent her from becoming pregnant. That was all there was to it. It eliminated and surpassed all other contraceptive methods.

As was true with all potent drugs, The Pill occasionally produced side effects in some people. A decade of studies of its effects in the United States and abroad had revealed there were some women for whom the oral contraceptive should not be prescribed. These included women who were unusually sensitive to its hormonal effects, women with kidney ailments, women with a history of migraine headaches, liver problems, clotting or circulatory problems, diabetes, or a family history of breast or cervical cancer.

But even if you subtracted these, The Pill was still a properly prescribed birth-control measure for millions of women. And you had to balance its risks against the hazards of pregnancy. Few women realized that during and immediately after a normal pregnancy there were also real risks of clotting problems and that even without the possibility of embolisms, pregnancy carried other risks associated with high blood pressure and kidney disorders. If a woman kept on having babies, there was also the natural wear and tear on the body which could result in bladder problems, varicose veins, a weakened uterus and cervix, hemorrhoids, not to mention such specific risks of pregnancy as hemorrhages, miscarriages, ectopic pregnancies, and difficult deliveries. Add to that the stress and financial havoc caused by overlarge families. It was easy to see that The Pill in its current form, or more sophisticated future chemical versions which might be taken less frequently or even injected or implanted, was going to be one of man's best hopes for improving world health and coping with the crucial population problem for a long time.

Henderson's patients in this period of transition ran the gamut. Many were taking The Pill regularly. Many more started, stopped, and then later returned to the method. Others vacillated between the oral contraceptives and diaphragms, condoms, spermicidal foams and tablets, and the IUDs—intrauterine devices. The younger women who had grown up with The Pill accepted it readily. Older women, such as Ruth Sinclair, could not make such an easy adjustment. They agitated themselves with complaints and anxieties about The Pill's side effects, and consciously or subconsciously resisted it by forgetting to take it as prescribed.

For Ruth Sinclair the problem was unending. She and her husband had agreed that they neither needed, wanted, nor could afford a larger family, but after a night of fire-fighting Bill Sinclair apparently found nothing so satisfying or relaxing as spending most of the day in bed with his voluptuous, passionate wife.

Not that Ruth Sinclair objected. "You know," she had once confided to Henderson with the sudden disarming candor that was so typical of her, "Bill really turns me on. You'd think after seven years of marriage and three kids we'd be slowing down, wouldn't you? Not us! We keep right on going. Better than ever. But Doctor, I simply can't have any more babies!"

Henderson had tried to help them with every bit of professional guile and knowledge that he possessed. With Ruth Sinclair it was no use. Advance preparations didn't suit her, and once aroused she had no inclination to pause for other available precautions. She had at one point decided to try an IUD, "because then I don't have to remember anything." But she soon rebelled against having to probe within the vaginal passage to reach the IUD tab in the cervix. This confirmed that the plastic loop that Henderson had placed within her uterus had not been spontaneously expelled. After her third child was born, she began taking The Pill, but soon gave up complaining that the oral contraceptive made her nauseous and brought on headaches.

After some prodding, Henderson had finally gotten the truth out of her. She was scared stiff of oral contraceptives. Her friends were always telling her about how many Pill-takers dropped dead, went blind, or suffered paralyzing embolisms.

"Listen," Henderson had said. "There's about seven million women taking these pills right here in this country. And there's millions more taking them all around the world. Do you know how many have serious side effects? About thirty out of every million. And some of those shouldn't have been on the pills anyway."

He tapped her chart which was on the desk in front of him as they sat in his office. "There's absolutely nothing in here—in your family health history—in your personal health history—or in your present physical condition to suggest that you are in any way prone to serious side effects from oral contraceptives. If there were, do you think I'd prescribe the pills for you?"

"But they make me sick to my stomach. They repeat on me all day."

"They're on your mind too much," Henderson replied. "I'll bet you take one and then sit around waiting for a burp or a headache or expecting to drop dead."

"Me sit around? Do you think we've got maid service? I'm going all day long. Some nights every bone in my body is aching. I'm a wreck!"

Two months after the birth of her third child she had gone back to the diaphragm method of contraception. Either it had worked—even with her batty, hit-and-miss approach—or else she had been lucky or less fertile. She had sailed along for nearly twenty-three months. Then, a matter of a month ago, she had called for an appointment "about something important."

"I don't know what's the matter with me," she had announced dolefully when she had disrobed, donned a minismock and permitted his examining room nurse to assist her to the table. "I was due for my period about three weeks ago, I think. Both of these," she clutched her ample bosom as she reclined on the examining table, "are bothering me. They're very tender."

Her breasts certainly were increasing in size. He could see the network of delicate veins becoming visible through the skin. The nipples were larger and more deeply pigmented.

"I hate that thing," she continued, eyeing the speculum that he was heating to her body temperature with the electric pad in the drawer by his elbow.

"It won't take a second," he replied soothingly. "You'll hardly feel it. It's even warmed up for you."

The value of the all-seeing speculum had been impressed on him early in his medical-student days—and not merely as a handy appliance for visualizing the vaginal passage to diagnose feminine ailments, minor and major, as well as the various stages and conditions of pregnancy.

While only a third-year student, he had landed "right

on the money" as the Ob residents of the big-city hospital used to call it. He had been examining an aged habitué of Skid Row when his insertion of the speculum had yielded a view of a mysterious mass which when probed readily dislodged itself. Very young and eager, he had immediately assumed that he had happened on an important discovery—a tumor which might be a matter of life or death for his patient. He had plucked it out, hustled it to the sink, rinsed it thoroughly, and discovered he was holding a roll of United States currency—$57.00 in small bills it was found later. The chief nurse who had let him go through the frantic bit of diagnosis without saying a word had crumpled with laughter. "There's a fortune walking the streets of this city," she had explained to him. "Thousands of these old dolls trust themselves a lot more than they do any bank."

Visualizing Ruth Sinclair's cervix, he, a month ago, had been gratified to find it remarkably free of erosions and lacerations from previous pregnancies. Its tissues were soft with a blueish tinge of color. Through his gloved fingertip he could feel her uterine arteries pulsing. The uterus was nearly globular and upon bimanual examination, his right hand on her abdomen and two fingers of the left hand within the vaginal passage, he could discern the soft, compressible isthmus between firm cervix and the elastic uterus: Hegar's sign that appeared usually about six weeks after a period. There was always the possibility that there might be a tumor of the tubes or ovaries but he was guessing that it was another pregnancy.

After he had completed his examination and she had dressed and joined him in his office, he had asked, "How would you like another baby?"

A wild stare and suppressed gasp as her hands shot up to her mouth and her eyes widened, "Oh, no!"

"I'm pretty sure of it."

"But I'm only a little late, Doctor Henderson. I've only missed my period."

"I think maybe you've missed two periods," he had said. "Do you keep a calendar the way I suggested?"

"No, I just remember."

"You must have missed a date. Probably during the Christmas holidays or around New Year's."

"But we've been careful!" wailed Ruth Sinclair. She had burst into sobs. "I swear I'll take that damned diaphragm and throw it out the window! From now on, it's going to be either the pills or no going to bed! That's it! Listen, Doctor, I just can't be pregnant again! I'm already killing myself with the other kids. It's too much. Too many responsibilities! We're broke and I'm exhausted!"

More tears.

He was studying her chart. "You know your fatigue is probably the real thing," he had said. "It may be caused partly by the pregnancy and you're carrying around quite a bit more weight than you ever did, too. Did you know that you've gained thirty-one pounds since you've been coming to me?"

Silence.

She loathed all their discussions about her weight.

"And besides," Henderson continued, "you may also be a bit anemic. You may have an iron deficiency which now with the pregnancy is even more of a problem. What are you eating these days?"

"Nothing! When Bill is working I eat with the kids."

He could guess what that meant. She was snacking absent-mindedly. Probably cleaning up what the kids didn't eat. Plenty of soup and peanut-butter sandwiches. Soda pop. Also pizzas, Chinese and Italian dinners, beer and ice cream when she and her husband went out on the town on his weekends off from work. She had once told him she was partial to all of these dishes and beverages. Although she had put on some weight, she was big-boned and tall enough to carry the extra curves.

"Look," he had said, trying to calm her down. "I've been wrong before. Don't fall apart about having a baby. Wait until we hear from the laboratory tests and don't forget it's not a new experience for you. You know what it's all about."

"I know we can't have another one. That's what I know!"

The tests had confirmed his preliminary diagnosis. For a while she had bucked like a wild horse, alternating between tears, fits of rage, and spells of depression which left Bill Sinclair exhausted.

"What'll I do with her, Doc?" he had asked in one telephone call. "She's really climbing the walls over this one."

"Hold on, Bill," Henderson had advised. "When she gets further along I think she'll knock it off. A lot of women in her spot tend to go through this same cycle." He had really been expecting to see an improvement but instead she had slid into a deepening emotional crisis which resulted in the hyperemesis, complete with nausea and the dry heaves. He had then admitted her to the Hospital for a complete workup, but she apparently was afflicted with nothing except pregnancy. When she had quieted down after a week in the Hospital, he had sent her home under an arrangement whereby she would see a staff psychiatrist, but that had been three weeks ago and now here she was, back in the Hospital.

The intensity of her distress about this pregnancy had puzzled Henderson until this morning when he had heard her sounding off about Bill Sinclair's fire-fighting and the big cave-in. Since then it had gotten through to him. This time there was just too much of a threat to her sense of security. It wasn't just another baby. It was another baby plus the enormous anxieties she had developed in the last year about the hazards in her husband's job. Why hadn't he, Henderson, or at least the damned psychiatrist, sensed the depth of the problem sooner? The trouble was that psychiatrists always seemed to have all the time in the world. But in obstetrics it didn't work that way. While they had all been expecting her to calm down or respond to treatment, the pregnancy was progressing. Now it was getting too late for a therapeutic abortion. True, only a few years ago, he would not have entertained such an idea so readily, in fact not at all. But that was because he had been taught otherwise when he was in medical school and it was only now that society and the medical profession were showing signs of coming to grips with the swiftly changing circumstances and mores of the late 20th century. The proponents of therapeutic abortion were gaining ground as birth control became a major factor both in family health and in the world population crisis.

In England a new law permitted physicians to consider such factors as overcrowding, inadequate housing, and the emotional tensions that might be created by too large a family when considering a medical abortion. In the United States, a leading group of obstetricians had declared that a doctor determining whether or not a pregnancy constituted a serious threat to a woman's health should take account of the patient's *total environment,* actual or reasonably foreseeable.

Ruth Sinclair, in Henderson's opinion, could qualify for abortion under these guidelines. Despite her protestations about financial hardships, Bill Sinclair's income and his access to accident, health, and pension benefits placed his family in a far better financial position to raise four children than many other middle-income American families. But her emotional vulnerability to stress constituted a threat to family health which would only be magnified by an addition to the family. Two children would have been ideal for her. Three were acceptable, and four were the absolute limit. But now that she was well along with this present pregnancy, Henderson would employ every bit of his professional skill and energy to protect the life of his patient and her baby, but before the nine months were up, he was going to have to plan some serious discussions with Mrs. Sinclair and her husband and the psychiatrist who was helping him cope with her hyperemesis. She was thirty-four and with three children to care for and another on the way she needed no further pregnancies. Abruptly, it occurred to him that even if it were too late to halt the latest pregnancy, he might at least be able to pull her out of her mental tailspin if he could offer her a guarantee that it would be her last.

Buzzing Martha Williams, his office nurse, Henderson said, "See if you can get me Marvin the Mind Bender on the phone."

Marvin Laden was probably the youngest of the rapidly growing number of psychiatrists who were opening practices in the community, but he was unabashed by his lack of seniority. Although he was keenly interested in building up a practice, he had no hesitancy in espousing radical political and professional causes. His fees were still low, his candor refreshing. His interest in patients as people and the scorn he displayed toward the more aloof and fee-minded members of his specialty had attracted Henderson. Together they had reached an easy and informal working relationship.

"Marvin," Henderson said when Laden was on the telephone, "if you can put your clothes on for a moment and get rid of that female 'sensitivity' patient, I'd like to talk to you about Ruth Sinclair."

"I only wish Sinclair was my 'sensitivity' patient,'" Laden replied. "All she does is come in here and leave her lunch all over my new furniture."

"I put her back in the Hospital this morning," Henderson said. "Did you get my message?"

"Sure. I was over there to see her only an hour ago. You've got her stabilized but I don't know where she's headed. Depression. Overwhelming anxiety. Some real panic."

"Particularly about the firehouse," Henderson said.

He briefed Laden on Ruth Sinclair's ramblings about her husband's job and added his conclusion.

"I think you're right," Laden said.

"How do you think she's going to hold up during the rest of this pregnancy?" Henderson asked.

"I'm not sure. It may have created a much more serious problem."

"She's too far along for an abortion," Henderson said. "If that's what you are suggesting."

"She wasn't right for it in the first place," Laden replied. "I discussed it with her during her first visits."

Henderson was startled. "I didn't know that," he said. "I ought to realize that some of you guys would abort the whole world if you had a chance. When I sent her to see you, all I wanted you to do was put her back together again so we could keep her out of the Hospital and support her through this pregnancy."

"Well, if it makes you feel any better," Laden said, "the talks about an abortion only made her feel worse. She's a little too old to accept it. Her background is too conservative. She'd be so full of fright, guilt, and confusion that she would have risked becoming a total and permanent wreck. But somebody has got to be sterilized—either her or her husband."

"That's what I called you about," said Henderson. "I'd like to submit a request for a voluntary sterilization to the Abortion-Sterilization Committee at the Hospital. Let's give her about a week in the Hospital and then we'll talk to her and to her husband about it. If they're both for it, we can submit the request to the Committee for consideration at their next monthly meeting. Are you with me?"

"Absolutely," said Laden. "I'll tell them that I concur with your opinion and her request in view of the patient's medical and psychiatric history."

"And from a psychiatric point of view," Henderson added, "it may stabilize her for the duration of this pregnancy?"

"I'd say it would work wonders," Laden replied.

"She will suffer no negative psychological side effects in your opinion?"

"Hell, no. She's ready for it. I only wish I'd thought of it before you did. But how about the Hospital Committee? Can we count on their approval?"

"No problem," Henderson answered confidently. "Out of the five on the Committee, we have two Catholics. They will probably vote no or abstain from voting.

But the other three, Stone, Crawford, and Harding will go along with us."

"A vasectomy for the husband might be easier," Laden said. "Then we don't have to fiddle around with getting Hospital approval to get the same result."

He was getting on to one of his favorite causes: birth control by vasectomy.

"Not on this one, Marvin," Henderson said. "It's such a new idea to people like the Sinclairs that it might spook them. I'm going to have her right there in the Hospital after I deliver the baby. Forty-eight hours later I'll pull her down to surgery and ligate those tubes in four minutes."

"*If* they let you do it," Laden said. "You're still thinking like an obstetrician. You've got to become more of a social scientist."

Laden liked to remind Henderson that in the midst of all the hullaballoo about population control, voluntary sterilization, which was the safest and most reliable method of achieving it, had not yet achieved the acceptance it deserved. With a snip of a scalpel and a few strands of surgical thread, any woman could be guaranteed permanent protection against pregnancy. By a similar but even simpler surgical procedure any man could be rendered sterile. Each method was close to one hundred percent effective, and both eliminated all problems related to the uncertainties, hazards, and side effects encountered with birth-control drugs and devices.

Viewed anatomically, the human reproductive system was not overly complicated. In a female, from the upper corners of the uterus arose the twin fallopian tubes which served as connecting passageways between the uterus and the two ovaries. Each fallopian tube was about four inces long and about the diameter of a soda-fountain drinking straw. Attached to the tubes were the two ovaries, almond-shaped and characteristically dull white and glistening.

In a woman of Ruth Sinclair's age there were still about 34,000 egg cells in each ovary. Each month a single ovum which had reached maturity was released by the ovary and drawn into the open end of the fallopian tube. There it was propelled along by rhythmic contractions of the tube's muscle tissues and thousands of hairlike cilia cells. If it met up with a live, male sperm within twenty-four hours, it might be fertilized and another baby would be on its way into the world. The fertilized ovum continued a three-day journey through the tube into the uterus and attached itself to the uterine wall for the nine months of pregnancy. In a single episode of sexual intercourse, a human male released about five hundred thousand sperm and only *one* of these had to make the trip through the uterus up into the fallopian tube and penetrate an egg to start adding to the population.

Most methods of birth control were aimed at preventing the rendezvous between sperm and ovum. When the male penis was sheathed in a rubber condum, none of the sperm was supposed to gain access to the female reproductive tract. Chemical agents employed by the female, such as vaginal foams, creams, and suppositories, were designed to knock out the sperm before they could begin their trek through uterus and tubes.

The diaphragm was supposed to bar the door to the uterus by capping the cervix. Followers of the calendar rhythm method, acceptable to the Catholic Church, avoided intercourse during periods of the month when there was most likely to be an ovum in the fallopian tube. The famed Pill prevented pregnancy because its synthetic hormones either halted the monthly release of the ovum from the ovary altogether, or brought about less receptive atmospheres in the uterus and cervix. The IUDs prevented the fertilized egg from passing down the tube or developing within the uterus.

All of these methods, however, were only relatively effective. For The Pill—the most reliable in the prevention of unwanted pregnancies—the "failure rate" was estimated at one pregnancy per thousand women. The IUD's failure rate ran around twenty to thirty pregnancies per thousand. The diaphragm's "failure"

was up to about one hundred to three hundred pregnancies per thousand, primarily because occasionally
someone like Ruth Sinclair took a chance on not using
it or didn't use it properly. The same chance-taking
among couples who relied on rubber condums resulted
in a failure rate of six to twenty percent. The calendar
rhythm method resulted in a failure rate of about twenty percent because of menstrual cycle irregularities and
human miscalculations. Spermicidal foams, creams,
suppositories, and other local agents were considered
generally less effective, particularly when used without
a diaphragm.

Thus, voluntary sterilization was the only certain
permanent method of birth control. In the human female all that needed to be done was to clamp, sever,
and ligate (tie off with knotted thread) both fallopian
tubes midway between the ovary and uterus. It could
be done as a separate elective surgery or during the
time that a woman was in the hospital after the delivery
of her baby or while undergoing a variety of other
operations. Until quite recently this way of controlling
the size of a family was sought by relatively few. Now
many more people were considering or requesting
voluntary sterilization. Some were motivated by reasons
of health. Others wanted to control the size of their
families for economic reasons. Still more were genuine-
ly concerned about population control.

Yet some segments of the medical profession were
not facing their responsibilities or keeping pace with the
times. In the United States, when a woman or a married couple requested voluntary sterilization, they were
frequently turned down by their physician. Across the
country many hospital committees on voluntary sterilization were composed of physicians who were still
clinging to outdated rigid criteria that insisted a woman
should give birth to four, five, six or more babies before
they would provide their consent.

The single largest stumbling block to far wider use of
sterilization continued to be the ignorance, prejudice,
and conservatism of many physicians and their tenden-

cy to "play God" with their patients in matters of birth control. If a doctor were connected with a hospital whose policies regarding sterilization were restrictive—as was still too often the case—he had added reason to discourage his patients from sterilization. If he were opposed to the idea of voluntary sterilization himself, he could be extremely negative in his interviews with the patient.

If the physician objected on religious grounds, he would not only be likely to refuse the operation, but more than that he might also try to talk the patient out of it and be of little help in referring a woman to a more liberal physician. Thus, the woman desiring sterilization ran an obstacle course of physicians' attitudes and hospitals' regulations, and no one knew how many thousands—or hundreds of thousands—of women had been deterred by them.

Of course, many doctors no longer felt this way and some hospitals, such as Henderson's, had taken steps to liberalize their regulations regarding voluntary sterilization. So far, however, these hospitals were a minority.

4

Night Rounds

When Henderson had seen his last patient he stretched, yawned, and then decided to drop by the Hospital to check on Barbara Michaels. He hoped to find her in active labor, but she was merely dozing.

"Not much progress, Doctor," reported the nurse who was watching her.

Barbara Michaels stirred, grimacing with pain. "It's no good," she muttered despairingly. "I'm tired of it!"

He confirmed the limited dilation of the cervix and listened to the baby's heart tones. They were still good and strong.

"Honey," he said. "I want you to hold on a little longer. You're really not ready for me to induce you yet and the baby is still all right. Just keep on resting as much as you can. I'll be back with you."

Picking up the evening newspaper at the newsstand in the Hospital Gift Shop he noticed a big heart-shaped box of candy, impulsively bought it, and headed home for supper.

The snowbound farmhouse was lit up in a way to bring joy to the Indiana Gas Company. How in Heaven's name, he wondered, was it possible for Mary and the kids to have every light in the place blazing at once? He braked to a halt as he encountered a stalled vehicle in the snow-drifted driveway and suddenly groaned, "Oh, my gosh. I forgot to get her damned license plates!"

Plowing through the drifts to the front door, he stepped inside quietly and paused for a moment, taking in the sight which still at times seemed slightly incredible—his four children, from his eldest girl Cary, 15, her sister Elizabeth, and the two boys, Charlie and the littlest one, Casey, just turned three, ranged around the huge table in the cedar-paneled kitchen.

And this wasn't all!

Upstairs were Pixie and Dixie, the white rats, Cary's cockatoo and Charlie's pet cat. Down cellar, along with a serpent and a batch of turtles, was José, a foul-tempered monkey. In the barn across the road was the pony, a large, noisy pet crow named Count Dracula, and the formerly stray dog Bingo.

He waded into the kitchen melee with Holly, the Great Dane, thumping appreciatively against him; Charlie, his six-year-old, tackling him about the knees; his ears deafened by a shrill chorus of reports about Mommy's stalled car, Casey's chicken pox, the shocking behavior of José in the basement.

He reached Mary, garbed in ski pants and sweater, busily forking barbecued chicken parts onto a platter, and gave her a kiss as he thrust the huge box of candy into her hands.

"The mailman brought you a valentine," he told her.

"Valentine candy in March?"

"Why not—if you've got the right girl?"

She smiled brightly and then, with the practiced practicality of marriage, switched the subject. "Did you get my car plates?"

"Not yet."

"But they'll give me a ticket," she wailed. "It's not fair!"

"You're snowed in anyway," he said. "What's the difference?"

"I'll tell you something," she said, gesturing emphatically with the big fork. "I'm busting out of here tomorrow if it takes a team of tractors to move that car! I've had it with this crowd. I'm getting cabin fever. How many babies today?"

"I delivered two, so far," he said. "I've got one still waiting. I'm going to have to do something about her later on this evening."

"Line up, kids," Mary said. "Come and get it!"

She forked out the chicken while the two girls standing beside her added the mashed potatoes and string beans, the whole thing somehow looking like an army chow line. He took his own plate and retired from the bedlam to his study off the hall. He shucked off his shoes, gazed at the walls hung with his skin-diving spear guns, blue-rubber feet flippers, fishing poles, and gun rack. Somehow they always made him feel momentarily better. He opened his mail.

"Join the new Pyramid Travel Club," urged the first letter. "Just send three dollars. Pass this letter along to six friends. In two weeks you'll be able to leave for Europe!"

Mary came in with pie and coffee, put his down next to him, and took hers to the chair in the corner. "What's your problem?"

"A girl in labor all day, if you can call it that. Seven hours of intermittent contractions. In between she's resting and sleeping."

"In bed all day resting? I could go for that myself."

"All you've got to do," he said, "is have another baby."

"And you, Buster Crabbe, can go jump in the lake!"

Their first child had come when he was still only a second-year medical student. Mary was having labor pains while Henderson was still insisting on searching through a stack of medical books to confirm that she really was in labor. When they finally got out to the sidewalk for the trip to the hospital, they found the lock on the car door frozen. There had been Mary, sitting on the curb, doubled up with labor contractions while he was running around with a pan of hot water trying to melt the ice in the lock.

Their life together had begun when they both were

college students attending a philosophy class. A group had retired to a nearby beer parlor to continue debating the classroom topic, "What Is a Miracle?" The other students were ribbing Mary who was stubbornly insisting that she believed in miracles.

"I think the birth of a baby is a miracle," she exclaimed defiantly. Henderson had been the only one at the table who didn't laugh at the lively, slim, fine-boned blonde who was taking herself so seriously. He walked her home that night. By the end of the week he was carrying her books to class and the next week they decided they were "engaged."

Their families exploded.

Henderson's father protested loudly that Mary was going to ruin his son's hopes of becoming a doctor. Mary's family, residing in an upper-income Chicago suburb, saw Henderson, a nineteen-year-old youth planning a ten-year medical training program, as a highly dubious choice for a husband.

An only child, Mary had grown up in Chicago and was pretty and talented enough to be singing as a supper-club soloist on weekends when Henderson came along and changed her mind about a career in show business.

The family pressure raised such hob with their romance that during the first summer, they broke up. Mary had quit college and gone to drama school in New York, feeling utterly miserable. She had later told Henderson, "It was the worst winter of my life."

He, glooming around the college campus, had begun to write to her, but her mother intercepted his letters and saw to it they never were forwarded. Finally, he reached her by writing her at the drama school. He wrote that he had just heard that he had been turned down by the medical school that was his first choice; but he added defiantly, "I'm going to get into medical school if I have to keep on going to premed classes for twenty years. I'm going to be a doctor no matter what happens!"

Mary had quit drama school and flown back to the

Middle West for a secret reunion. The stew had hit the fan when their families found that they were back together again, but this time there was no stopping them.

Mary demanded, and received, from her family grudging approval for the marriage, followed by a fancy June wedding that was flawed only by the fact that Henderson had time for no more than a weekend honeymoon before returning to his classes.

Finances were tight—both families still frowned on the marriage and were not being much help with money. They lived mainly on Mary's weekend supper-club singing and Henderson's endless series of after-class, part-time jobs that ranged from sandwich-counter clerk in a five-and-dime to medical-school laboratory technician. They lived in a tiny apartment where Mary spent much of her spare time typing up Henderson's applications to medical schools. When the acceptances began to come in along with the rejections, he selected a school in Chicago. It had a good rating and besides they didn't have enough money for moving.

During that period, when Henderson was still in his residency in obstetrics, they had accepted the offer of a house from Mary's family. It was a large home in an upper-class suburb of Chicago and, as they soon discovered, a mixed blessing. Mary had the space and comfort for their first babies, but she spent most of her time battling people from the utility and phone company who were always threatening to turn off their lights or yank out the telephone unless the Hendersons could catch up with their bills. A well-established surgeon who lived down the block was overheard complaining to neighbors, "I spent fifteen years building up a practice to afford this neighborhood and what do I find living next to me one morning? A goddamned interne!"

The pressure of living so far beyond their means had almost torn Henderson apart. Even Mary admitted that she hadn't realized how much it hurt him until a long time later. Whenever Mary, driven to distraction by his commitments to his patients and the jumbled night hours that he kept, would cry, "doctors like you should never get married!" Henderson could only reply, "damned right!"

There really never was any end to the conflict if a man loved both his profession and his family. You just went on coping with it. He believed Mary when she told people that she had not minded being alone so much with the children, or resented it as much as some people might think. Together they had found their own style of having a life together—Mary napping after the last child was asleep and then getting up to cook something when he finally did come home and sitting down to talk with him late into the morning—Henderson always coming home for even an hour or less no matter what the time of day or night to talk and be close to her with moments of overwhelming passion. Out of it there grew a complete and enduring companionship.

There was no doubt that the sacrifice Henderson had to make for his medical practice had been hard for his children. They were starved to have him around more than he possibly could be, even though he tried to make it up to them with frenetic weekends and stolen vacations, both winter and summer. Henderson still made a habit of taking at least one of his children, or perhaps two of them, with him to the hospital on Sunday when he made his rounds. They would sit patiently in the waiting room looking at magazines and then go with him on treats for hamburgers and malteds and to visit the shopping center malls which now were open on weekends. Along the way they talked things over.

There were also the times they spent together with the pets. Henderson's early love of animals was still strong. A wish to encourage and share with his children the curiosity and warmth that he felt toward all manner of living things had transformed the farm into a menagerie. Over the years there had been some spectacular successes and failures. A brace of Mexican burros had become so belligerent that the cry, "The burros are loose!" was enough to send the whole family fleeing for cover. Easter chicks grew from fluffy, yellow balls into huge aggressive roosters that dwelt in the trees and swooped down on unsuspecting visitors. When Mary had wanted to get rid of them, Henderson had argued that they be kept for protection. "Imagine any prowler that comes to this house being attacked in the middle of the night by squawking chickens . . . "

José, the spider monkey now residing in the basement, had such a nasty disposition that no one in the family could even tame him. He had bitten Henderson on the hand one night and made him so angry that he had punched the monkey in the nose—and then had a terrible time stopping the nosebleed. He had decided that the only solution was to pull all the monkey's teeth. Everyone had gathered around while Henderson gassed José and took him into his study with a pair of dental pliers and shut the door. For a long moment there was silence. Then Henderson had emerged, admitting sheepishly, "I just can't do it. He looks too much like a helpless baby."

The anesthetized ape slept for two solid days with everyone taking turns shaking him and shouting, "José! Wake up! Don't die! Wake up!"

When he was a resident "sleeping in" at the Hospital, Mary would drive downtown in the evening or on weekends and they would have coffee or a drink together at the small restaurant near the Hospital. Their closest friends were the other internes and residents and their wives who were in the same fix. Mary used to say the whole period of his interne-residency had reminded her of the labor of childbirth—you could only bear it because you knew it couldn't go on forever.

She hadn't realized then—and certainly neither had he—that their social life would be mostly a matter of eating sandwiches together in the kitchen after midnight. Mary had abandoned dreams of becoming a gracious hostess early in his medical career when she arranged a New Year's Eve party for fifty people. Just before the stroke of midnight, Henderson had received a telephone call and left the party.

"He rushed off to take care of a little old cleaning woman he had known at the hospital," Mary was fond of telling the children when she was warning the girls against marrying a doctor. "She had gone into a diabetic coma and I didn't see him again until the next day. Happy New Year!"

Henderson had become so wound up in his work that Mary had actually kept one of her pregnancies a secret for five months, "just to see how long I could go before you'd notice it." Finally she put a Father's Day card at his place at the supper table with the baby's due date on it. Henderson's eyes had nearly popped out of his head and he had chased Mary all over the house and embraced her until she gasped for mercy for herself and the baby.

He finished off the pie, drained the coffee, and reached for his coat.

It was time for night rounds at the Hospital and after that it would be time for Barbara Michaels to have her baby. He found her groggy from the hours of unproductive, mild, pre-labor pains.

"What time is it now?" she mumbled wearily, uneasily shifting her position.

"The middle of the night," he answered, gazing at the chart the nurses had been keeping and then examining her himself, confirming lack of progress. "Your baby is all right but you're still dilating awfully slowly."

"Are you going home now, Doctor?"

"Don't be silly," he said. "I'm going to stay here with you and help you have this baby."

Sitting on the edge of the bed, he felt the fatigue of the last twenty hours dragging at him and thought, "I'll grab a nap in the doctors' bunkroom and then we'll stimulate her labor."

"Excuse me," said the nurse, "but Emergency just called. They've just had an incomplete miscarriage come in. She seems to be hemorrhaging."

"Where's her own doctor?"

"In Chicago. She was just out here visiting when it happened."

"I'll be right down," he said. "Call the lab and tell them to do a blood count and blood-matching on her. Prepare for transfusions. Call surgery and tell them we may want to do a D&C."

As soon as he saw the patient his professional instinct sensed a crisis and he felt a sudden surge of strength blotting out the fatigue. She was a thin, blond girl in her late twenties, deadly pale, hollow-cheeked, her skin cold and clammy, barely able to speak to him in a tearful whisper.

"It came right out of me, Doctor. And then I began to bleed. The pain was worse than having a baby."

Swiftly he confirmed it. She was bleeding all right— from both uterus and cervix. A steady crimson flow that had to be brought under control quickly.

"Your baby must have passed, Honey," he said. "But there's still some tissue left in the uterus and it's making you bleed. We'll take you into surgery, give you a whiff of gas and get you fixed up." She nodded.

"My heart, Doctor," she whispered faintly. "I had an operation last year. My husband knows about it."

He was examining the curving scar beneath her left breast when her husband, back from parking the car, told him. It sounded like they'd gone in to correct a faulty valve.

"For Pete's Sake!" he told himself. "That's all I need to hear. This is turning out to be a great night! A hemorrhaging uterus and a heart condition. I'm going to need help with this one."

To the Emergency Room nurses he said, "Tell surgery we have an incomplete abortion that needs a D & C. She's a heart case and we'll need the heart monitor and an E.K.G. stat!"

A lab technician came in with a bottle of matched blood. "Start that into her," he told the Emergency Room crew. "We've got to get some more help in here."

From the Floor Desk he rang the home of Donald Hopkins, the Hospital Staff Cardiologist. "Don," he said, when Hopkins' voice answered, "it's Bob Henderson. Are you awake?"

"I'm sound asleep," said Hopkins.

"I'm over at the Hospital. We've got an incomplete abortion here in the Emergency Room. A girl from Chicago. She's hemorrhaging, her cervix is lacerated. It looks like someone tried to abort her and did a half-assed job. I'm going to have to go in and do a D&C and put her back together. The hooker is that she's had heart surgery. From what her husband can tell me it sounds like a mitral commissurotomy but she's still in chronic failure. Can you manage to come over and help me out?"

"I'll be there in about ten minutes," Donald Hopkins answered.

Henderson hung up and rejoined the nurses. "Did you get the transfusion started?"

"Not yet. She still has her blouse on."

"Forget the damned blouse," he said sharply. "Get it off later. I want blood started into this girl now."

In the corner of the Emergency Room an elderly alcoholic half rose from her stretcher.

"What are you boys and girls fooling around here at this hour for? Why aren't you out dancing?"

"That's what my wife keeps telling me," he said. "Take her into Surgery while I get dressed. Tell the anesthesiologist that Dr. Hopkins is on his way over."

In the Surgery locker room Henderson switched from his white maternity outfit to sterile green pajamas and jumper and was putting on his cap and mask when Don Hopkins came in, still yawning.

"Robert, you baby doctors may enjoy these weird night hours but you're going to ruin me. How much trouble are we in?"

"She's in there on the table," he said, tossing him a suit. "Let's take a look."

They went through the swinging doors and found the Night Operating-Room staff had tabled the patient.

They had rolled in a heart monitor and connected the electrodes to her wrists and ankles. A yellow dot danced, zipped, and looped erratically across the viewing screen.

Hopkins, eyeing the dot, was suddenly wide-awake, his voice carefully matter-of-fact. "Pretty chaotic pattern," he observed. "We're going to need a couple of minutes, Robert, before you can get started. You'll have to do it with a local. Go ahead and scrub while I see if I can find out what's involved here." He took the stethoscope the nurse handed him and bent over the patient. Scrubbing, Henderson could hear the anesthesiologist saying, "I don't like her blood pressure. It's still dropping," and Hopkins replying crisply, "I think it's simple blood loss causing that irregular pulse, not a new heart problem. We've got to get more blood into her fast."

Henderson cut the scrub short and stepped back into the operating chamber, thrusting out his arms for the knee-length, green gown and gloves the circulating nurse was holding, feeling her bow-knot it tight. As he watched Hopkins work rapidly to hook the second bottle of blood into the patient's other arm, he noted her pinched, chalky-white face, the anesthesiologist intently scanning his instrument dials, the yellow dot on the cardiograph machine looping unbelievably erratically.

"No blood pressure now," the anesthesiologist said. "She's fading," and then tautly, "her breathing has stopped."

"Give us a hand here, Bob," said Hopkins coolly.

Henderson stepped quickly to the transfusion apparatus and with his gloved hand began squeezing the rubber pressure bulb. The new blood boiled up darkly in the clear saline solution, flowing under maximum pressure through the plastic tube into the patient.

"Keep it up," Hopkins said. "Get it into her. Her heart will take it."

They stood squeezing rhythmically. The rest of the Operating-Room team stood poised, eyes flashing from the patient to the yellow dot. Silence held the room as moments crept by. Gradually the wild dipping and zooming of the dot slackened. It traveled in a more rhythmic ripple across the screen.

"She's coming back," Hopkins said. "Okay, Robert. She's all yours. Get going."

The nurse was ready with a fresh pair of gloves. Henderson punched his hands into them, dropped down on the low stool and went to work, packing the uterus, suturing a tear in the cervix that was adding to the hemorrhage.

"How is she?" he asked.

"Holding okay," said the anesthesiologist.

"She just didn't have enough blood left in her," Hopkins said, "but she'd better find a way to stay unpregnant—or find a better abortionist."

An estimated million American women were having abortions each year. Most of them were performed illegally, without proper medical supervision or hospital protection. Several hundred thousand of such women wound up in the hospital, and countless others died, as this patient tonight might have died right here on the table.

Some of the old-fashioned legislatures and private pressure groups who were resisting liberalized abortion laws could profit from a few minutes with a case such as this one. Yet you couldn't blame the legislators and lobbyists entirely.

"Regardless of the law," one doctor had pointed out, "there is a tremendous inner resistance within the medical profession to overcome. It is difficult for many physicians, conditioned by a lifetime commitment to preserve a life, to change their sights and practices so suddenly." The day when older and conservatively educated doctors would view an abortion as they did an appendectomy was simply not in sight.

But across the nation, the reform and repeal of outmoded abortion laws was underway. Reforms were being demanded by women's groups, social scientists, and a growing number of doctors and clergymen. The decision for an abortion, these groups believed, was a private matter to be decided by a woman and her doctor. Even the conservative American Medical Association went so far as to approve abortions for other than strictly medical reasons providing it did not violate the doctor's "good medical judgment" or "personally held moral principles."

But reforms were coming too slowly to prevent the birth of thousands of unwanted children, and injury or death to untold numbers of women. Even in states where abortion was legal, most hospitals were virtually unprepared to meet the expected flood of demands for abortion. The majority of medical societies had done little to help their physician-members cope with these anticipated demands. The wealthy and better educated would find a way. Some were even flying to Europe for an abortion—paying more than $1000 in air travel and medical costs for a $50 procedure. The poor and less well educated paid a higher price in greater risks of injury or death from the illegal backroom abortionists. In some of the larger U. S. cities there was a likelihood that a crime syndicate owned a piece of the action. They rented the apartment, financed the abortionist, and took a cut of his fee. And so long as the fee was paid, they cared nothing about the patients.

When Hopkins and Henderson had finished it was 3:20 A.M. Henderson headed for the Maternity Wing and found Barbara Michaels tossing, bathed in perspiration, wide-awake, bewildered, exhausted, angry, and still no nearer to giving birth.

"This is for the birds!" she panted. "I'll never go through this again, never. I swear it!"

"Come on now," he said, coaxing gently. "You told me all along how much you wanted this baby."

"Not now I don't," she said. "Get me out of here, will you?"

Under his hand palpating the abdomen, the uterus felt soft and boggy. What was the aphorism that his first obstetrics professor had been so fond of? "We seek to determine *not* what a woman can endure, but what she can accomplish."

"Right you are, Honey," he said. "I'm not going to let you go any longer."

In the corridor he said to Nurse Bates, "She's had it. Start the IV, Pitocin—and call me with the first pain. I'm going to flop on this stretcher. Watch the heart tones!"

"I'll start calling you in ten minutes," said Bates. "I know you. You sleep fast but wake up slow."

He seemed only to have been on the stretcher in the corridor an instant when the nurse was prodding him. "Heart tones are dropping. Down to 100."

He rose and swung his feet off the stretcher and sat for a moment, shaking off the fog of sleep. "What about the contractions?"

"No good. They last only about thirty seconds."

"Take her into Delivery," he said. "I'll be right with you."

He went into the lounge, cooled a cup of coffee with cold water, swigged it down, scrubbed up, and joined the team in the Delivery Room.

"Barbara," he said, gazing down at his patient. "What do you say—let's have this baby right now?"

"You said it, Doctor," she murmured.

He dropped to his stool and rolled in for a last-minute estimate of his situation.

The baby's position, he determined, was good enough, engaged in the pelvis, stuck at Station Plus One. There were no obstructions. The cervix was completely dilated, but the uterus was no help, even with the priming of the Pitocin.

"Make it twenty drops a minute to kick things along here and get me a forceps pack," he said. "Heart tones?"

"Down to eighty," Bates said.

Time to get the baby out now and no more kidding around.

"Oh, my!" gasped Barbara Michaels as the Pitocin hit her. "I'm getting a bad one!"

"That's good," he said. "That's what we want. Now push. Brace your feet in those stirrups and push—just like you were rowing a boat. You'll feel a sharp stick, now, Barbara, I'm putting the Novocaine in."

The anesthesiologist carried her through the contraction and the baby moved down a bit. Henderson slid the forceps in, guiding them with his hand over the head, and locked them.

Through the mist of fatigue Barbara Michaels moaned, "It's too much for me."

"Steady, gal," he said. "You've done it. You're all finished."

Guided by the forceps, the baby came out, pale blue, limp, almost lifeless.

In an instant he had clamped the cord, severed it and had the baby on the table, suctioning out the breathing passages, slipping a thin plastic tube into its mouth, down its throat and into its trachea. Bates, anticipating him, was there with the portable oxygen set. He took the aspirator between his lips and puffed into it gently as Bates aimed the stream of cool oxygen into his mouth.

Puffing, he watched the tiny infant's chest inflate and deflate. How many hundreds of times had he done this at Cook in similar crises with the voice of the instructor dinning in his ear!

"Not too hard, Henderson. Remember you're not blowing up a balloon. Those lung tissues rupture very easily!"

Never would he forget the night at Cook when he had bent over the perfectly formed newborn boy, puffing ceaselessly at the catheter, inflating the tiny chest for half an hour, blindly refusing to give up until the Senior Resident gripped his shoulder.

"Bob, quit it. You can't do any good. The portable X ray shows the kid's lungs never grew properly. There's just not enough tissue there to support life."

Now he felt the first tremor in the tiny limp body, swiftly withdrew the aspirating tube and let Bates squirt the stream of oxygen into the baby's mouth. A sudden gurgling gasp, flexing of the crumpled, ridiculously little limbs and then a real breath, and the doctor sat back, tingling with relief, feeling the exhilaration of observing the ever-miraculous gift of life.

"Here she comes," the nurse said. "Look at her respond!"

The infant was really squawling now, clenching and unclenching its tiny fists. "You took a beating, Honey," he said to the baby. "No wonder you're angry."

"Barbara," he said, "are you with us? You just had a little girl."

The nurse rolled the table over and Barbara Michaels managed to turn her head. Her eyes focused slowly, "She's beautiful," she murmured, "just beautiful."

Buoyed up by the oxygen the anesthesiologist had given her, suddenly revitalized despite her ordeal, in the wondrous way in which a woman who has just given birth comes back, she exclaimed exuberantly, "I wanted a girl and I got one!" and then swiftly changing the subject, "Doctor, did I tell you my husband has a new franchise for Chevrolet? He's doing very well."

"Hey, that's wonderful," he said. "I'll get him some customers."

"You'd better get a new car yourself, too," she said, and fell sound asleep.

He remained hunched on his stool, shoulders sagging, feeling the fatigue draining him again, waiting until the placental stage of labor had passed and he had the episiotomy sutures in. He removed the gown and gloves and mask. Crossing the corridor to the deserted doctors' lounge, now dimly illuminated by the graying dawn of another day, he sank into a chair to initial the delivery forms and certificates on the Michaels baby.

"I don't know whether they really drink any coffee in here or just sit around here all night spilling it," grumbled the attendant who was cleaning up.

"Neither do I," he said, propping up his legs out of the way of the man's mop. He wrote another note—to himself: "Don't forget those car plates!" and fell asleep.

5

That Miller Girl

His office nurse came and closed the door.

"That Miller girl is here again," she said in a low voice.

"Does she have an appointment?"

"No. She just walked in and took a seat. She's in for a long wait."

"No," Henderson said. "Let's get it over."

Once again the girl who called herself Audrey Miller was ushered into his office. She sat across the desk from him, visibly pregnant and smoking with a studied unconcern. It had begun exactly like this when she appeared two weeks before.

"Helen Marks sent me," she had said.

He remembered the Marks girl. She had lived in the area long enough to have him deliver one baby and had then moved into the city.

"Oh yes," he'd said. "How is she?"

"All right. She's moving to California."

"Well, what did you want to see me about?"

She exhaled a casual smoke ring. "I don't have any money and I'm pregnant."

"Well, that's not too unusual. Are you married?"

"No, but I know who the father is. But I don't want to keep the baby."

"You mean you can't get together? Is he married?"

"No, I just don't want to marry him. I just want to have the baby and get it adopted."

"How old are you?"

"Twenty-five."

She could be a few years either way. She was a big sexy-looking girl with a fall of false hair and plenty of makeup. Accentuated full lips. Well-bosomed. Earthy good looks. A maid of many beds.

"Well, let's see how you're coming along," he'd said, noting the nurse had an examining room ready.

"I make it about seven months for this pregnancy."

"That's about right."

"And you've had another baby?" He knew she had. His pelvic examination told him that.

"I had a couple," she said. "But I didn't keep those either."

He'd run into this kind before but they still bothered him. He busied himself with filling in the chart while she discussed her previous adventures.

"I was working at ... " She named a well-known department store in the city. "I was engaged both times it happened. I got sick leave and had them and they were adopted."

She was telling the whole thing with utter detachment. He could fill in the rest blindfolded. A high-school dropout who had taken the bus to the big city escaping a home life that was certainly no bargain or it wouldn't have had such devastating effects. You could call her ignorant and irresponsible or accept the word of the psychiatrists that she was leftover wreckage. Within her she carried her own self-destruction and a vindictive compulsion to create human beings who would help her strike back at society and retaliate against her own parents.

There were millions like her. Some got married. Some just drifted. They produced unloved children and these unfortunates, in turn, would breed a new generation of disturbed individuals.

This one seemed, somehow, sinister. Why, he wondered, had she not had abortions? Certainly not because of scruples! Or had she held up some married man for the price of the abortion and then not gone through with it? That guess seemed closer to the truth.

"We'll need some laboratory tests," he said, "but I'd say you're having a normal pregnancy."

"Do you think it could be arranged—the adoption?"

"Sometimes it's possible through the Hospital. I'll refer you to the social worker that handles your sort of request."

"Is this the only hospital in town?"

He was puzzled by the question. "Yes, it is."

"So the baby would be adopted locally?"

"I really don't know what the arrangements would be."

"Do they check to see if the people who get the baby have enough money?"

There was something about the question that raised his guard a notch higher. These were not the usual questions you were asked by unwed mothers. Usually it was, "Can you find someone who *really* wants a baby?"

"I'm sure the social workers look into all that," he said.

"In case there was any damage, they would handle that?"

"Damage?"

She lit another cigarette. "Well, when I first found out for sure that I was pregnant this time, I tried to stop it. I mean my boy friend tried to stop it. He didn't want me to be pregnant and he didn't want to pay for me to have anything done. So we—he tried to stop it."

"How?"

He listened impassively while she described the attempted abortion. Together she and the boy friend had positioned a rubber catheter tube into her cervix. Then they thrust a long knitting needle up the tube until it was inside the uterus.

"What happened?" he said.

"Nothing. Well, there was some blood, bright red

blood, on the needle when he took it out but I didn't feel anything. And nothing happened afterwards."

She paused for a puff on her cigarette. "So I think I ought to have a record. I mean a medical description from the hospital."

"What sort of a medical record?"

"Well, like if there was any damage done at that time. If there were holes poked into the baby by that knitting needle or into the afterbirth, wouldn't that show there was an attempted abortion?"

"What if it did?"

"Well, I've been told. A friend of mine said I could take him to court."

"Who?"

"The one who did it. I mean he did give me some drinks first before he tried it. It was done while I was under the influence. It was an assault on my unborn child my other friend said. Just for the record I ought to have something from the hospital. In case I wanted to go to court."

To himself he thought, "Lady, you are really something different! I've met a lot of bad-news types but there's always something new coming in that door."

"I'll have to look into that," he said aloud. "You'd better talk to Mrs. Dugan at the Hospital about your adoption." He scribbled a note. "Talk to me again after you've seen her."

At the Hospital a few days later the social worker caught up with him in the hall outside the cafeteria.

"That Miller girl. What do you think?"

"Why?"

"Well, I'll tell you what I think. I think that girl is dangerous."

"To whom?"

"I don't mean mentally. I mean I think she's up to something with some lawyer."

"I had the same feeling," he said. "She's too curious about the adoption, isn't she?"

"She certainly is, Doctor. I think she's out to grab the baby back. Or at least hold the adopting couple up for ransom. She has a six months option to change her mind you know."

"You got the word," he said. "Same as I did."

"I'd be afraid to put the child into the hands of anybody she could get at."

He nodded. "I suspect she may have pulled some fast ones before," he said. "When I see her I'm going to close her out."

Now as she took the seat across the desk from him, he felt the same wave of revulsion within him and an anguish for the baby that was coming. He suppressed it.

"I've spoken to Mrs. Dugan," he said. "She recommends that you get in touch with one of the large adoption agencies in the city. I think so, too."

She stared at him. "Those places are all down in the city," she said. "There must be a lot of people out here looking for kids, too."

"There probably are," he said, "but that's the way we prefer to handle it. I'll deliver the baby for you without charge, but that's all. Unless you want to be sterilized. I can refer you to a psychiatrist who would probably recommend it."

The stare she gave him was a complete blank. It must have taken her years to perfect that look.

"I'll let you know," she said.

"You do that," he said. "You've got a couple of months yet to make up your mind."

He doubted if he would ever see her again. Her lawyer friend, he reflected, would keep her busy shopping around. The black market in babies was still a lucrative business. The skies were full of lawyers jetting back and forth to arrange for babies born in one city to be "bought" for a childless couple in another. "Airmail Babies" was what they called them. For the right price, Audrey Miller would waive all rights including the six months option to recover the infant. When she came out of the hospital, there'd be a lawyer waiting at the airport. By nightfall the newborn babe would be with its new "parents" in another part of the United States. A neat, tidy day's work for a certain kind of lawyer.

6

"Chinese Gordon"

"Dr. Laden is calling," his secretary said.

"Good evening, Marvin," Henderson said, picking up the phone. "Where are you calling from—a drive-in-movie? I hear that's where a lot of you mind men go to peek at the latest Swedish sex films. Sneaking in under the cover of darkness instead of standing in line downtown where one of your patients might see you?"

"My patients bring their own films to show me at my office," Laden said. "I'm an expert on Polaroid closeups. As a matter of fact, I've just spent an hour with a patient who wants to rob a bank."

"Helping him get into the vault?"

"He doesn't need help. He works there. To wind up my evening office hours I'm going to persuade a nice little secretary that she doesn't have to shack up with some meatball she met at a weekend psychodrama."

"You call that work?" Henderson asked incredulously. "Taxi drivers give those pep talks to women passengers all day long. For fifty cent tips."

"Never mind," Laden said. "I'm calling because I thought I'd be hearing from you today about what gives with Mrs. Sinclair."

"She looked great when I saw her the other day," Henderson said.

The Sinclairs had responded enthusiastically to the proposal that Ruth Sinclair be sterilized. After talks

78

with Henderson and Laden, they had signed the request that Henderson would submit to the Hospital Committee. Buoyed up by the prospect of no further pregnancies and rested by her stay in the Hospital, Ruth Sinclair had calmed down and her hyperemesis had completely subsided.

"She's really pulled out of that depression," Henderson continued. "No more complaints. I haven't even had a call from her in a couple of weeks."

"That's what's bothering me," Laden said. "I hope we haven't built her hopes too high about getting sterilized. Did you happen to notice the new lineup on the Hospital Committee that has to approve it? I got my copy of the bulletin in the morning mail."

Henderson pawed through the stack of correspondence on his desk. Either Laden was not leading as hectic a life or, more probably, he was less disorderly.

"I didn't get to mine yet, Marv," he admitted. "What's with the committee?"

"They've rotated in some new faces for the summer season," Laden said. "Your man Stone went off and who do you suppose was appointed to take his place? None other than Lum Fong."

"Gordon?" Henderson said, startled. "Your Berkshire Institute guy?"

"That's right," said Laden. "The Imperial Wizard himself. He may give us some headaches. When can we talk about it?"

"I'll be closing down over here for the night," Henderson said. "By then it will be ten o'clock and I'd like to eat. Mary and the kids are away for a few days so how about meeting me over at the Club Car for a steak?"

"I'll be there," said Laden.

Considering Laden's news about Gordon as he drove to the former village railroad yards, Henderson was struck by the parallels. Where else but in the United States would some entrepreneurs realize that it would be profitable to convert a string of abandoned railroad dining cars and junked Pullmans into a complex of

Victorian-style restaurants? And where else also could an old fogy like Gordon, a Freudian psychoanalyst left over from the Twenties, be operating his updated computerized nut lodge for wealthy neurotics with equally spectacular success? America of the 1970s was a bonanza business for the Cult of Nostalgia and the Cult of the Expert. The major difference was that the gaslit restaurants and restored country inns provided their patrons with substantial servings of food and drink. Whereas patients of the Berkshire Institute would part with large sums of money for tests, consultations, and therapy and, save for the euphoria aroused by temporarily being the center of a great deal of attention, would then be sent on their way to resume driving themselves and the rest of the world crazy.

J. Arthur Gordon, M.D., Ph.D., was a tall, white-haired gent whose restrained dignity and courtly manner suggested either a long career in international diplomacy or years of playing the butler and the governor who wouldn't commute James Cagney's death sentence in old Hollywood movies. A longtime figure on the psychoanalytic scene, world traveler and professor emeritus at a couple of universities, Dr. Gordon was also widely known as an international authority on Chinese philosophy, a collector of Asian art, and a connoisseur of Chinese cooking.

The Director of the Berkshire Institute and Chairman of its Department of Psychiatry, he was also known to younger and less reverent members of the psychiatric fraternity as "Chinese Gordon," "The Grand Oz," "Oriental Arthur," "Chinese Meatballs," and "Lum Fong."

About ten years earlier, Dr. Gordon had turned up as the purchaser of a private mansion outside of town that was a perfect replica of a stone-walled French château. With a walled private courtyard, secluded landscaped lawns and gardens, wood groves, and fifty-two rooms, it was perfectly suited for transformation into the Berkshire Institute with a staff of psychiatrists, psychologists, and technicians. Patients usually remained for brief periods because, as Marvin Laden explained to Henderson, "The old Doc was smart enough to realize the time had come to get out of the sanitarium business—too many headaches with hired help. He switched over to where the big money is: psychometric testing, patient evaluations, staff conferences about referring patients to Encounter Groups— Marathon Psychotherapy—and the Mind Growth Colonies that suddenly are all over the place, and especially 'consultations.' That's his bag!"

The Institute had been humming along for years before Henderson, immersed in his practice, learned much about it. Gordon had staff privileges at the Hospital but seldom used them. Most of his patients were from the city or other parts of the country. They were flown into the International Airport and driven to the château in a limousine, and they departed in the same fashion. It wasn't until Henderson became well-acquainted with Marvin Laden that he learned about the place.

Laden knew a lot about the Institute because as he put it to Henderson, "I'm a fugitive from that dump."

Educated and trained in medicine and psychiatry at an Eastern university, Laden elected to seek a psychiatric post in the Middle West "because I wanted to be as far away from New York as I could get but not too close to California. With the salary they offered me at the Institute, I figured I could fly out to the Rockies to ski on weekends, but since I only stayed three months all I've got is the Ford camper that will get me up to Wisconsin."

Considerably put off by the brand of psychiatry he had encountered in New York and Boston, Laden had been stupefied by what he found going on at the Berkshire Institute.

"I thought I'd met some of the biggest frauds back in New York," he said, "but in the pure swindle, Gordon makes those Park Avenue guys look like guess-your-weight hustlers on the Coney Island boardwalk. And the thing that drives you absolutely crazy is that he's still got some sort of a reputation that dates back to the people he was associated with before the Depression."

In his early years Gordon had served on the staffs of some of the most prominent psychoanalysts in the country, but had never blazed any trails himself. Before long he was operating his own private sanitarium. With the financial assistance of a wealthy patient, he undertook his first field trips to China and carried out the studies which led to doctoral degrees in Chinese art and philosophy. In World War II he was appointed a Commander in the United States Navy Medical Corps, and, because of his special knowledge of China, was assigned to liaison duties with the Office of Strategic Services in Chunking and Shanghai. After the war he served in an advisory capacity to innumerable missions and committees of the United Nations. Presently, while serving as Director of the Berkshire Institute, and at a point in life when many of his contemporaries were under the sod or lapsing into nostalgic reveries, Gordon was circling the earth in jet airliners like a satellite.

"Why does he do it?" Henderson had asked Laden.

"Extraordinary ego drives," Laden had said. "Or to put it another way, simple greed and vanity. Where in the world can you be the center of so much deferential treatment, pampering, and solicitous attention as Lum Fong gets in the first-class seat of a jet plane bound for Tokyo and Hong Kong? All those stewardesses in kimonos! When he lands, there's always a committee bearing gifts and escorting him off as the guest of honor at tea ceremonies, and Geisha girl hangouts, and performances of the Kabuki Theater. When he leaves, he is given a farewell party and another trunkful of antique loot for the château."

Gordon returned from each visit to the Far East with further acquisitions—for what apparently was a most extraordinary private collection of rare Oriental art. Those who had glimpsed it reported that the château's library, which served as Gordon's private study, was an overpowering blend of medieval Gothic and centuries of Asian cultures.

The terra-cotta tile floor of the massive chamber was strewn with Persian carpets. The walls were hung with 15th Century Flemish tapestries, but in recessed niches between the ceiling-high windows were Chinese tomb figures: prancing horses with vermillion saddle cloths, tiny bronze and ivory miniatures of musicians, dancers, warriors, and jungle beasts that had amused the court followers of the Ming Dynasty.

Here, wearing a Mandarin coat of smoky blue silk, Gordon sipped tea and, with carved ivory chopsticks, sampled Chinese dishes prepared for him by his personal Chinese chef. "And that guy doesn't have to scrounge around downtown for Chinese beansprouts or Japanese seaweed," Laden had told Henderson. "Crates of the stuff are flown in from Japan and Formosa every week. The same helicopter that shuttles Gordon back and forth to the International Airport lands on that helicopter pad he installed on the château lawn. It swoops down to drop off live carp from Hong Kong or pick up Gordon for one of his global mystery trips."

"How come he still rates so high overseas?"

"Because they think he's got such great connections in Washington. He's heavily funded and he always lets them know it. How many financial grants have you received lately? From the Government or private foundations or a drug company?"

"I never had one," said Henderson.

"Well, Lum Fong is a leading authority on how to get grants," Laden responded. "He's always being funded by somebody for some damn project. That's one of the prime functions of the Berkshire Institute. That château is a very impressive place to visit—whether you come to bring money or as a patient. But the patients don't get to see much of Gordon. First, they have to work their way through his defense in depth, or pay their way might be a better way of describing it. They're interviewed by case workers. Then they're tested by psychologists. Later they may be seen by one of his staff psychiatrists. But not by Lum Fong unless they're in the real upper money brackets. All most of them see of him is the Blue Light."

"The Blue Light?"

"It's a blue panel with his name on it and it's in almost every room in the château. Even in the toilets. It flashes like a call light at the hospital when there's a message for you. All day long it flashes three or four times and then plink! Suddenly it flicks off."

"Because Gordon has answered the call?"

"Hell, no. He's not even there. It's programmed on tape to flash intermittently and then quit."

"Even when he's out of town?" Henderson asked.

"Out of town!" exclaimed Laden. "It flashes even when he's out of the country. He could be in Outer Mongolia but that blue light flashes. To reassure the patients that the Grand Oz is not far off and all is well."

Henderson ended his reflections about Dr. Gordon as he reached what at one time had been one of the busiest railroad junctions in this part of the Middle West, with steam locomotive repair shops, freight yards, and passenger and baggage depots. The tracks that had once thundered with transcontinental expresses now led nowhere. The yards and shops had been converted into a railroad museum and complex of cheerful Gay Nineties restaurants.

In the parking lot Henderson's car was taken by a teenager dressed in a brakeman's outfit and waving a red and green lantern. He went into what had been the round house for the engines, now the main restaurant and called The Round House. In the center of the huge structure a majestic mountain locomotive, completely restored, brass fittings gleaming, rotated slowly on a turntable moved by hydraulic power. A plume of steam wafted from its boiler. In the sunken repair pits chefs, wearing blacksmith aprons, tended broiling steaks and barbecued roasts. Surrounding the old steam king of the Rockies was a sea of dining tables. Canopied entrances led to the antique cars that were now restaurants: The Parlor Car; The Observation Car (specializing in color

TV sets for viewing sports events); The Mail Car (for men diners and drinkers only); the Kiddie Car (junior-sized portions and high chairs) and the Caboose.

Henderson mounted the steps to enter The Club Car. At its far end, in a red-plush banquette, amidst potted plants and vases of red roses, Dr. Marvin Laden sat sipping a Scotch and glancing through papers from his attaché case. The dining steward escorted Henderson down the car aisle lined with booths and banquettes, the walls hung with tasseled velvet drapes and reproductions of oil paintings of the Post-Civil-War Period.

Marvin Laden, wearing a "Stop at Two" button in his lapel (as part of his personal battle against the population explosion) was just ordering a caesar salad from a waitress in a black mini and net stockings.

"May I take your order, too, sir?" she said as Henderson sat down, proferring him a parchment paper menu.

"Yes, thank you," Henderson said, handing her back the menu. "But I don't need that. I'll have a double martini on the rocks, shrimp cocktail, sirloin steak, medium rare, a dish of sliced tomatoes, strawberry shortcake, and coffee."

Noting Marvin Laden's evil grin, he exclaimed, "Marvin, do you mind? I haven't eaten since lunch. At midnight my partner goes off call and I may spend the rest of the night at the hospital with labor and deliveries. This may be my last square meal for the next twenty-four hours—except for those saran-wrapped so-called sandwiches that come out of the machines. Now tell me. Why do you see your old pal Gordon as a problem in the Sinclair case?"

"Reprisals," Laden said. "Against me. Don't forget I yelled my head off before I quit out there. And he may know about the long report I filed with the Grievance Committee of his psychiatric association. As far as Gordon is concerned, I'm dead professionally, and if he can make me more dead, he'd like it."

"What are you suggesting?"

"Let me withdraw from the Sinclair case before her sterilization application comes before the Committee. You'll stand a lot better chance of getting approval. We can find another psychiatrist who will go along with that tubal ligation as soon as he's reviewed her case, seen her and her husband, and consulted with you about it. With my name off the application you shouldn't have any problem."

Henderson took a gulp from the martini the waitress had brought him and sat back to think it over. "It's hard to believe Gordon would be that petty."

"You can believe it all right," Laden said. "You've seen plenty of it yourself in Ob-Gyn and Surgery. You know what prima donnas some of those guys are. And Gordon is the worst."

"He's such a silly faker," Henderson commented.

"If he were only that," said Laden, "I wouldn't mind. We all know the world is full of thieves, nuts, and fakers. But Gordon is evil. He's immoral. He's not distracted by other people's problems because he himself is devoid of humanity. He's destructive because his kind of permissive therapy creates dissatisfaction and arouses false expectations in men and women who are emotionally disturbed or mentally ill.

"Wealthy couples with marital problems are one of his specialties. After he's put the husband or wife through a string of psychiatric tests and consultations with his staffers, which costs them plenty, he usually advises the patient to consider a divorce to achieve fulfillment and retain one's integrity—and drops the word that he happens to know a crackerjack lawyer in the city."

"Did you say 'crackerjack'?" inquired Henderson incredulously.

"That's his very word," Laden said. "Now you know I can't be making *that* up. Old Oriental Arthur really dates back quite a bit but he's still the swinger. Don't forget his computer facilities at the château are generously donated by a big data processing company. As part of a deal for some goddamned study he's doing for them."

"And the lawyer?"

"He's real, too. Probably the highest-paid matrimonial lawyer in this part of the country. And of course, the lawyer refers his freaked-up rich clients to Gordon for psychiatric guidance and therapy so it's a beautiful arrangement. Between them they must have split enough fees to buy a couple of Swiss banks."

Henderson shook his head. "How the hell do you collect all this stuff?"

"I know even more," Laden said. "I've got one of his secretaries for a patient. She quit the château after one of their teen-aged patients knocked himself off. Fong telephoned long distance to commiserate with the father and mother and after he hung up reminded her to be sure to add the cost of the telephone call to the family's final bill. I could keep on going but we'd be here for breakfast."

"But Gordon won't vote against Ruth Sinclair's sterilization," Henderson said. "Why would he do that? There's nothing in it for him. And it's right down the line with the latest psychiatric thinking all over the country."

"That doesn't make any difference," Laden said. "I predict that he'll cast a vote against it for several reasons. First, he'll see my name and recommendation on the application when it comes before the Committee. He knows I don't like him, but even more important he'll feel he'll have to vote against it to assert his seniority over me. Actually, Sinclair would be better off if I had been against it. Then Gordon would have been for it. He's too much of an egocentric not to take the opposite point of view from a disrespectful young punk like myself. In fact, he'll welcome the opportunity to put me down in the eyes of the Committee. Second, I suspect that he's probably ambivalent about women anyway. So what does he care if Sinclair or any other woman has to undergo the risks and discomfort of another pregnancy? Let them suffer a bit. Secretly, it might make him feel better. Of course, if Mrs. Sinclair is awarded any money in that auto accident case, he'd probably become a lot more interested. He might even have her hustled out to the Institute for some consultations and evaluations."

"Like hell," said Henderson. "And even if he wanted to knock you down out of pure malice, would he pull a trick like that on me? I've been around this town for a long time, you know."

"I know it," Laden said. "And I know that you were Chief of Ob-Gyn at the Hospital even before he bought the château and opened the Institute. You're one of the busiest guys in town. Top man on the Hospital staff. But have you ever sent Gordon a patient?"

"Christ no," Henderson said. "I never even met him. When he first came here, there were some invitations to visit his Institute but I was too busy chasing patients and delivering babies."

"He's probably huffy about that, too," Laden pointed out. "And he also may have checked you out and found you have too many ordinary patients. Not a heavy-fee practice with an office in the city. You're not his kind of bird."

"Well, I've got to be convinced," Henderson said. "This Sinclair sterilization is much too simple a case. I wouldn't consider for a minute taking your name off that application."

"Okay," Laden said. "You submit the application and see what happens. Maybe I'm just an alarmist or just obsessed about Gordon. I guess you don't want to settle for a vasectomy for her husband?"

"Bill Sinclair?" Henderson said. "No, at any rate not yet, Marvin."

"Well, it would be a hell of a lot simpler," Laden said, "and I hate to see Mrs. Sinclair get her hopes up so high and then have them cut right out from under her. Then we might have to worry about a really serious postnatal depression."

7

A Day in Court

"Do you swear to tell the truth, the whole truth, and nothing but the truth, so help you God?"

"I do," Henderson replied. He lowered his right hand and settled himself in the witness chair, glancing about the courtroom, conscious of the same sense of uneasiness he always felt in courtrooms.

He had not been convicted of any offense since he had been caught speeding during his college days, yet deep within him he carried mingled fears, distrust, and hostility toward American courtroom justice.

He neither liked nor trusted most of the lawyers he had met, and he felt the same way about the majority of judges. He considered them lazy, inept, egocentric political hacks. The United States jury system often seemed to him to be rigged for disaster. Here he was in a modern, exceptionally well-designed and furnished courtroom and he hated it. He found it oppressive. On the wall hung a plaque: *"IN GOD WE TRUST."* After numerous court appearances as a medical witness in injury and accident cases, in which he had been badgered, patronized, insulted and manipulated by lawyers, Henderson had concluded it should be changed to read, *"God Help Anybody Who Gets Dragged in Here!"*

Today he was a prisoner of his patient, Ruth Sinclair. A few days earlier he had been summoned to testify in her accident case. Together with one of his office nurses, Martha Williams, he had driven into the city with a box full of files and patient records. The jury had been hearing evidence all week and his appearance was supposed to be brief. "Just routine," Mrs. Sinclair's lawyer had assured him. Nevertheless, it was a nuisance and an aggravating pain in the neck. As luck would have it, Ed Russell, Henderson's partner, was out of town and Henderson had been forced to cancel a double load of office patients and hope that half a dozen others who were nearing term would not go into labor.

The jury regarded him with interest. Obviously to them he was an interesting specimen. A live obstetrician whose presence in the witness chair might add some spice to a trial that had been dragging along all week.

Approached now by the Sinclairs' attorney, Henderson began to suspect that he was viewing the cause of the slow pace. Certainly this member of the bar looked like a sane and fairly respectable citizen, but what was the matter with his clothes? His necktie was too loud and his suit was baggy. The trousers sagged in clusters around his ankles. Why was he so sloppy looking? Was his thinking equally untidy? Did he think he was Clarence Darrow?

Withholding judgment, Henderson answered patiently as the lawyer led him through a recitation of his education and medical training. Seven years after her accident, and after endless haggling and legal shilly-shally between her attorneys and the lawyers for the insurance company, Ruth Sinclair was finally having her big week in court. Henderson wasn't going to detract from it if he could help it.

Today Ruth Sinclair, though perhaps a trifle pale, looked even more smashing than usual. Her reddish-gold hair luxuriantly framed her face. She was outfitted in a navy-blue-and-white suit and, with her long-white-gloved hands folded carefully in front of her, managed to radiate dignity, motherhood, and voluptuous sex.

With her sat her husband in his blue fire-department uniform and their three children. Why in God's name was the whole family including the kids there? To testify about their mother's miscarriage? To gain the sympathy of the jury and enhance the possibility of a verdict or financial settlement in her favor? Legal maneuvering of some tawdry sort, no doubt, Henderson concluded.

Henderson responded dutifully as "Baggy Pants," in direct examination, brought out that he had been called to the Hospital Emergency Room where Mrs. Sinclair had been rushed by ambulance after her accident. He confirmed her injuries—numerous bruises and contusions of both knees and elbows—and her condition—approximately three months pregnant. He confirmed that he had immediately admitted her to the Hospital for further observation.

"Did you fear a miscarriage—an aborted pregnancy?" Ruth Sinclair's lawyer asked.

"Yes."

"Why?"

"Because there is always a danger that a severe physical shock may precipitate an abortion—miscarriage."

Henderson reached for a chart that he had brought with him, anticipating that he would be requested to describe the state of growth of a three-month fetus in the mother's womb. But to his surprise "Droopy Drawers" did not see fit to pursue the point. Instead:

"On March 15 you discharged Mrs. Sinclair from the Hospital?" was his next question.

Henderson felt let down. He had been prepared to provide the jury with at least a condensed summary of vulnerability of the plus-three-months pregnant female. Judging by their expressions the jury was disappointed, too. He leafed through his sheaf of aging Hospital records and found the March 15 date scribbled on a chart.

"Yes." he said.

"But you readmitted her to the Hospital on April 4, just two weeks later?"

"Yes."

"Why?"

"She had telephoned me from her home to report she was 'spotting.' That is, she had noted evidence of some sort of internal bleeding. I confirmed it with my own examination at the Hospital and admitted her as a patient with an imminent threatened abortion. The bleeding persisted and the pregnancy was terminated by an abortion—the layman's term is miscarriage—forty-eight hours later."

"She lost the baby?"

"That's right."

"In your professional opinion, could the automobile accident of February 28 have caused Mrs. Sinclair's miscarriage?"

Henderson paused. He wanted to choose his words carefully.

"Yes."

He waited for the next question which he presumed would be, "Why?" It didn't come. He looked at Mrs. Sinclair's lawyer but all he was doing was hitching up his sagging trousers and staring at the ceiling. Was this his idea of an impressive silence? Henderson looked at the Judge. The Judge aroused himself and addressed the Sinclair lawyer.

"Counselor?"

"No further questions, your Honor."

For God's sake, man! Henderson exploded to himself. You're missing your chance to get some information out here! Don't tell me you dragged me away from thirty patients for those questions!

But that was apparently all the attorney had in mind. And now the lawyer for the company that had insured the driver of the other car was approaching the witness stand. Henderson eyed him warily. This one was a sleek and well-tailored reptile. His shoes gleamed. In what looked like a $15.00 haircut not one hair was out of place. The suit was expensive and sagged not a quarter of an inch.

"So, Doctor, you think that this miscarriage was definitely caused by the automobile accident that occurred nearly a month earlier?"

"No," Henderson replied. "I think there is a possibility that it was caused by the accident."

So now the term "possibility" was being explored by the opposition. Already, it seemed to Henderson, that thanks to Mrs. Sinclair's inept legal representative, *he* was being put on the defensive. This was the explanation that he had been prepared to give to *her* attorney.

"Doctor, have you personally published reports in medical journals relating to spontaneous abortion, or miscarriage as we laymen know the term?"

"No," Henderson said.

"No, but as a practicing obstetrician . . . "

He was interrupted by the lawyer. "Excuse me, your Honor, may the witness be directed to answer the questions."

"You may just answer the question with a yes or no, Doctor," the Judge said.

Henderson nodded. "The answer then is no," he said.

"Isn't it true that many pregnant women suffer injuries in automobile accidents and other injuries of an even more serious and traumatic nature without losing a baby in a miscarriage?"

"Yes."

That was a point he had wanted to elaborate earlier under direct examination. Some women could fall off the roof and not abort the pregnancy.

"And," pursued the insurance lawyer, "when you examined Mrs. Sinclair after the accident were there any signs or symptoms or any other evidence that suggested that her pregnancy was threatened as a result of the accident?"

"She had suffered a severe shock," Henderson said. "She was emotionally upset. She was subject to a great deal of emotional tension."

"But were there clinical signs or symptoms of a miscarriage?"

"No."

"You hospitalized her merely as a precautionary measure?"

"Yes." Henderson answered. But he was thinking to himself: what's not being brought out by this line of questioning is that in my professional opinion she was just the type of patient who *might* abort a baby.

"I would like to add to that," he said. "May I say . . ."

The insurance-company lawyer pounced on him. "Excuse me, Doctor, may *I* ask the questions?"

"Henderson looked at the Judge, who shook his head.

"You may just answer the questions, Doctor," he said. "The attorney is directing his examination in a perfectly proper manner."

Henderson nodded. All right, you pompous fathead, he said to himself. You'd rather play around with procedures than bring out the whole story! He shoved himself back in the chair, controlling his blood pressure and concealing his wrath. Cool it, he told himself. Wait until the oaf representing Ruth Sinclair comes back for a second round of questions. Perhaps then there will be an opportunity to bring out the relationship between tension and spontaneous abortion.

"During Mrs. Sinclair's extended stay in the Hospital you did not encounter any evidence that her pregnancy was threatened?"

Henderson hesitated. How was it possible to explain to the jury that as a physician you developed certain intuitive feelings about certain patients?

"Doctor, would you please answer the question. I say again, as the weeks in the Hospital passed"—now there's typical lawyer baloney, Henderson thought to himself. It was just about two weeks. He makes it sound like she was in for months!—"you did not find any evidence that her pregnancy was threatened?"

"You may answer yes or no, Doctor," the Judge said.

Henderson shrugged. "No," he replied.

Now the lawyer flipped open his fancy leather loose-leaf notebook in which he seemed to have Xerox copies of Hospital records. These days everybody had Xerox copies of everything!

"You have testified that on March 15 you discharged Mrs. Sinclair from the Hospital. Could that be an error?"

Ah, now what do we have here? Henderson was thinking to himself. Some sort of a trap, no doubt. He fumbled through the sheaf of six-year-old medical records: Hospital Chart notations jotted down with good and bad pens at all hours of the day and night, pale fuzzy carbons of typed Hospital forms. He knew that whenever he had been at the Hospital during that period he had dropped in to see Mrs. Sinclair to check her condition and note her progress. Whatever the time, midnight or high noon, he had scribbled notes on her chart, not always being careful about his penmanship. And the typing that had been done by the Hospital clerks and his own staff would not have won any prizes. Some of the pages would have to be sent to an FBI laboratory if you wanted a real verbatim transcript.

Rather than come up with the wrong answer he took his time. Silence descended on the courtroom. Everybody was watching him and waiting and Henderson realized that the insurance company attorney, smoothie that he was, was deliberately letting him fumble. Obviously the louse had the correct discharge date right there in his fancy looseleaf notebook, but he wasn't going to bring it out. He was enjoying letting Henderson appear to the jury as a fogbound fumbler: why, this quack can't even read his own records! How can he possibly have an opinion that's worth a nickel. Probably, if the truth were known, he himself is responsible for the miscarriage. Begrudgingly, Henderson admired the way the slickster was handling the case. He was playing it according to the set of rules endorsed by the American judiciary, the adversary process! What a heap of hypocritical bull!

Finally he found a chart notation that appeared to be related to Mrs. Sinclair's discharge from the Hospital. Wasn't it the 15th of March? No, sure enough, Mrs. Sinclair's Perry Mason had pinned the donkey's tail on him! He had said the 15th and Henderson had foolishly gone along with it and now he could see that the seven-year-old date actually was the 12th.

"Yes," he replied to the lawyer, "I think the correct date was March 12." So here he was, caught with *his* pants down by this lizard who was obviously setting him up some more good zaps.

Holding the notebook in front of him, the attorney nodded and then said, "I see here that someone wrote on Mrs. Sinclair's chart that she was to be permitted limited smoking. Is that your notation, Doctor?"

Henderson examined his blurred records. Those were his initials all right.

"Yes."

"Why?"

"Because at that time Mrs. Sinclair was still smoking cigarettes regularly. She had felt the lack of cigarettes since she entered the Hospital and she requested that she be permitted to resume smoking on a limited basis."

Actually she had been bitching and yelling for a week about his keeping her off cigarettes.

"Are not cigarettes considered a possible hazard to pregnancy?"

"Yes."

"You are familiar with the research studies that deal with the adverse effect of cigarette smoking by pregnant mothers on unborn babies?"

"Yes."

"Do you agree that an unborn baby may develop less completely if his mother smokes? That he may weigh less at birth, for example?"

"Yes."

The lawyer displayed a Xerox of a research paper from an eastern medical research center. "Are you familiar with this research report by Doctor Karlis Adamsons and doctors Terusada Horiguchi, Arsenio C. Comas-Urrutia, Kotaro Suzuki, and others?"

"Yes," Henderson said. He again had to admire the way this character sang out the names of those researchers. The skunk must have practiced them in his bathroom for a week.

"I would like to read from this report to the jury, your Honor," the insurance-company attorney said.

"Permission granted," the Judge replied.

"The use of radioactive nicotine," the lawyer read from the report summary, "enabled the scientists to show that nicotine introduced into the mother's bloodstream, swiftly crosses the 'placenta barrier,' reaching a plateau in an (unborn) baby monkey fifteen minutes after the injection. Dr. Suzuki estimated that a pack of twenty cigarettes could yield one milligram of nicotine per each kilogram of body weight in an average American expectant mother, depending on how much she inhales."

He paused to let the emphasis of the report have a maximum effect on the jury.

Henderson decided to put an oar in. "May I comment, your Honor?"

This time the Judge nodded.

"I take no issue with the report the attorney is quoting from. In fact, I now encourage and advise all my patients to give up smoking and in some cases, *forbid* my pregnant patients to smoke. But I would like to emphasize that Mrs. Sinclair had been in an automobile accident that caused a shock to her nervous system. She was anxious and nervous, which is not an ideal condition for a pregnant woman. The sudden deprivation of her cigarette smoking certainly was making her more tense. It was a matter of permitting her to smoke but only to a limited degree—a few cigarettes a day."

"You say that she is extremely emotional?" the lawyer quickly noted.

"I mean she is normal but emotional. The accident had increased her tension."

"No further questions," said the insurance-company eagle.

He folded his leather notebook and glided back to his table with a satisfied glance in the direction of the jury.

Congratulations to you, brother! Henderson thought to himself. So now you've presented a picture of Ruth Sinclair as a cigarette-craving, emotionally unstable patient. You've done your job well. The jury can now consider whether she lost the baby because she smoked cigarettes or was a nervous wreck without dwelling too much on the contributory aspects of being tossed in a heap in a jolting, terrifying car smashup. Well, if he could enlarge on the role of tension in pregnancy and spontaneous abortion he might give them a more balanced picture. He waited for Mrs. Sinclair's lawyer to pick up the leads he had given him, but to his astonishment, he heard him say, "No further questions."

"That will be all, Doctor," the Judge said. "Thank you for your testimony."

Henderson sat for a moment, absorbing his own shock and outrage at what appeared to be the laziness or ineptitude of Mrs. Sinclair's counsel. This goat was actually going to rest on his laurels without engaging Henderson in a further discussion! Why? What was his strategy? Why let the insurance company have the last word? Or did this guy feel that all he had to do was plant Ruth Sinclair and her fireman husband and children in the courtroom and there would be an automatic financial settlement in her favor? Had, in fact, the two lawyers already reached some sort of understanding and was all this a charade—on *his* time? He had wanted to help Ruth Sinclair and present a fair picture to the jury of how tension might contribute to a miscarriage, but that apparently was not what either side particularly wanted. Another memorable day in court!

Now his mind automatically went back to his own schedule. It was three P.M. by the courtroom clock. As

he went up the aisle, he nodded to the Sinclair family—
you weren't supposed to be too friendly with anybody
in court, motioned to Martha Williams to join him with
the box of reports and charts that he had thought he
might need for his educational lecture, and exited from
the courtroom. His eye went for a phone booth so that
he could check in with the answering service and hospital but there were legal indians in all of them. He
escorted Martha Williams into an elevator and fingered
for a dime in his pocket. He would make the calls from
the parking garage.

He handed Martha Williams the parking-garage ticket and a five-dollar bill.

"You pay this thing and ask them to get us the car in
a hurry," he said. "I'll telephone to see what's been
going on."

It always bothered him to be completely out of touch
with his answering service for more than an hour. He
wanted to know what was happening at all times. At
the garage he found a booth, sat down, dialed the
answering service and got a long series of rings. They
were so busy they needed a new switchboard and more
girls. He would raise more hell about it tomorrow.
While he was waiting for an answer he reached into the
adjoining phone booth and dialed the Hospital. Holding
both phones he found himself getting no answer on one
and a busy signal on the other. More switchboard
problems! The whole goddamned system was breaking
down. He redialed the Hospital Maternity Floor on a
direct line—busy too! He reduced his respiration to
slow deep breaths and shut his eyes, testing his sanity
and waiting to see who would answer which phone
first. Opening his eyes, he saw a stranger ogling him
curiously. Here he was with two phone booths and a
phone to each ear—the guy probably thought he was a
horse player or a bookie.

The answering service came through while the Hospital line was still ringing busy.

"Oh, yes, Dr. Henderson. I was just going to try to
reach you. I have the husband of one of your patients

on another line. A Mr. Burton. He says his wife is having contractions every seven minutes."

"Seven minutes!" exclaimed Henderson. "Why didn't she call me sooner?"

"Her husband says she wanted to have time to fix her hair before going to the Hospital."

Henderson had risen hastily from his seat in the phone booth and was craning his neck to see if Martha Williams had the car yet. She was just standing there. There was no sign of the parking attendant.

"You tell her to forget about that hairdo and get started for the Hospital right now. Tell her I'll meet her there. She's to go directly to the Maternity Floor. They will be expecting her. I'll hold on while you give her those directions. Then plug me in to Maternity at the Hospital."

He stood half in and out of the phone booth, watching for the car, feeling himself responding to this bit of news with quickening pulse and rapid breathing. He hadn't counted on delivering Mrs. Burton until later in the week. Now here she was in full labor and it was a third child that was coming. With a "multip" (multipara—a woman who had had two or more pregnancies resulting in viable offspring) you could never tell how fast a third child might move through labor. When patients fooled around at home until their contractions were only seven minutes apart, they were apt to be delivered in the car or on the Hospital sidewalk. And here he was, twenty miles away! He *might* make it, but he could take no chances. With his partner on vacation he would have to grab whoever was on the Maternity Floor and ask them to hang on until he got there. A voice came on the Hospital line, crisp and businesslike. He recognized it as Weaver, the Day Supervisory Nurse of Maternity.

"Hello, Weaver," he said and then to put her on the defensive, "what's all the gabbing on the house phones? I couldn't get an open line to you."

"Dr. Fowler is here," Weaver replied smoothly. "He's been busy with several calls from patients."

Weaver was always good with the counterjab.

Fowler, able and energetic, was one of Henderson's chief rivals in the local Ob group. Weaver would enjoy letting Henderson know that Fowler was busy and making money while he was monkeying around a courtroom.

"Fine," Henderson said, aimiably. "Can you get him on the line? I'd like to talk to him, too. And Weaver, I've got a patient coming in. Mrs. Burton. She's a multip with good contractions. Take care of her yourself until I get there. You'd better have a cart (wheeled stretcher) ready for her."

"Will do," Weaver answered in her best Air Force Nurse manner. "Here's Dr. Fowler."

"Afternoon, Bob," Fowler said. He had a way of sounding so relaxed and casual that Henderson suspected he could put a patient to sleep without benefit of anesthetic.

"Hello, George," Henderson said. "I know you're busy but I was wondering if you could cover for me for about half an hour. I've got a multip coming in with seven minute contractions and it's going to take me that long to get over to the Hospital."

"Sure thing," Fowler drawled. "I've got two going here this afternoon but I don't think it will be until after that. I'll have Weaver call me for a look when she gets here. What's her name?"

"Burton. Weaver will get her 'ready file' for you. I'm on my way."

The parking attendant was stepping out of the car and Martha Williams was getting in. Henderson handed the attendant a tip and slid in behind the wheel.

"Well," he said, easing the car out into the street traffic, "I just checked the Hospital and wouldn't you know we have a baby coming."

"Oh for goodness sake!" exclaimed Martha Williams fervently.

"We'll be all right, I think," Henderson said. "Dr. Fowler happened to be on the floor and he's going to cover for me. With a little luck I'll get out of this town without any mistakes and I just might make the delivery. Watch those overhead signs for me."

He threaded his way through the city traffic and shot up a ramp to the southbound expressway out of the city. There was no time for conversation about the courtroom and the Sinclair case. Martha Williams knew him well enough to know that when there was a delivery coming, he always wanted to concentrate; to summon up a clear picture of the patient, her specific condition, the possible complications, to gather himself together for a focus on this woman and her child and the climactic moments of a human event that had been nine months in preparation.

Now, as they slowed to pass through one of the expressway's tollbooths, he was seized with an inspiration. A State Highway Patrol car was just pulling through, headed in the opposite direction. Leaning from his window, Henderson called, "Officer, I'm a doctor. I've got a baby to deliver at Valley Community Hospital. Can you give me a little help with this traffic?"

He had flipped open his wallet to display his County Medical Society ID card and handed it to the toll-booth man. The toll-booth man passed it to the policeman who examined it quickly and handed it back.

"How about the Fremont exit?" the policeman said. "I can take you that far without calling another car."

"Many thanks," Henderson called. "That will do it."

To Martha Williams he said, "Here we go. You'd better check your safety belt!"

He pulled on through the toll gate and in his rear-view mirror saw the police car making a sweeping U-turn through the traffic lines. The red beacon on the roof of the car had begun to rotate and as the car swept past them, the cop switched on his siren. It had a nice, satisfying, ear-piercing shriek. Henderson put his foot down to the floor and stayed right behind the police car as the traffic parted to let them through into the fast lane of the expressway. Beside him, Martha Williams sat speechless, feet braced against the floorboards. She was getting more out of their day in court than she had expected.

Zooming along at eighty miles per hour, Henderson began to feel more relaxed. He had a clear picture of his patient in mind, and with the speed the cop up front was providing he stood a good chance of getting to the Hospital ahead of the baby.

"Did you get that lawyer's name?" he asked.

"You mean Mrs. Sinclair's lawyer?" Martha Williams said. "I think it's Davis. William Davis."

"No, not him," Henderson said. "I mean that wise guy from the insurance company. He's the one *I* want if I ever get in a jam. God knows where Sinclair got that saphead Davis but I wouldn't hire him to get me a dog license. What time is it?"

"Three-twenty-five," Martha Williams said. She was trying not to gasp as the speedometer crept up between eighty-five and ninety and the cop's siren screamed a little louder.

"If I don't get to deliver this baby," Henderson said, "and Fowler does it for me, I'll have to pay him a fat fee. I'll send the bill to that genius representing the Sinclairs, for dragging me down to the city."

They were nearing the Fremont exit. Henderson could see the village water tower and estimated the Hospital was only three minutes away.

"You'd better slow down," Martha Williams said between clenched teeth. "Fremont happens to be the next exit."

"I know it," Henderson said, "but I like this cop. I hate to leave him."

He flicked on his signal blinker for a right turn, rolled down his window and waved a salute of thanks to the trooper, braked hard and zipped down the ramp off the expressway.

"I'm going in the back door," he said as he turned off the road to bump across the ruts of a farmer's field and then through an unplowed, snowbound parking lot which put him in the rear of the Hospital.

"You keep the car. I'll see you later at the office."

He unsnapped his safety belt, slid out of his seat, raced in a service-entrance door and through the cafeteria kitchen. Smiling brightly at the cooks and dishwashers he took the backstairs route to the Maternity Floor rather than wait for an elevator.

He emerged from the stairway just as Weaver was passing. She immediately pounced on him.

"Hey, what's the big idea of waiting until the last second with this one?"

"Believe it or not, Weaver," he said, "she just called me from home a moment before I called you. How is everything?"

"Dr. Fowler is ready to deliver her."

Weaver, despite her professional calm, was nonetheless flustered. "She's eight centimeters dilated," she snapped, as if Henderson were personally responsible, "and her bag of waters went while we were prepping her."

"Keep cool, Weaver," Henderson said, dodging into the doctors' locker room. "I can't afford to pay Fowler. If I don't make it, you catch the baby for me."

He stripped down to his shorts and yanked on a fresh white cotton jumper and trousers and thrust his bare feet into blood-spattered shoes. When he came out his patient was still in the labor room wearing the indignant, ruffled-feathers look of a woman who has been hurried.

"Is it a boy or girl?" he asked mischievously, picking up a rubber glove from the tray for the examination.

"It's going to be a boy, Doctor," Mrs. Burton said defiantly, "but I don't know what this rush is all about. I know the baby isn't coming yet. That's why I didn't call you earlier."

Now that he had her there safely on the Delivery Floor he could grin back at her. His gloved hand had found the baby: Station Plus Three. Right on the perineum. The cervix fully dilated.

"Honey," he said, "that hair style looks great but it's a good thing you didn't decide to give yourself a permanent. You might have had this baby in a snowdrift. It's here—right now."

She stared at him in disbelief. "I don't believe it," she protested. "It hasn't hurt that much yet. I've always been *much* later than this, Doctor. You know that."

"I know you've got a baby coming. That's all I know," he said. "Roll her in, Weaver, while I get scrubbed."

At his word, the Delivery Room Nurse, fidgeting in the doorway, shot away to marshal her forces: "Multip coming! Let's go, everybody!"

The corridor flurried with activity. As he scrubbed, the stretcher whizzed by behind his back, and when he stepped into the Delivery Room they were swirling around the table, positioning his patient. He knew it was close—as close as Weaver, a pro from Cook herself, had known, but he couldn't resist pausing deliberately to adjust his mask and ask in mock surprise, "What's everybody so shook up about? Didn't any of you ever see a baby born before?"

"Dr. Henderson," said his patient, still protesting as they positioned her in the stirrups. "I'm *sure* I'm not ready!"

He stood gazing down at her, thrusting out his arms for the gown and gloves the nurses were holding. "I don't think you are either," he said solemnly.

Glancing at the wall clock which pointed to 4:26 he said to the Delivery Room team, "I'll bet you all steak dinners we don't have a baby here before four-thirty."

The anesthesiologist, on his perch beside the patient's head, was laughing behind his mask. "Do you see what I see, Bob?" he asked. In the overhead mirror the anesthesiologist had a sharply focused view of the patient's perineum and could see it dilating.

He dropped on his stool and rolled in close, swiftly clamping his instruments on the thigh drape. Before him his patient's hip rose suddenly in the stirrup to the accompaniment of a wail of shocked surprise, "Oh God! Now I *am* getting an awful pain!"

"Keep your bottom on the table, Honey," he said,

and then to the anesthesiologist, "give her a whiff, George."

The baby was coming. There would be no need for an episiotomy with this one. As Weaver pitchered the soap over his hands, the perineum continued stretching beautifully. The baby's head was nicely positioned. Through his rubber-gloved fingers he could feel its pulse beating strong beneath the fontanelle membrane of its head.

"Honey," he said to the patient, "you're doing fine with this baby. When you get the next pain, give me one more real push."

The gas was blurring her as the contraction overwhelmed her. "Okay . . . okay," she gasped. "Okay!"

"Here we go now," he said. "A real push. That a gal! Go to town!"

He had the baby's head in his left hand. There was no cord problem and while he was still suctioning out the mouth and nasal passage, the pale blue corner of the right shoulder thrust out. He grasped its rubbery corner and the baby, rotating, dropped out into the crook of his left arm, trunk, arms, legs, and feet in one continuous motion. A gush of fluids and Bingo! It was all over.

He was still snapping the clamps on the umbilical cord when Weaver, never one to ease up, was peering triumphantly over his shoulder.

"You lose, Dr. Henderson. The time is 4:29. It's a girl and I'll bet she's under six pounds."

"Give her a tickle, Weaver," he said, scissoring the cord and chuckling. "Make her squawk. She sure wanted out fast."

The nurse tapped the baby expertly and in an instant there was the familiar gasp and exhalation followed by the thin cry and then the wails of the squirming, miniature human.

"She's going to be a real tiger, that one," he said. "How's her mother?"

"Doing okay, Bob. Blood pressure 130 over 80. Pulse 100."

"Let her sleep while we wait for the placenta."

The placenta passed normally and then the circulating nurse was back with the baby, sponged clean and ready for finger-printing.

"Miss Weaver was right about the baby's weight, Dr. Henderson," she was giggling. "She might have made six pounds but she piddled a bit as I carried her down the hall and came out five pounds, 15 ounces."

"All right," he said, laughing. "Well I owe you all steak dinners. It was a terribly difficult delivery and I couldn't have done it without you."

8

A Pain-Free Birth

Henderson had finished showering and shaving and was brushing his teeth. He expected to spend the rest of the night wide-awake at the Hospital. He had been plotting that if this Gibson maternity case went well, he would casually invite Henry Palmer or any of the other skeptics and holdouts in the local obstetrics group who happened to be at the Hospital to observe his patient as she was supported through labor and delivery by paracervical anesthesia and pudendal block. And he intended to be crisply shaved and lotioned for the occasion, rather than sporting a fuzzy overnight growth of whiskers.

There was still some resistance and disapproval to the use by Henderson and his partner of the paracervical anesthetic procedure. Henderson wanted to gather more disciples as he demonstrated how remarkably effective this local anesthetic approach could be. Let the word get back to some of the old coots who ran the County Medical Society! Now, in his mind as he brushed, swished, and rinsed, he pictured the grudging shrug and the admission, "Well, Henderson seems to be getting some pretty fair results . . . "

If the paracervical method he was using continued to bring an unbroken string of relaxed, pain-free deliveries, he might even be invited to address some state medical meetings. He raised his hand with a flourish to acknowledge the imaginary applause and beamed into the bathroom mirror. The toothbrush shot from his grasp, caromed off the tiled wall and plopped into the cat's box of Kitty Litter.

He snarled a silent oath. This wasn't the first time the cat's box had swallowed up his toiletries. He had previously lost soap, shaving brush, toothpaste. To hell with the toothbrush! Let it lie there among the plastic sand and lumps of cat dung. Why was a cat defecating in the bathroom when she had the run of the great outdoors? Because, his wife had explained patiently, she—the cat—preferred to "go" in the house.

Between him and this cat there existed a silent, undeclared cold war. It was sheer endurance with him sometimes sitting on the toilet and the cat sitting in its Kitty Litter box, both moving their bowels and scowling at each other, vowing to fight to the finish.

The cat would no doubt discover his toothbrush in her litter box. She would go to work to oust it, vigorously pawing urine-soaked granules of plastic sand around the bathroom floor for all the little bare feet to step in first thing in the morning. There would be shrill, childish voices piping amidst the pre-school bus and breakfast melee, "Mommy, look at the mess Daddy and the cat left in the bathroom!"

He retrieved the granule-coated toothbrush with a wad of toilet tissue, packaged it in a paper towel and thrust it deep down in the waste basket.

Completing his dressing he stepped out the front door and found himself shivering in a breeze that was still full of winter on this April night. He moved across the lawn, stepping lightly and cautiously, on the lookout for small boys' forgotten bicycles or skunks that might have emerged from winter hibernation to raid the garbage cans. From the barn came the mournful halloo of Bingo, now properly incarcerated with the pony, and from the porch rafters a muffled squawk as Count Dracula, the crow, acknowledged his departure. Further away in the darkness he could hear what sounded like the engine of a farm tractor. What was his farmer neighbor doing at this ungodly hour? Spring plowing? Burying his wife? Bulldozing her deep in a cornfield after a family argument?

Henderson slid into the icily cold car and positioned a sheepskin beneath his buttocks: an indulgence he permitted himself against chilly drafts while driving to and from the hospital.

"You'll freeze your behind in this job," one of his colleagues had warned him when he first started his suburban practice. There were physicians who seemed to have no difficulty managing the practical aspects of their life. They had tidy heated garages which they entered from within their domiciles and electric eyes which opened the garage doors on signal when they returned. It was his fate—and his own fault—that such was not the case here. The barn-garage had become the pony stables. They had not added a garage to the old farmhouse.

"It would be silly to be always opening and closing those doors," was the way Mary had dismissed such a project. "Besides, you'd be constantly waking us all up the way you come and go at all hours of the night."

He had put off the garage addition and every winter slithered over ice and through slush and snowbanks to climb into the cold car, vowing to get something built during the spring and summer but never quite getting around to it. Often at such moments he had marveled at the physical stamina of firemen such as Bill Sinclair. One moment they were asleep in their warm beds on the second floor of the firehouse. Then the bells began to bang out an alarm. Almost as one man, the hook-and-ladder company flung back blankets, swung feet around into sock-draped trousers, and moved swiftly across the room to slide down the brass poles. Within fifteen to twenty seconds, they were rolling down the street in zero weather, clinging to the sides of the big hook-and-ladder truck. Two minutes from the instant they had swung out of bed, they might be scaling aerial ladders, racing up fire escapes or flights of stairs, subjecting their bodies to maximum stress from violent exertion, heat, smoke, and flames.

As a physician, Henderson had long been fascinated by the physiology of firefighting: sudden maximum stress, adrenalin pouring into the bloodstream, pulses pounding around 140–160, blood pressures zooming.

He had often mused over what a stress study one might make if you wired a bunch of firefighters with biosensors and radio telemetry gadgets and followed the various pulse, blood pressure, and body-temperature readings through a major big-city fire. Just a study of their exposures to heavy smoke inhalation—"taking a bad feed," Bill Sinclair called it—would be well worth undertaking.

Henderson had always been fascinated with not only the stamina but the super-human discipline and self-control that certain professional career types developed through long periods of learning, training, and facing up to unpredictable challenges. It was the sort commonly ascribed to master crooks and sheriffs in films and novels, yet it actually did exist in individuals in many kinds of work: concert artists, professional athletes, firemen, astronauts, military men, journalists, circus acrobats, pilots, surgeons and, he supposed, even certain politicians and actors. He had concluded it was nourished by the self-esteem, satisfaction, and sense of fulfillment they received from whatever they were doing.

Tears need not be shed for the ones who risked their lives or frequently pushed themselves beyond the extremes of endurance. The real victims were the ordinary men in ordinary kinds of work, trapped in a bewildering bind of family pressures and finances, undergoing all manner of stress before they even got to a job they didn't particularly like.

At the Hospital he changed into his whites and listened as his partner reported that his paracervical-anesthesia patient, Mrs. Mary Gibson, was progressing satisfactorily in her period of labor.

"I gave her a second needle about thirty minutes

ago," he told Henderson. "She really wasn't feeling any pain yet but she was dilating nicely and I thought I'd stay a little bit ahead with this one as you suggested."

"Fine, Ed," Henderson said. "That's the way I want her. I want to roll her into Delivery as fresh as a daisy. And then invite some of the brothers in to watch. Did you notice who's going to be around?"

"You've got Henry Palmer for sure," his partner said. "He's got a patient that's due about an hour after yours. He ought to be on the floor."

"He'd better be," Henderson said, "or I'll have him paged all over the place. I'm going to invite him personally. No more peeking in the door like some of them."

"Good luck," his partner said. "If you can make Henry see the light, the rest of them will go down like dominoes."

"Why don't you stick around?" Henderson suggested. "We'll trap him together. You can stand at the door and keep him from sneaking out when I'm busy. I'll have a live witness besides the nurses that he saw the whole thing."

"Not tonight," his partner replied. "I've got that surgery case first thing in the morning. I'll be home in bed in ten minutes."

He disappeared in the direction of the locker room. Henderson sat glancing over Mrs. Gibson's chart and then went to the labor room in which she was resting. He found her sleeping so quietly and soundly that she barely stirred when he confirmed with a manual examination that she was about five centimeters dilated. He sauntered back down the corridor and met the floor nurse coming to get him.

"Your answering service wants you," the nurse said. "I told them you were here for a delivery. They asked that you call them back right away."

Henderson dialed and got the same girl who had left the message. "You had a call from Wisconsin," she said. "They said it was an emergency. You're to call this number . . . "

"A doctor calling?"

"No, a Mrs. Quoddy."

He sat for a moment thinking about the name Quoddy but it struck no note in his memory. He dialed the number and got an answer on the first ring. An excited Mrs. Quoddy. "My sister is your patient, Doctor. She's taken an overdose of the pills you gave her."

"What's her name and what were the pills?"

"Her married name is Cochran. Ruth Cochran. She just came up to stay with us yesterday . . . "

He remembered Ruth Cochran. Marital problems and a baby he had delivered several months before, but sitting there in the Hospital at midnight he couldn't begin to recall what medication he had prescribed for her.

"We don't know what the pills were," Mrs. Quoddy was saying. "But she got them from you."

Always, he reflected, there was that note of accusation: "she got them from *you!*"

"Where is she now?"

"At the hospital. My husband drove her there right away but now she's unconscious. And the hospital wants to know what you gave her."

"You say an overdose. What do you mean exactly? What did she do?"

"Well, you know she hasn't been getting along with her husband . . . "

"Yes. I know."

"Well, yesterday she had another fight with him so she got the kids in the car and drove up here to stay with us. When he found her note, he called her up and told her not to bother to come back. Right after the phone call she ran into our bathroom and locked the door and took all the pills she had in her handbag."

"What about the labels on the bottles?" he asked, hoping that would help.

"They're smudged. I can't read them. Except your name."

"When did this happen?"

"About half an hour ago. My husband had to get a

ladder and climb in the bathroom window to get her out."

"I'll have to check my office records," he said. "Then I'll call the hospital myself."

He got the number of the hospital from her, hung up the phone, and sat looking at the clock. It was 1:20. There was certainly no one at his office. The Gibson girl was five centimeters dilated but she wasn't going to have that baby for a while yet and the analgesia Russell had given her would keep her comfortable. He ducked into the doctors' dressing room, snatched his sports jacket from his locker, and threw it on over his white suit.

"Going to my office for a few minutes," he told the Floor Nurse. "Call me if something comes up with Mrs. Gibson but I should be back in twenty minutes."

"You'll surely get pneumonia going out dressed like that."

"You're right," he said. "I'm going to need something to warm me up when I get back here. Call that all-night place that delivers. Get me a sausage pizza and a malted milk. Get yourself one, too. In fact, ask all the girls on the Delivery Room floor how many pizzas and malteds they want. Tell them I'm buying. The sky's the limit."

He took the backstairs to the doctors' parking lot and gunned the cold engine to try to coax a bit of warmth out of the heater as he drove the half-mile to his office. He left the car lights on and the motor running so the police would see it was his car and not come busting in with drawn guns to foil a night holdup. Fumbling with his key chain, he found the office key, shoved the door open, flicking on the lights. The cleaning women weren't due to come through until early in the morning and the place was a shambles from evening office hours. He knelt beside a filing cabinet and flipped the folders, hoping that the patient's file wasn't fouled up. There it was: *"Cochran, Ruth."*

He sat on the floor reclining against the file cabinet and glanced swiftly through it, noting with relief that he had prescribed no barbiturates for her. She had had dexamyl for weight control during her last pregnancy and a tranquilizer to help her through her marital storms and elixir of terpin hydrate of codeine. Why the hell had he prescribed that? Oh yes, here it was. Cough and cold. The prescriptions were for limited doses and she hadn't requested a reorder on any except the tranquilizers. He heaved himself to his feet and sat down at the desk, making the long distance call to the Wisconsin hospital's emergency room. The resident who was taking care of Mrs. Cochran was quickly on the line. He read him the medications and dosages.

"That fits with what we've found," the resident said. "We did a gastric lavage and got some of the dexamyl capsules out of her. She's got a respiration of fifteen and a pulse of eighty-two. Blood pressure's holding up well, too. She's nowhere close to being comatose. So long as there were no barbiturates I'm not worried. I think she just took a handful of the tranquilizers."

"So do I," Henderson said. "Would you give me another report on her in the morning? I'll want to talk to her husband."

He dialed the Hospital and got Nurse Bates.

"How is everything?"

"Mrs. Gibson is playing cards with her husband. Couldn't be more cheerful and relaxed. You'd better get back here to pay for those pizzas. We gave the place such a big order that they telephoned back to check it out. They thought somebody was putting them on."

"I'm on my way," he said. He waited until she had hung up, then dialed his automatic recording service and dictated the details on Mrs. Cochran. In the morning, his partner would play back the tapes so that he'd be filled in on the night's events for all their patients. It gave them both twenty-four-hour coverage on the whole range of their practice.

By now the car heater was blasting out plenty of heat and he drove back to the Hospital at a more leisurely pace, relieved that Mrs. Cochran was alive and kicking, wondering again what *was* the answer to suburbia's marital problems. The vast, neat villages that sprawled across the landscape with the station wagons, splendidly equipped high-pressure schools, homes crammed with electronic gadgets, and the combination of tension, boredom, monotony, and frustration ripping family lives to pieces. Psychiatrists and lawyers reaped a rich harvest.

The women raised the most emotional hell, but the men actually committed more suicides. The women by and large took the overdoses of pills and ran off to the lawyers. But the pills were not often fatal. Somehow they almost always managed to call a girl friend or a neighbor or a relative so there would be time to save them ... even though they swallowed a handful. And how many actually seriously intended suicide? It was hard to tell. It was easy to flush half the bottle down the toilet before taking the rest and lying down on the bed or the bathroom floor.

The men, on the other hand, usually went all the way with a gun. Once they had made up their minds, there was no turning back. Boom! There was Daddy on the floor and nothing to do but bury him.

The most desperate men, it seemed to him, were the middle-to-upper-middle-class white-collar workers. And of all these, the junior executive was in the worst bind. The competition pressure on his office job was total. The cost of raising and educating a family stunned him. Psychologically, he was castrated. The office in which he worked was full of mini-skirted lasses who were beyond his reach unless he demeaned himself with an affair that was bound to be costly, stressful, and lead nowhere.

The American accent on youth constantly reminded him that he was an outsider. And when he reached home at the end of the day, where was he? In too many instances, he was aware that neither his wife nor his kids were waiting breathlessly for his arrival. Television, teenagers, and a wife who was either nonreceptive or obviously disdainful of his notions about sex did nothing to bolster his own self-image. But when a male is plunged into self-doubt, despair, and black depression it is not his nature to seek solace or advice. Privately pondering his present and future, he may see only one escape and take it.

The women, Henderson thought, seemed to survive by their penchant for distractions. Here in suburbia, he met them first as mothers-to-be and observed them as they coped with babies, children, social cliques, and themselves, a subject which forever fascinated them. Yet, did they really like each other? Not that much, it seemed to him. At least not in groups. They competed with each other, confided—to a degree—in each other, and together restlessly tackled Cub Scouts, cocktail parties, weight watching, bowling, gardening, and home remodeling. Yet so many of them were dissatisfied and restless. And once they were "bored," trouble ahead. Sometimes, it was the novelty and excitement of a flirtation or an affair with another man. Sometimes it became more complicated. Long hours of listening to the tribulations of the unhappy female had provided him with a finely tuned ear. You would sit and listen and wait and hear about the husband who "didn't care any more" and wasn't sexually responsive—Doctor, could there be anything wrong with him?—and finally there would be enough clues to complete the picture. She'd found a "friend," another woman who was an "afternoon" partner, who was perfectly "safe" to be seen with and freed her from the threat of pregnancy. It was still a minor problem in the suburbs but it was happening.

A good many of the women you found in suburbia, he had concluded, probably had never belonged there in the first place. Many of them would have been better off in the city where they could more easily pursue careers, if they so desired, and still bring up babies—a feat that was difficult if not impossible in the suburbs. He considered a paradox of the times: here were our schools and colleges turning out women who were just as well educated as men, just as competent as men, and yet once their schooling was over they were rudely shoved aside and given substantially the same choices given to their grandmothers. It simply was not enough for them.

And even those women who simply wanted to be wives and mothers sometimes went a little nutty. Many of them saw little beyond their day-to-day routines and began losing the community of interest that had existed between themselves and their husbands. The men, for their part, began spending more and more time in the more sophisticated environs of the big city, and once such a chasm opened, it was exceedingly difficult to breach. And even devoted families had their problems. "Women," Henderson had told one confused husband, "can't stand too much 'calm.' They take it as indifference to themselves and their problems."

Back in the locker room on the Delivery Floor he shed his sports jacket, scrubbed, and pulled on a freshly laundered jumper. The counter in the staff kitchen was lined with pizzas and malteds. The girls were munching and gabbing and they greeted him with a chorus of thanks.

"Doctor, I want you to know that's the first pizza I've really enjoyed in a long time," one of the nurses said. "I didn't have seven kids fighting for it and a husband who chomps holes in it along with the kids. Gosh, was that good!"

He tasted the sample she gave him. "You've got a date for another," he said. "That place must be under new management."

He ate the sausage special that Bates had saved for him, followed it with malted milk and coffee and with Essie Bates went back in to see Mrs. Gibson.

"She just dozed off, Doctor," her husband said. He was reading a paperback in the chair beside the bed.

"She been getting along all right?"

"So comfortable she can't believe it. Not at all like the first baby. She has the contractions but she doesn't feel them."

"That's the way this new cervical anesthesia is supposed to work," he said. "It's taking all the hell out of labor. Let me see how she's coming along."

With the husband outside, he checked Mrs. Gibson's progress. The baby had moved down to Station Two. Its heart tones were good.

"Essie," he said to the nurse, "I think we're in luck here. No problems. But I want to give her one more needle before we go into Delivery."

He took the Kobak needle from the nurse and guided it up into the vagina between his thumb and forefinger.

"Hold it, Honey," he said to Mrs. Gibson who was stirring. "You're coming along fine. Just lie still while I get this anesthetic in to you."

He found the lateral fornix of the vagina and defined the space between the baby and pelvic wall with his finger. He directed the needle into the tissues of the broad ligament, penetrated slightly, aspirated for signs of bleeding, got none, and injected a small amount of the anesthetic. Then he repeated the procedure to anesthetize the nerves on the other side of the cervix.

"How do you feel now?" he asked.

"Like I'm home in bed. I just fell asleep. Is the baby all right?"

"As far as I can tell, the baby couldn't be better. And it won't be too long now before we deliver you, so just lie there and rest."

"From now on I'm going to have all my babies this way," she said.

"It's a coming thing, I think," he said. "I told you it's even surprised me."

At this same moment, he knew from reading the reports in the medical journals, hundreds of other women in hospitals scattered from Hawaii to Maine would be having their babies painlessly and safely through this relatively new procedure. In the first of the two stages of childbirth, their doctors used what was generally called paracervical block anesthesia. They usually combined it with pudendal block anesthesia to eliminate pain in the final phase. Importantly, both were done with a local anesthetic.

Medically, a "block" means a temporary deadening of the nerves that communicate pain impulses to the brain. Paracervical means "around the cervix." In paracervical anesthesia, the cervix, or neck of the uterus, was anesthetized with small doses of a local anesthetic drug in the same manner that a portion of your gum is anesthetized by a dentist for a tooth extraction or the filling of a cavity. In fact, the same drugs might be used in both procedures.

The pain in childbirth was associated primarily with the stretching of the birth canal and particularly the dilating of the cervix. Normally and during the nine months of pregnancy, the cervix was tightly contracted and could be felt with a finger as a muscular bump on the roof of the vagina just a few inches inside the body. It contained a tiny canal that connected the vagina with the uterus. Through this canal the baby within the uterus reached the outside world.

When an expectant mother went into labor, the first rippling muscular contractions of the uterus exerted pressure on the baby and on the "bag of waters" (in which it floated) to push the baby downward into the cervix. As labor progressed, the cervix gradually opened until it fully dilated to a diameter of about four inches to permit the passage of the baby.

In the earliest stages of labor, the discomfort was usually mild. The pains were about fifteen to twenty minutes apart and usually lasted for about one minute. They were somewhat similar to the abdominal cramp that may accompany menstruation and were easily alleviated with tranquilizers and injections of pain-relieving drugs. As labor progressed, however, the contractions of the uterus became much stronger and closer together. As the descending baby exerted increasing pressure on the cervix, the pain increased.

This was the time when most women reacted to the increasing pain of the steadily stretching cervix by becoming tense, fearful, anxious, frightened, or hysterical.

As the contractions continued toward a climax to expel the baby, the pain became extreme. It was this that could lead to extreme suffering by women in childbirth.

To offset this pain, the majority of American women until lately were treated with a wide range of drugs and various forms of gas or spinal anesthesia. In recent years a limited number tried having their babies by natural childbirth or hypnosis.

With paracervical block anesthesia, the increasing pain was abruptly halted—dramatically swept away— by injecting small amounts of fast-acting local anesthetic directly into the tissues and ligaments surrounding the cervix.

Mary Gibson, Henderson's patient tonight, was expecting her second child. She had been admitted to the Maternity Wing in the early stages of labor shortly before noon.

"You're on your way," Henderson had told her after he had examined her in the bedroom that served as a labor room, "but it's going to be a while before you have your baby. I'm going to give you a tranquilizer to help you rest here comfortably. Later on, when you need it, I'll put in the block that I've been telling you about."

For the rest of the afternoon Mrs. Gibson had dozed and read a magazine while the Ob nurses kept track of her progress. Toward evening, when the uterine contractions came closer together and the pain increased, Henderson reappeared accompanied by a nurse carrying a tray with antiseptic solutions, hypodermic needle, and a small bottle of local anesthetic.

"Stay right there in bed," he had said. "This should only take a minute."

He snapped on rubber gloves, swabbed the interior of the vagina and cervix, which was now about halfway dilated, with the antiseptic solution and filled the hypodermic syringe with anesthetic. With his gloved left hand he located and felt the head of the baby as it pressed down against the cervix. Then, using his forefinger and middle finger as a guide, he inserted the

needle and injected the anesthetic at four separate
points on opposite sides of the cervix, slanting the
needle away from the baby's head and the mother's
blood vessels. If you looked at the expanding circular
ring of the cervix as a clock face, you would say that he
injected the anesthetic at "three o'clock and nine
o'clock" and then at "five o'clock and seven o'clock."

"That's all there is to that," he said to Mrs. Gibson.
"What did you feel?"

"Nothing much."

"That's just right. Now let's see what happens to the
pains during your next contraction."

He sat with her beside the bed, one hand resting
lightly on her abdomen, glancing at his watch.

"I think the contractions have stopped," said Mrs.
Gibson about five minutes later.

"No, they haven't," Henderson answered. "You're
starting to have a contraction right now. A good strong
one."

"But I feel as if nothing is happening. Just a feeling
of pressure," Mrs. Gibson said.

"That's fine," Henderson said. "That's just the way
we want you to feel. You can keep track of your
contractions if you like by resting your hand on your
stomach."

Using a stethoscope, he checked the baby's heartbeat.

"Your baby's doing fine," he said. "And so are you.
I don't think it will be more than a few hours now. I'm
going to stay right here at the Hospital with you until
you've had the baby."

For the next hour, Mrs. Gibson rested, free from
pain. The tension and anxiety that she had begun to
feel as the pain increased subsided. ("I felt," she told
Henderson later, "as if I were just floating along. I was
wide awake but I wasn't scared about what was happening to me.") Her husband arrived, looking concerned and then vastly relieved when he found his wife
greeting him with a wave and a smile.

"Are you *sure* you feel all right?" he inquired incredulously.

"Just like I was home in my own bed," she answered. They sat talking about what to name the baby. About an hour after the first injection Henderson repeated the procedure. Now, at one-thirty A.M. Mrs. Gibson, as Henderson examined her, was through labor and about ready for the Delivery Room without having suffered any major discomfort.

There was a time, Henderson reflected, as he watched her resting quietly, when this stage of childbirth would have had her twisting and shrieking like a wild animal. Her great-grandmother certainly hadn't been so lucky!

The first medical efforts to ease the pain of childbirth began in Scotland in 1847. A Scottish physician, James Y. Simpson, introduced the use of chloroform to render women in labor unconscious. Simpson persisted even though he was denounced by clergy, the public, and even fellow doctors for interfering with a "natural process." Later, the further development of general anesthesia gases and numerous new drugs made possible the procedures still commonly followed today. In these, the mother is made as comfortable as possible with sedatives, tranquilizers, and pain-killing drugs which are administered in the early stages of labor. Then, as the birth of the baby approaches and the pain becomes severe, she is taken to the Delivery Room where an anesthetist administers enough gas anesthesia to render her unconscious as the pain of each contraction mounts to its maximum. At the moment of birth, the anesthesia may be so deepened that the mother is completely unconscious. Or by using combinations of gases and drugs which obliterate the memory it is possible to maintain the mother in a semiconscious state. She can then respond to the physician's directions to "bear down" during the contractions. Although she may cry out and writhe with pain, she will awaken later with no memory of the ordeal and swear she "never felt a thing" or was "sound asleep" the whole time.

Although the development of general anesthesia seemed to have made childbirth as free from pain—or at least the memory of pain—as was medically possible, disturbing discoveries were made about the effects of the gases on both mother and baby. The gases, it was found, tended to depress the respiration centers of the brain. After being inhaled into the mother's lungs, the gases were carried to the unborn baby via the bloodstream of the mother. They reduced the amount of oxygen that reached the baby's brain and tissues. They might also interfere with the baby's ability to breathe properly after it was born. Lack of oxygen before, during, and after birth might create a hazard to the baby's life or cause brain damage which would affect the child's growth and achievement in later life. This breathing depression made general anesthesia particularly hazardous for small or premature babies.

One of the most dangerous situations for gas anesthesia was the "full stomach," patient whose body may react to the anesthetic gases with nausea or vomiting. Regurgitated food particles may then be inhaled into the air passages of the lungs, causing choking, suffocation, or chemical pneumonia. Women in childbirth fitted into this category because they might well have eaten a full meal just prior to the onset of labor.

For these reasons there was an increasing body of medical opinion that was solidly arrayed against using gas anesthesia in normal childbirth and that believed that it should be reserved for deliveries with complications. Some doctors went so far as to state that they considered general anesthesia the *very worst* anesthetic for obstetrics.

Another factor that counted against general anesthesia in childbirth was the lack of competent anesthesiologists. In the national doctor shortage, there was such an acute lack of them that non-doctors administered more than half of all anesthesia. While large medical centers and training hospitals might have anesthesiologists available around the clock, suburban and rural hospitals were less fortunate. Here anesthesiologists might be only "on call" or even completely unavailable.

Seeking other means of relieving childbirth pain, modern medicine had developed spinal and caudal regional anesthesia. In these procedures solutions of pain-killing drugs were introduced by hypodermic needle into the interior spaces of the spinal column, either in the small of the back or at the tip of the spine. The drugs temporarily deadened the nerves that relayed pain sensations from the birth canal to the brain. The mother was completely conscious but felt nothing.

Many doctors employed spinal anesthesia in childbirth, but others contended that it had formidable drawbacks. One was that introducing a needle into the spinal column called for highly specialized skill. Some hospitals permitted only anesthesiologists to administer spinals. Caudals could cause convulsions, drops in the mother's blood pressure, and other serious complications. More frequently employed was the spinal anesthesia known as "saddle block" but this, too, occasionally resulted in neurological complications that affected either the mother or baby or caused post-birth headaches that might last from a few hours to a week. Another objection to spinal anesthesia in obstetrics was that the mother's control over her abdominal muscles was rendered so limited that she could not assist the doctor by "bearing down" during contractions. There might also be a slowing down of the uterine contractions, prolonging the period of labor. In preference to using any anesthetics, some doctors relied on natural childbirth, hypnosis, or combinations of pain relieving drugs. Both natural childbirth and hypnosis, however, proved effective with only a few patients.

As for drugs by themselves, one doctor had observed, "Despite the use of sedatives, tranquilizers and narcotics even to the point where maternal disorientation and infant depression occurs, pain relief is often imperfect. Fear magnifies pain. The amount of systemic sedation (drugs) needed to overcome a vicious cycle of fear and pain is often dangerous to the baby, particularly if the baby is premature."

Thus, although the 20th century has seen continuous advances in anesthesia techniques for relieving pain in childbirth, none of these remedies has turned out to be sufficiently safe, simple, and effective to be the ideal answer.

Curiously, while most of the extreme pain that is experienced in childbirth originates in the slowly dilating cervix, no one gave much thought to the possibility of reducing the pain right where it started. This remained true long after it was known that the nerves of the uterus, and particularly the cervical portion of the uterus, follow a sensory pathway through the tissues and ligaments surrounding the cervix and are easily accessible to the hypodermic needle of a physician via the vagina.

Then, from Germany, in the 1920's and 1930's, came the first published reports of injecting a local anesthetic to block out these nerves during the pain of childbirth. Nothing more was heard of this procedure in the United States until 1945 when Dr. Samuel Rosenfeld of New York became the first American physician to recommend its advantages in a medical journal.

Rosenfeld's report of his success in reducing pain in one hundred patients apparently didn't strike many sparks of interest among United States obstetricians but it *was* read with interest by two young doctors, Donald Freeman and John S. Gilam, who were completing their training in obstetrics at the University of Minnesota.

"We were looking around for a research project during our residence," Dr. Freeman later explained. "We began to conduct some trials along the lines that Rosenfeld recommended. The relief from pain that our patients experienced was remarkable."

This the two young doctors reported in a local Minnesota medical journal in 1950. After helping Freeman design a long, hollow needle guide to inject the anesthetic solution into the cervix, Gilam turned his interest to other areas in medicine but Freeman, with two other Minnesota doctors, continued to study the matter.

Interest in paracervical anesthesia slowly spread. A team of Iowa doctors reported favorably on the procedure. At the University of Illinois in Chicago, Dr. Alfred J. Kobak conducted studies that confirmed the safety and effectiveness of the technique; he also designed a special tubed needle with which to administer the local anesthetic.

Commented Dr. Kobak, "The patient is relieved of pain without the disadvantages of general anesthesia; and now we have finally, the long-sought answer to the question raised by a famous obstetrician, 'What is the sense of putting the entire body to sleep when you want to operate on only a small part of it?' "

Henderson had first seen the technique demonstrated while he was still in medical school. Then it was such a novelty that none of his class really bought it. It seemed to work like a charm in some cases and not so well in others. They hadn't then understood the reasons for the failures. For one thing, there was no opportunity in a large hospital clinic to explain to patients what it was all about. You were getting them a few hours before delivery, when they were well into labor. Already they were in pain, often scared out of their wits, jumpy if not hysterical. And, at that time, the local anesthetics didn't last as long as they do today. Now one injection will totally anesthetize the cervix for more than an hour.

And also, in the intervening years, groups around the nation had demonstrated the effectiveness of the pudendal block—locally anesthetizing the rim of the vagina so it, too, was desensitized to the stretching as the baby was delivered.

Henderson had begun trying it in his own private practice about six months before. After about twenty-five patients whom he had helped along with the assistance of an anesthesiologist, he had learned to gauge and time the injections. The results were remarkable.

The patients with whom he was using it were experiencing practically painless childbirth.

Now he sat with Mrs. Gibson, feeling the powerful movements of the uterine muscles as she went through another contraction.

"This is real second-stage labor, Essie," he said to his nurse. "She's six centimeters, nearly fully dilated. Tell them to get going in Delivery."

As soon as they were back with a stretcher, he left to scrub and then walked into the Delivery Room to thrust his arms into the long white sterile gown the nurse was holding out for him and snap on the rubber gloves. They had Mrs. Gibson on the table, her blue-draped and elevated thighs and legs in the stirrups, but her hands free. He dropped down on the stool and rolled into position to prepare the perineum with green soap and an antiseptic solution.

Two white-gowned delivery nurses darted about assisting him as he positioned himself on the low stool. There was no anesthesiologist, no gas cylinders. The room was quiet and free from tension.

What a contrast to the past, Henderson reflected. Here was a mother-to-be, neither writhing in pain under the restraining leather straps nor woozy, semiconscious, or entirely unconscious from drugs or general anesthesia. She was fully conscious, relaxed, and keenly aware and interested in what was going to take place as her baby was born. During this climactic moment of her pregnancy, and in the midst of one of the most memorable and dramatic experiences of her life, she would be wide awake and conversing with him and the nurses.

Everything was clearly going to go smoothly with this one and he remembered his hope for an audience.

"Is Dr. Palmer around?" he asked.

"I believe that he's gone," a nurse responded.

"Didn't he have a delivery?"

"Yes. But it came a little sooner than expected."

So Palmer had escaped. He had probably got wind of Henderson's plans and dodged down the back stairs as soon as he had his patient safely stabilized. Palmer would have hated coming in to observe Henderson. The rule with his kind of doctoring was never to permit the staff to see you learning anything new. Palmer was just the type to slip out of town and pick up his instruction in paracervical block technique in a hospital in California or New York, well away from his own practice. Then he could return as an expert, with no loss of face.

"Gosh, those lights are bright," Mrs. Gibson said. "Were they that bright last time?"

"They sure were," he said. "Only you were out like a light with the general anesthesia you'd had to keep you from squirming off the table."

"I'm not squirming now," she said.

"Right," he said. "I'm giving you your last needle now so you won't be uncomfortable when the baby is delivered."

He took the syringe for the pudendal block, extended the needle through the rubber diaphragm on the protective sheath and filled it with anesthetic. He palpated the ischial spine through the vaginal wall with his middle finger. Then he directed the needle sheath directly toward the spine with his index finger, and then slowly injected 10 cc's of anesthetic.

Now the nerves that supplied the lowermost part of the vagina, the vestibule, the labia, clitoris, perineum, and lower anal region were deadened as the anesthetic fluid spread rapidly through the tissues of the region. He felt as if he had hit the pudendal nerve with just the right penetration of the needle. She wouldn't feel the tremendous distention of the vagina and perineal structure as the baby was born. He could even do an episiotomy—enlarging the opening a bit with scissors—without her feeling a thing. He tapped the perineum and pinched it without a sign she felt it.

"You're stone cold dead in the market," he said. "Now the contractions are coming up. The important ones. You won't feel pain but push down—bear down good and hard when I tell you."

"I'm doing it!" she gasped. "Is that right?"

"Keep it up," he said.

He had the baby's head in his fingers. The cord was clear of the neck. He was rotating it.

"Now another one. We're on our way here."

"Boy, this is work!" she gasped. "Is it coming out?"

"Would you like to see the baby born?"

"Sure."

"Swivel that overhead mirror for her girls."

Suddenly she glimpsed a glistening wet brown object in Henderson's gloved left hand.

"Is that it?" she cried.

"That's your baby's head," he replied.

"Oh my gosh!" exclaimed Mrs. Gibson. "It's wonderful, isn't it? It's coming! I see what to do!"

She kept bearing down when he asked her to push during the contractions, working with him, then resting and turning her head curiously to watch the nurses preparing for the baby's birth.

Again the massive contraction. He had the baby's shoulder now. How different it was from the deliveries of the past!

"Is it a boy or girl?" asked Mrs. Gibson. She was sweating, panting, and out of breath.

"I can't tell yet," he said, "but now we're going to know . . . "

The baby was in his hands.

" . . . and the answer is a boy. No doubt about it."

He made his first swift inspection and found the infant normal. He cleansed the mouth and nasal passages, clamped the umbilical cord, severed it, and lifted the baby who was already squirming and kicking. No gas anesthesia hangover for this kid!

He handed the newborn to the nurses and they exclaimed over it with Mrs. Gibson while he sat waiting, watching intently for any untoward developments when she passed the placenta.

"Let me see his hands," Mrs. Gibson was saying.

"What are you doing, checking him for mongolism—reading his palms?"

"Well, I've read you can tell by looking."

"That's right. You usually can," he said. "Boy, today you girls know everything!"

He rose and peered down at the baby. The nurses had bathed it pink and clean, wrapped it in a blue blanket and rolled its "warmer" up beside Mrs. Gibson.

"He looks like a real tiger to me," he said. "If you'll excuse me, I want to see how my other patients are doing."

Reviewing the case as he drove home, Henderson felt that he was on solid ground. There was good reason to believe that he and so many other obstetricians would soon be using paracervical anesthesia in the majority of their normal birth procedures. He now had used it in more than 150 cases. He liked it and felt there was certainly less risk of problems than with gas or any other kind of local anesthetic. Of course, you were still using a drug and whenever you introduced any drug into the human body there was an element of risk. You might always encounter the rare individual who was hypersensitive to the anesthetic but this could even happen when you used penicillin and it happened occasionally in dentists' offices. If you were properly alert and prepared, you should be able to deal with the problem.

There were occasions when the heartbeat of the baby dropped slightly just after the cervical anesthetic was administered, but it returned to normal within a few minutes and there was no evidence that this temporary drop represented any real threat to the baby. When the procedure was first introduced, there were more reports of these heart tone changes, but now there were fewer of them and it was probably because techniques were improving and obstetricians were using smaller dosages of anesthetic. One thing that could certainly be said for it was that it did not cause the potentially dangerous respiratory depression common to most drugs used in labor.

If paracervical block continued to gain in popularity, what would be the reaction, Henderson wondered, of all the anesthesiologists who usually assisted obstetricians during deliveries which employed gas anesthesia?

There would be some, of course, who would resent being eliminated and miss the fees they usually received for their services. There would be others who would be skeptical about the effectiveness of the procedure and some would publish warnings about its safety. But he suspected a lot of them would take the transition from gas to local anesthesia in the same manner as his anesthesiologist friend Herb Goodman. As Goodman gradually became convinced that the procedure was having no ill effects on the mother or baby, he stopped complaining that Henderson was trying to put him out of work. He knew damn well that if there were complications Henderson would want him right there working with him, but that normal deliveries were another matter.

9

An Office Call

"You have a telephone call from Mrs. Sinclair," his office nurse, Martha Williams, said.

"Sinclair!" he exclaimed. "Don't tell me they want me back in that courtroom!"

"I don't know. But I'm sure not going down there with you in that car again. That ride back finished me off. We'll take the train into the city or I won't go."

"How did she sound on the phone?" Henderson asked. "High or low?"

"Neither. Just ordinary. Cheerful. Here, I've got her on the line for you now."

Ruth Sinclair's tone was conversational.

"I've been staining," she announced casually.

"Since when?"

"Well, actually since yesterday. I was just working around the house doing some of the wash. I felt something warm and wet on my leg. And when I looked there was a trickle of blood. Tiny. Not much. Hardly worth worrying about."

Henderson felt the rise in his blood pressure that often resulted from a conversation with Ruth Sinclair. Here she was losing blood. Hemorrhaging of some sort. And she doesn't bother to call! She could be headed for another miscarriage!

"You should always call me immediately when you find you're staining," he said sharply.

"I know." She was mildly apologetic. "But then I sat

down to talk to somebody on the telephone about my accident case and forgot about it and when I remembered again, it had stopped."

"But now it's started again?"

"Yes. Slightly."

"Have you got someone who can drive you to my office right now?"

"Yes I have. My sister is here. Oh, that reminds me, Dr. Henderson. I was going to call you anyway to tell you about the settlement. We got the news yesterday."

"Good. Tell me when you get here. Come right away."

Henderson hung up the phone and sat for a moment breathing deeply. That explained her attitude, of course. She'd gotten some kind of money out of that accident case despite the fouled-up manner in which that lawyer had presented the case, probably just because of showing up with her husband and three kids, and she was so busy yapping on the telephone about it that she forgot she was staining!

Sure enough, ten minutes later she was telling him all about it while he had her on the examining table.

"Of course, ten thousand dollars isn't much, considering what I went through, and we have to pay Mr. Davis his fee out of that, but you see I *was* right to keep fighting that company for my rights."

"You certainly were," said Henderson. He was examining the sanitary pad she had been wearing. There was blood on it all right. Along with some dark red clots.

"You've got something going on here," he said.

"Could it be my period . . . late?"

So that was it! Boy, what wishful thinking!

"I would say no," he answered.

"Well, I wondered if it might be that. I'm really not very far along you know. Only three months."

"Four months, the way I figure it," he said.

"You're really sure it's pregnancy?"

"That's what I've been telling you," he said. "I think you ought to give up the idea that you are anything but pregnant. Did you have any cramp or pain when this staining started?"

"Not a thing. Not yesterday or today either."

He considered the possibilities. "Staining isn't uncommon at this point in a pregnancy," he said. "It may subside completely."

"What does it mean if I am having a baby?"

"It may subside without bothering the baby. You may still have a perfectly normal child."

"I suppose it might be just emotional—from my being in court and testifying."

"Possibly."

"Is there something that you can give me to stop the bleeding? A pill or an injection or something?"

"No. There's nothing like that for this kind of thing. If you were going to have a miscarriage, anything I gave you would only delay it. Did you notice these dark spots?"

"Yes I did . . . sort of."

"I think they are from the edge of the placenta," he said. "You know as the baby grows inside your uterus, it's attached to the wall by the placenta. And the placenta has cells that burrow into the wall of the uterus to get a good grip so that they can build up a system of blood vessels to nourish the baby. As they grow deeper, they sometimes rupture a small blood vessel in the wall of the uterus. You may have this sort of bleeding."

"Do I have to go to the Hospital?"

"No. I just want you to stay off your feet for a few days until we see what happens. I want you to rest, read, sleep, watch TV, but stay quiet. And be sure to let me know if you feel any pain or cramps or if the bleeding increases."

He had glanced at the chart that an office nurse, Dottie Kimball, had handed him. Mrs. Sinclair's weight was up again. Obviously she hadn't been following the diet he had given her. But no wonder, if she was still so nonmotivated about this pregnancy that she was kidding herself into believing it was going to be a mistake and wind up with her having a late menstrual period.

There was no point in bugging her about the weight gain now. If she did abort the baby, she might later develop guilt feelings about not having followed the diet.

"Just go home and lie down and think about your accident money," he said. "What are you going to do with it?"

"Put it in the bank," she said. "We might use part of it for a new car, a station wagon or one of those campers, but if I'm really going to have a baby, I don't know . . . "

Her voice trailed off. She certainly wasn't happy about the baby but at least she did have some sense of relief from the family financial pressures. That ought to keep her calmed down and if he could keep the pregnancy going, by about the seventh month, she would begin to come on strong with a surge of natural maternal motivation.

"Bill and I both want to thank you for testifying in court for us," she said. "You certainly explained everything to that jury."

Henderson sighed. "I tried" he said, "but I would have liked to have had more time to talk to them."

"Oh you told them plenty," Ruth Sinclair said. "You fixed that other lawyer. That's probably why they gave me the money."

"Thanks," Henderson said. So he had fixed that lawyer! Golly Jesus!

After she had departed with her sister he sat musing over Mrs. Sinclair's newest problem.

When you had spotting or staining in the early months of pregnancy, it either stopped with the proper bedrest or it went to abort the pregnancy. Ruth Sinclair was so busy thinking about her accident money that she had forgotten that the miscarriage which was or was not related to the accident also had occurred in her fourth month of pregnancy. Threatened miscarriage must never be underestimated. Premature birth was still the major problem in United States obstetrics. And hemorrhages had become the predominant cause of serious complications and death in childbirth.

Was it possible, Henderson wondered, that his patient, Ruth Sinclair, was prone to placental problems which might mean slight or big trouble early or late in her pregnancy? Had the miscarriage she suffered actually been caused by an abnormally situated placenta?

You couldn't tell much about the position of a placenta after a miscarriage had occurred and you had done a D&C.

The blood clots now coming from her placental site, while not necessarily ominous, were not to be dismissed lightly. The placenta, a large, liver-colored, disk-shaped organ, was little known to most women, yet it played the key role in the growth and development of the baby within the uterus. For nine months the placenta functioned as a lung, gastrointestinal tract, and kidney, providing the baby with food and oxygen and carrying away gases and waste materials.

The human embryo was no chicken egg with an abundance of yolk to sustain and nourish it. All its nourishment had to come from the mother. As soon as the fertilized egg descended from the fallopian tube and implanted itself in the lining of the uterus it began to develop tiny but extremely active cells called "trophoblasts" which spread like plant rods to tap the mother's blood vessels.

By the third week of pregnancy the embryo had formed its own blood vessels which were linking up with the uterine wall through the long cylinder of tissue known as the umbilical cord. The cord contained two arteries which carried blood away from the baby and a single large vein to return the blood to the baby's body. As the cord reached the uterine wall its arteries divided into hundreds of minute branches which became the placenta. Here, too, were developing a network of blood vessels from the mother's circulatory system. And within the placenta occurred the wondrous exchange between mother and baby.

The maternal blood vessels received the waste materials from the baby's bloodstream. At the same time, the baby's blood vessels received nutrients and oxygen from the mother's blood to be carried back to the fetus. There was *no* direct connection between the bloodstream of the baby and bloodstream of the mother. They continued as independent circulatory systems, but the intricate thin-walled network of capillary vessels within the placenta allowed the exchange of waste products and nutrients and oxygen by a process of chemical diffusion.

The total area of these capillary surfaces in a human female had been calculated and its extent was astounding. One researcher estimated a total surface area about the size of a nine by twelve foot living-room rug.

So here the scene was set for plenty of action. For not only was the placenta making possible the continued life and normal development of the baby, but also through its system of blood vessels might pass other substances that happened to be in the baby's or mother's bloodstream, such as bacteria, viruses, protozoa, drugs, anesthetic gases, and chemical agents.

A truly marvelous organ, the placenta endeavored to be selective about what filtered through the membranous walls of blood vessels. Nutrients such as calcium, iron, and hormones, and a multitude of other nourishments passed readily through the "placental barrier" and into the fetus.

The size of the molecules had much to do with it. The smaller the molecules, the more rapid the transfer. Larger molecular substances passed through much more slowly or not at all.

But the agents that carried measles, mumps, chicken pox, polio, malaria, syphilis, could cross the placental barrier and damage the fetus. So could ordinary aspirin. If overdoses were taken by the mother, it might interfere with the ability of the baby's blood to clot after delivery. So also could the nicotine in a cigarette smoked by a mother. Its adverse effects, researchers had recently demonstrated, depressed the heart rate and blood pressure of the baby.

The placenta could also be the cause of a miscarriage or a serious delivery problem at birth. If the fertilized ovum was not well-anchored to the endometrial tissue lining the uterus, it would not develop into a strong, normally functioning placenta. Improperly or insufficiently nourished, the fetus would not survive or it might be born with defects. A weak placenta might break down and hemorrhage and the mother might lose the baby. Or a fetus could bleed to death if its placental blood vessels sprang a leak into the mother's blood supply system.

Until recently one of the most common and catastrophic events in a pregnancy was the passage through the walls of the placenta of the virus that caused rubella, or German measles. If the disease developed in an expectant mother in the first three months of pregnancy, the virus, traveling through the placenta, might attack her unborn child's developing organs, especially his ears, eyes, heart, or brain. One-fourth of these babies died before birth and about half were born with birth defects. During the last great epidemic of German measles to sweep the United States, in 1964, an estimated ten million Americans developed the disease. The toll in babies was set at about 20,000 born dead and 30,000 born with some sort of handicap.

Now millions of doses of a new vaccine for German measles were being distributed in a national mass immunization program which could protect both pregnant women and their babies.

In the first four months of pregnancy, the most frequent causes of a lost baby were spontaneous abortion, or miscarriage, and ectopic or tubal pregnancy. In the second half of a pregnancy one of the most dangerous life threats to the baby were hemorrhages related to the placenta. And hemorrhage was becoming the predominant cause of death in childbirth.

In middle-class Americans prenatal care during the nine months was drastically reducing the cases of toxemia. Eclampsia, with its terrifying and frequently fatal convulsions, was almost eliminated. You could keep a

close watch on expectant mothers by frequent laboratory urinalysis and weight checks and the toxemias
didn't build up until they were out of control.

But in the later months of a pregnancy you had to be
constantly on the alert for signs or symptoms relating to
two conditions of the placenta known as *abruptio placenta* and *placenta previa*.

Both posed a risk to the life of the mother and the
life of the baby. Abruptio placenta was the premature
detachment from the wall of the uterus of a normally
implanted placenta. It could be partial or complete. It
could cause a minor or massive hemorrhage. If you
delivered the baby within six hours, by the vaginal
route, or by a cesarean section, and treated the mother
with liberal blood transfusions and the administration
of fibrinogen for clotting, you could reduce the maternal death rate to one percent or less. The mortality rate
for the baby ranged from thirty to forty percent.

But as far as Ruth Sinclair was concerned, Henderson was thinking mainly about *placenta previa*. While
its cause was unknown, two factors seemed to be related
to its occurrence: age and multiparity, or having borne
several children. It was only about half as frequent with
a first baby and it was about three times as likely in
women of thirty-five years or older.

At thirty-four, and with three children, Ruth Sinclair
certainly fitted into the placenta previa-prone category.
Moreover, the chances were about twelves times as
great if placenta previa had occurred in a previous
pregnancy. Henderson wondered if it *had* occurred in
her previous pregnancies. Indeed, might it have caused
her miscarriage after the automobile accident? Although placenta previa was not usually diagnosed until
the seventh month, it was deemed probable by many
obstetricians that many miscarriages of the earlier
months of pregnancy might be due to this abnormality.

In some patients the complication of placenta previa
was surmised by some physicians to be a result of its
not getting enough nutrients from the maternal blood
vessels. To increase its supply the placenta spread itself

over a larger area of the uterus, and in so doing its lower portion overlapped the internal mouth of the cervical canal. In other cases the ovum simply seemed to find the lower portion of the uterus rather than a higher portion more acceptable for implantation. In any case, the placenta previa, instead of being implanted high up on the anterior or posterior wall of the womb, was implanted so low that it overlay or reached the vicinity of the cervix. It could overlap or obscure the internal entrance to the cervix, marginally, partially, or totally.

The most characteristic event in placenta previa was a painless hemorrhage. It often occurred while a pregnant woman was apparently in perfect health. She might be fast asleep in her own bed—taking an afternoon nap or sleeping through the night—when she would suddenly awaken to find herself lying in a small or large pool of blood. The hemorrhage could be slight or sufficient to cause death unless dealt with swiftly.

A placenta-previa hemorrhage also might not occur until the patient was in the midst of labor, when there would be a sudden profuse discharge of blood. This was a hemorrhage of the maternal blood vessels as the placenta separated from the wall of the uterus. The inability of the enormously stretched fibers of the uterus to contract and compress the torn blood vessels posed an obstetrical problem during the third stage of labor. Or profuse hemorrhage might occur after the birth of the baby and even after delivery of the placenta. Then to save the mother's life you had to act quickly to stop the bleeding and replace the lost blood with transfusions.

At this point—in her sixteenth week of pregnancy—Mrs. Sinclair's placenta should be implanted in the upper wall of her uterus. It should have already grown from a few tiny blood vessels to a large round organ through which coursed the bloodstreams of both mother and child, busily exchanging oxygen and nutrients from the mother with carbon dioxide and other metabolic wastes from the fetus. But if the placenta had taken root poorly or incompletely, it could cause an abortion and she would lose the baby. If only a few of its blood vessels were ruptured, however, you might get the intermittent spotting which might cease by itself.

Even if he could see inside the uterus, there was nothing Henderson could do except to increase his vigilance. In most of the separated placentas in these early months, there was no chance for a normal live baby. If it hemorrhaged later on, it might cause a sudden massive escape of blood. He would have to know about it quickly and move like lightning to prevent a tragedy.

10

Emergency Room

Dimly, as Henderson groped toward consciousness from deep slumber, he sensed that the muffled knocking at the front door was becoming more insistent. When he heaved over on his side the luminous face of the bedside clock told him it was two-thirty A.M. He lay motionless, convincing himself that he was awake and not dreaming, trying to think of what could be happening. The children, so far as he knew, were all in bed and his wife slept soundly beside him. None of his patients were scheduled to go into labor.

The muffled thumping continued. Prowlers? Boozed-up trouble makers? He had recently had a run-in with a Mafia-type who didn't want his wife to stay in the hospital. When Henderson refused to sign a release for her, the husband had come around at night and taken her out at gunpoint. He had left a message with a nurse that he would "see" Henderson later.

Henderson slipped out of bed quietly. He got his vest-pocket automatic pistol from a corner of the closet where none save Mary knew it was hidden and moved warily through the dark hall into the living room. Once again there came the insistent muted rapping and thumping. Henderson closed the hall door behind him to protect his wife and children and debated his next move. Should he let the intruder know he was inside, ready and armed? Open the door and whack him with a

143

golf club? Ambush him from the kitchen side entrance? Inevitably, each choice would lead to violence. Someone was going to get badly hurt. He decided to put in a call to the police. Keeping low by crawling across the kitchen floor, he reached up for the wall phone, placed it to his ear and heard nothing. The line was dead. They must have cut the wires! Well, whatever happened next was going to happen *outside* his house.

He ducked low beneath the level of the kitchen counters and windows and crept over to the kitchen side door. From here he could hit them with the beam of the big flashlight and shout, "Reach! Get em up!"

A red glow flared suddenly on the kitchen ceiling above him. "Christ! What were they doing? Setting fire to the house?"

He fumbled for the big flashlight on the wall near the kitchen door, found it, quietly unlocked the door, and flung it open. Focusing the beam of the flashlight on the front door with one hand and aiming his gun with the other, he shouted, "All right, you, hold it right there!"

... and was immediately blinded by the glare of a searchlight ten times brighter than his own light.

A familiar voice, registering startled amazement, replied, "Hey, Doc. It's me. Sergeant Buck."

"Oh, Bucky!" Henderson exclaimed. "I'm sorry. I thought I had some freaks prowling around out here."

Now he could see the police car parked in the driveway. The rotating red beacon on its roof sweeping across the side of the house had reflected the red glow on the kitchen ceiling which he had mistaken for arson.

"These days," he said apologetically to Sergeant Buck, "you never know what kind of nuts may be after you."

"You're right," Sergeant Buck said, eyeing Henderson's weapon and his fighting regalia—pyjama top, undershorts, and bare feet. "I didn't want to raise the whole house but nobody was answering your phone. The Hospital and your answering service both have been trying to reach you. They asked me to check you out."

"My telephone line has been cut," Henderson replied.

"Cut?"

"Well, I thought so. I was sound asleep. I certainly haven't been getting any calls and just now when I grabbed the phone to call you, the line was dead. But wait a minute . . ."

He padded back inside the kitchen in his bare feet and looked over the wall phone. Sure enough, somebody had pulled out the jack.

"Godamnitall!" Henderson muttered.

He knew it must have been Mary who had disconnected the phone. He stood there, breathing deeply, fighting off the urge to bound into the bedroom and start yelling. It had happened once or twice before. She meant well enough. She had just wanted him to get some sleep. Staying up to watch the late TV, she must have pulled the jack so the wall phone wouldn't ring and any incoming call would have registered only as a flashing light on top of the TV set. But then she must have forgotten all about it when she had switched off the television and come to bed. Fortunately, the switchboard girls at the Hospital and the answering service were so damn sharp that they had called the police and asked them to check his house. Now he replaced the phone jack and dialed his answering service, saying over his shoulder to Sergeant Buck, "It's okay now, Bucky. Grab a couple of cold sodas from the refrigerator while I call in and see what's up."

The answering-service girl came on, "Oh, Doctor Henderson," she said. "I'm glad they found you. Mr. Frank Jordan wants to talk to you right away about his wife, Dorothy."

He took the Jordan number and dialed. Dorothy Jordan had been in to see him about having a baby but so far as he knew she wasn't even pregnant yet. Or could she be?

He listened intently as Frank Jordan told him what had happened to his wife.

She had awakened to go to the bathroom and while there had suddenly felt faint. The room had begun to spin. She had called out to her sleeping husband but he had really been awakened by the crash when she passed out cold and fell to the floor, fortunately knocking over a towel rack instead of striking her head.

"Is she fully conscious now?" Henderson asked.

"Just barely," Frank Jordan replied. "I got her back into bed and I've been bathing her face while they tried to reach you but she's still weak and dizzy."

"Does she have any pain?"

"Yes. She had a sharp, stabbing pain in her right side. Low down on the right side, just before she fainted in the bathroom and now she's had some more pains since I got her back into bed."

"Hold the phone a moment," Henderson said.

Turning to Sergeant Buck, he said, "Bucky, where's the rescue-squad ambulance?"

"At the fire station," Buck said. "Do you want me to check? I'll call in on the car radio."

"Yes, please," Henderson said.

Buck went out the kitchen door. On the telephone Henderson said to Jordan, "What's your address?"

"160 Palmer Drive," Jordan said. "It's the third house on the right. Are you going to come over?"

"Just a moment," Henderson said. He had scribbled the address on the pad beside the wall telephone.

Sergeant Buck was back. "Ambulance is standing by," he said. "One of the firemen can drive it."

Henderson handed him the paper with the address. "160 Palmer Drive. Third house on the right. Tell them to lift her from the bed to the stretcher cart and roll her in at the Hospital Emergency Entrance."

To Frank Jordan he said, "Put your front porch light on, Mr. Jordan. We're sending an ambulance over to pick up your wife. They'll bring her to the Hospital. I'll meet her there and examine her. You ride with her.

Don't let her get out of bed. They will lift her right on to a stretcher."

"She's been to the Hospital once," Frank Jordan said. "They sent her home."

Henderson drew a deep breath. "All right," he said. "Tell me about it when I see you. The ambulance should be there in five to ten minutes."

He hung up and said to Sergeant Buck who was coming back in the kitchen while his partner relayed the ambulance call on the police-car radio. "I'm glad you got me up, Bucky. I may have a hot one that has to be opened up for some surgery."

Buck looked gratified. "Glad we could help," he said.

"Always come and get me like you did tonight," Henderson said. "That phone is supposed to be answered day or night unless I've told the answering service and the Hospital where they can find me."

"You bet." Buck said. "You want an escort to the Hospital now? You can make it a little faster and safer with us out in front."

"I sure would," Henderson said. "Let me grab some clothes."

He hurried into the bedroom, putting the gun back in its secret hiding place and snatching up shoes, socks, shirt, and slacks. Back in the kitchen he took the wall phone and dialed the emergency room at the Hospital on a direct line.

"Henderson calling," he said. "I have a patient coming in by ambulance. A possible ectopic. Can you get me a scrub team ready? Also, check Maternity and see who's up there who might assist me."

He flicked out the kitchen lights, went out, shutting the kitchen door quietly behind him and slid into his car. Sergeant Buck already had wheeled the police car around and they both shot out the driveway and down the highway with the police car's red beacon flashing and Buck's partner screeching the siren as they streaked through stop streets and stop lights.

Henderson could hardly wait to get to the Hospital

and find out what had been going on. He was sure
Dorothy Jordan was suffering from a ruptured fallopian
tube as a result of an ectopic pregnancy—the embryo
had developed in the tube instead of the egg descending
into the uterus—but who was the melonhead who had
seen her at the Hospital and sent her home? And why
was it he had not been informed until the middle of the
night? Not only was he now wide awake, he was in an
uproar, pumping adrenalin, raging at his well-meaning
wife, Dorothy Jordan, and all others who might have
been involved in this incredible bit of bungling. Fuming,
he tramped down on the accelerator, tail-gating the
speeding police car as if they were both in a stock-car
race. At the entrance to the Hospital, he clicked on his
blinker lights to signal his thanks to Sergeant Buck,
who was probably relieved to get out of his way,
swerved into the parking lot and then, purposely
slowing down, strolled with professional aplomb into
the Emergency Room.

Dorothy Jordan was just being transferred from the
ambulance stretcher to a table in one of the examining
rooms and Henderson was gratified to note that the
Emergency-Room crew was exercising extra care with
her. They must have found his partner, Ed Russell, up
on the Maternity Floor because he was already on hand
to supervise the procedure. The young fellow nervously
coping with the Hospital admission forms was the husband.

"Doctor Henderson?" he inquired anxiously as soon
as he saw Henderson walk in. "I'm Frank Jordan."

"Morning Frank," Henderson said quickly, grasping
his hand. "Let us take a look at your wife, then I'll be
right out to see you."

Now that he had his patient within reach, the anger
drained away, replaced with an intense concentration.
At a glance he could see that Dorothy Jordan was in
trouble. A slim brunette in her early twenties, she was
pale and glassy-eyed with pain, bewilderment, fear, and
shock. He wasn't going to get much of a story from
her, but that didn't make too much difference because

he had the husband. The sheet from the ambulance stretcher showed evidence of some retching: regurgitated stomach contents that looked like scrambled eggs, toast. Nothing more ominous.

"Save that sheet for us, please," he said to the Emergency-Room Nurse. "We'll want to look at it." And then to his partner, "Morning, Ed."

"Morning, Bob," his partner said.

"She fainted at home in her bathroom about an hour ago," Henderson said to Ed Russell and the Emergency-Room nurses. "She has had intense stabbing pain in the lower left quadrant accompanied by nausea. Apparently she's been having cramps for a couple of days."

Without further conversation, they moved swiftly to get along with the examination. While Russell was adjusting an arm cuff and getting her blood pressure and temperature, Henderson stripped off his sports jacket, slipped into the white coat a nurse handed him and bent over Dorothy Jordan, saying, "It's Dr. Henderson, Honey. Just lie still while we look you over."

Her pulse was weak. The blood pressure reading low enough to cause them to exchange glances.

"You can cross-match 1,000 cc's for us," Henderson said to the laboratory technician who was taking a blood sample.

He took a rubber glove from a tray for his left hand, lubricated it and dropped down on a stool as Russell and the Emergency Room nurses gently lifted her legs into the table stirrups, and rolled in close for a pelvic examination. Palpating the abdomen with his right hand, he said to Russell, "There is tenderness and some muscular rigidity on the lower left side. I might say ovarian cyst or P.I.D. (pelvic inflammatory disease) if I hadn't seen her less than two months ago. There is very slight vaginal bleeding." Then to Dorothy Jordan as she gasped and writhed away from his left hand, "That's all right, Honey. No more. That's all there is to it."

And then to Ed Russell again, "Well, we have a very tender cervix which completes the picture. I'd say the pre-op diagnosis is a left ectopic, probably within the isthmus. There has probably been a partial tubal rupture accompanied by at least one episode of hemorrhage, and probably more than one, progressing to a more severe rupture within the last hour."

"I'm with you," Russell said. "Her blood pressure is moving up a bit. Close to seventy. But I'd guess it was down to around fifty-five."

"You bet," Henderson said. Then to the attending nurse, "Please tell the OR we will want to proceed with an immediate laparotomy."

Rising from the stool, he stripped off the rubber glove and bent over Dorothy Jordan.

"Dorothy," he said. "This is Dr. Henderson. Can you understand me?"

"Yes," she whispered.

"We think we know what your trouble is," Henderson said. "We're going to perform some surgery because we think you're losing some blood internally and we want to stop it."

"Are you going to operate on me tonight?"

"Yes—right away. It's not a big operation but the sooner we do it, the better. And you'll feel a lot better as soon as it's over."

"I bumped my head in the bathroom," she whispered. "Everything is spinning around."

"I know," Henderson said, quickly examining her head to see if she had suffered any injury. But it wasn't the fall in the bathroom that was making her dizzy— she was in shock in the critical stage of an ectopic pregnancy.

Ectopic means *outside*. In an ectopic pregnancy, the fertilized ovum did not follow the normal course of moving through the fallopian tube into the uterus. Instead it implanted itself within a portion of the tube, on an ovary, or even in the abdomen. The majority of ectopic pregnancies occurred within the narrow isthmus of the fallopian tube that immediately adjoined the uterus. Some localized condition prevented or retarded the ovum's passage into the uterus.

As the placental roots sent out by the ovum developed, it increased rapidly in size, distending the fallopian tube. The normal tube was only about four inches long and its interior diameter was only about the size of a drinking straw. Usually the ovum's pressure ruptured the tube in the first few weeks of pregnancy, often before the patient or her physician knew she was pregnant. The rupture could be brought on by any sort of sudden muscular stress such as might occur during the lifting of furniture, opening a window, sexual intercourse, or even a heavy sneeze, fit of coughing, or the contractions of muscles during a bowel movement. How Dorothy Jordan's tube had ruptured Henderson didn't yet know. He might get a clue when he talked with her husband. But her signs and symptoms—pain, dangerously low blood pressure that had brought on shock and dizziness, and a very tender cervix—indicated there had been an internal hemorrhage.

Usually when the tube ruptured there was slight vaginal bleeding, then sharp stabbing pain or cramps. The rupture could be a slight tear or hole in the tubal lining which might cause only a seepage or dribble of blood. But if it blew wide open, there might be a major hemorrhage putting the victim into shock so that she fainted. Unless she was treated immediately her life was in peril. Meanwhile, any movement or examination of the patient had to be conducted with extreme care to avoid causing a spasm that might increase the rupture and bring on another massive hemorrhage.

Even now, although she was in the Hospital, it was a tricky business.

"Let's get her on the cart together, Ed," Henderson said.

Russell nodded and they slid their arms under her hips and shoulders, holding themselves rigid, and drew her off the table onto the wheeled stretcher.

"You take her into the OR," Henderson said to Russell. "I'll be with you in a minute. I want to talk to her husband."

In the waiting room he found Frank Jordan and

said, "You told me on the telephone that your wife had been to the Hospital. When was this?"

He listened quietly and when Frank Jordan was finished, told him about his wife's condition and the need for the operation.

"I suggest you stay right here," he said. "When you finish up with those forms, you can get yourself a cup of coffee in the cafeteria. I'll be out to see you as soon as we finish."

He went into the doctors' dressing room and started changing from street clothes into green jumper and cotton pants. Ed Russell joined him. He also had to change from his Maternity whites into OR greens.

"How are we coming?" Henderson said.

"She's still stable," Russell said. "Herb Goodman is with her." He drew a paper cup of coffee for himself and handed one to Henderson. "Did you get a good story from the husband?"

"I sure did," Henderson said. "You'll love it. She was trying to get pregnant but she didn't know she had succeeded. She's only about two weeks past her due date for her period. Two days ago after breakfast she was doing some early morning exercises on the living room rug."

"Exercises?"

"That's what her husband says. She was watching one of those morning TV exercise programs. She felt a sharp pain in her abdomen. So what do you suppose she did?"

"More exercises?"

"No. Worse. She went to see 'Dr. Kronkite'!"

"Oh, brother!" Russell exclaimed.

"Dr. Kronkite" was the name they used when they referred to the local chiropractor.

"But Kronkite didn't cure her. All he did was give her a 'manipulation.'"

"For Christ's sake!" said Russell fervently. "She could have blown the whole tube right in his office. She would have been a goner."

"Right," said Henderson. "But she didn't. She went

home and had some more cramps so last night she had her husband drive over here to the Hospital."

"Why the hell didn't they call you?"

"Because they thought she might have appendicitis. It never occurred to either of them that she might be pregnant. So she walked into Emergency last night and the jackass who was on duty told her she didn't have appendicitis. He guessed that it might be an ovary problem."

"Who was it?" Russell asked.

"I don't know yet," Henderson replied. "But I'll find out. So he gave her a prescription for an antibiotic and get this—told her *not* to be examined for three days. Meanwhile, that tube has been busting."

"I'll bet she's got a quart of blood in her belly," Russell said. "That's what I told Herb Goodman."

"That's what I think too," Henderson said. He had finished changing into the OR greens. He rose, swigged down the last of his coffee and they both went from the dressing room into the Operating Room.

"Wash your hands, boys," the Chief Nurse, Lottie Novitska said. She was a seasoned OR nurse who had come back to the hospital when her kids had grown into their teens. A big blond cheerful Polish woman, she was not the least awed by surgeons. "Your patient is ready in Number Three. How's that for service in the middle of the night?"

"Real groovy," Henderson said. He poked his head in the door of Number Three and saw that they had draped Dorothy Jordan for a laparotomy. Anesthesiologist Herb Goodman was visible amidst a forest of IV stands, dangling plastic tubes, and his array of oxygen and anesthesia gas tanks.

"Morning, Herb," Henderson said.

"I wish it were morning," Goodman said. He was afflicted with his usual midnight blues but he was performing like a miracle worker. Henderson considered him the best anesthesiologist he had ever worked with. Although Goodman had only had Dorothy Jordan as an emergency patient for a few minutes, he already had her under a light anesthesia. He had both her arms taped to IV boards and had her started on a bottle of saline solution. Two 500 cc packs of whole blood were suspended from overhead racks. The electrodes of a portable electrocardiograph were connected to her wrists and ankles.

"How's her pressure?" Henderson said.

"Up to seventy-five," Goodman said. "I'll put her to sleep as soon as we get a little more blood into her."

This was the crucial lull that frequently occurred in an ectopic pregnancy crisis. When Dorothy Jordan's fallopian tube ruptured, the ensuing hemorrhage had dropped her blood pressure. Then, after the initial loss of blood, the dropping pressure had slackened the hemorrhage.

"We're on our way," Henderson said. He stepped over to the scrub sink where Ed Russell was completing his scrub and pressed the water valve with his knee, soaping from fingers to elbows with the antiseptic detergent solution. He completed the scrub, thrust his arms into the long green gown that the nurses were holding for him and extended his hands for the rubber gloves they were waiting to snap on him. He moved into position opposite Ed Russell at the table. The P. A. system was playing "I Wonder Who's Kissing Her Now." It sounded like an orchestra led by Sammy Kaye or Lawrence Welk.

"Where do they get those corny tapes?"

"What do you want to hear?" Henderson asked, " 'Alice's Restaurant'?" He was palpating the exposed abdomen that had been swabbed with the golden-brown povidone-iodine solution. It was non-stinging and non-irritating, yet was such a powerful antiseptic that it killed all microorganisms—bacteria, viruses, fungi, protozoa—within seconds. It was the same stuff that was sprayed on the astronauts when they came back from lunar missions to kill any moon bugs that might have hitched a ride back to earth.

Even though he was exerting the most minimum gentle pressure with his fingertips, he could discern a boggy mass in the pelvis to the left of the uterus. Around it the abdominal muscles were in spasm.

"Can you relax her a bit more, Herb?" he said to Goodman. "She's still a bit tight."

Goodman adjusted the valve on one of his tubes that led to the IV system and injected a muscle-relaxing drug.

"Much better," said Henderson. He took the first knife from the scrub nurse and glanced to make sure that Ed Russell had the suction tube on the stand ready for instant use.

"Suction on?" he asked. "Now let's see what we've got."

He made the midline incision for a laparotomy, drawing the knife lightly over Dorothy Jordan's distended abdomen. The skin parted under internal pressure and as the peritoneum came into sight, they could see blood beneath it, filling the abdominal cavity.

"There it is, Herb," Henderson said to Goodman. "She's got a belly full of it. More than 500 cc's. You'd better hit her with both packs as soon as we get a clamp on it."

Goodman rose from his stool at Dorothy Jordan's head and peered over the top of his white screen at the dark shadow beneath the glistening, transparent peritoneum.

"All that and peritonitis, too," he said.

"I think you're right," said Henderson. He and Russell had tied off the few oozing capillaries. With her blood pressure so low, there were fewer bleeders than usual.

Ed Russell picked up the plastic suction tube. Henderson nicked the peritoneum and as the blood gushed upward, thrust his gloved hand down through it and grasped the uterus. He held it steady as Russell worked to empty the abdominal cavity so that they could see what they were doing. The blood was still flowing upward. Russell's suction tube gurgled noisily as it pulled into the collection bottle beneath the table.

"More sponges, girls," Henderson said. "Let's not be stingy."

Holding the uterus, he thrust the additional gauze packs around the incision. "Drop her head a bit, Herb," he said. "The whole cavity is full of it."

Now he could see enough of the left tube to make out the rupture. It was in the isthmus but whether it had involved the ovarian supply, he could not yet tell. The field was still too occluded.

"Clamp, please," he said.

The scrub nurse handed him the large instrument they used in ectopics. He slid it into the incision and clamped it to the uterine end of the left fallopian tube. Moving slowly and gently he lifted it upward and clamped the other artery. There was the rupture, more clearly visualized, and now it was not hemorrhaging.

"I think I've got it," he said.

As Russell continued to suction, he sponged off the fallopian tube until they could make out the embryonic sac within it.

"Go ahead with the blood, Herb," Henderson said.

Goodman adjusted the valves on the IV tubes and stood up to squeeze the bulbs to increase the speed with which they got blood back into Dorothy Jordan.

Russell was daubing with his sponges and picking up more blood from the base of the abdominal cavity but there was none getting through the clamp.

"I think you've got it, Bob," he said.

As Henderson continued, the rest of the team watched and waited. After a long moment Herb Goodman reported from behind his screen, "Her pressure is climbing. I've got eighty-five . . . ninety . . . still climbing . . ."

"That's it, all right," Henderson said. "Just keep it coming."

With the blood loss controlled, there was a sudden drop in tension in the group around the table. Once again Henderson could hear the P. A. music. The tune was "Dancing in the Dark."

"I'm going to take this left tube," he said, "but

there's a shadow right across the field. Shoot the light in here, girls."

"That's your big balloon head," Goodman said. "Step back a bit and let us aim that light past it."

He rose from his stool and helped the nurses focus the bright overhead lights more directly into the incision.

"Can you feel that heat now?" he said. "Are you warm, Robert?"

"Hotter than hell, Herb," Henderson replied. "Inside this gown it must be 110."

"That's what I've been trying to tell you," Goodman said. "This is the only combined operating room-sauna in the country. Every night I yell my head off and all the engineer does is send some guy around to kick the pipes. Why do you run a place like this?"

"Nag . . . nag . . . nag," Chief Nurse Novitska said. "You could all lose a few pounds. It would be good for you."

"Look who's talking," Goodman said. "Either you're getting fat or the population of this room is due to go up by one."

Lottie laughed. "You'll be the first to know," she said. "If that happens to me with three teen-agers, my husband will throw me out the window."

She peered over their shoulders at the incision. "Wouldn't you like a Balfour retractor in there?"

"That's just what I was thinking," Russell said. With Henderson holding the uterus in one hand and the clamp in the other, he was working alone and could use a larger field to move around in.

"We couldn't find one when we set up," the scrub nurse said.

"Let me look in Number Four," said Lottie.

"I wonder if Lottie would let us deliver her, Ed," Henderson mused.

"Never," Herb Goodman said. "Do you think any of these girls really trust us?"

"We certainly do," the scrub nurse said. "Dr. Russell

delivered my baby girl and my sister's little boy, didn't you, Dr. Russell?"

"My pleasure," Russell said. He was still sponging away to clean up the field while he waited for the retractor.

"That's just because you girls are too young to know any better," Goodman said. "If you'd sat here and watched them for years the way I have, you'd run to the nearest Ukrainian midwife."

Nurse Novitska was back with the retractor.

"It was in a sterile pack," she said to the scrub nurse, "on the top shelf of that cabinet in Number Four."

"We thought you'd gone to the store," said Goodman. "At least you could have got them to turn down the heat or switch off that dipsy-doodle music."

"I don't even hear it," Lottie Novitska said. "I'm deaf from those records the kids play at home. We had fourteen of my daughter's friends over the night before last for a slumber party. Two A.M. and the Big Sound was still going strong until the neighbors called the cops."

"The music is nice on the morning shift," said the scrub nurse. "You get sick and tired of hearing those orthopedic guys scraping and hammering away on their bone cases like a bunch of carpenters."

"That I wouldn't know about," Goodman said. "Ever since I started giving those anesthesiology lectures at the university, my status has sunk to a new low. I never get called for a morning case around here because everybody thinks I'm too busy. I keep telling them I only have three classes a week, but they keep putting me on these night-duty rosters."

"But now you're Professor Goodman," Henderson said. "Not just a lowly physician and anesthesiologist."

"Low!" exclaimed Goodman. "Listen, I've gone from obscurity to oblivion. Just as I got to be a college professor, they started the campus riots. Over at the med. school I've got a class of thirty who have to listen to me. When I go home at night and switch on the TV evening news, there are *my* students being interviewed —talking to an audience of millions! Her blood pressure is now 110. Pulse steady at 85. Temperature 100."

"Very good." Henderson was relieved. He had been holding the uterus and the clamp while Russell got the retractor positioned so they could widen the incision. "How are you making out, Ed?"

"I hope to get some help from the anesthesiology department," Russell said. "Can you drop her head a bit more, Herb?"

He wanted the table tilted so that Dorothy Jordan's abdominal organs would fall back a bit toward the chest cavity.

"Much better," he said when Goodman spun the wheel that dropped the table. He and Henderson scrutinized the uterus and the right fallopian tube. They dabbed and sponged until they could examine both ovaries. Henderson passed the clamp he was holding to Russell while he fingered the left ovary thoughtfully. Ordinarily, he would have tried to leave the ovary even if he had to take most of the left tube, but its blood supply had been involved with the ectopic—he didn't like its color or consistency.

"What do you think?" he asked Russell.

"It looks like trouble if we leave it that way."

"I think I'd like to get rid of it," Henderson said. "The right side is still clean. The uterus is in good shape."

To Nurse Novitska he said, "You can write it up as a left ectopic requiring a left salpingectomy and oophorectomy."

Together he and Russell dissected out the left tube and ovary. They performed a cornual resection to prevent any chance of a recurring pregnancy in the stump of the tube.

"Bowl ready for specimen?" Henderson asked.

"Put it right in here, dear," Nurse Novitska said.

Into the stainless steel bowl she was holding Henderson dropped the ruptured fallopian tube that might have meant the end of Dorothy Jordan. Within it was the sixth-week embryo. The Hospital Pathology Department would study it to try to determine why the ovum had not descended in normal fashion into the uterus. Perhaps they could produce some clues about defects that might have kinked up the passageway.

Dorothy Jordan would be out of the hospital within a week and could try for another pregnancy within six months. She would have to be watched carefully because the rate of recurrence of another tubal pregnancy was estimated at about fifteen to twenty percent, but he wouldn't have to worry about her fooling around with chiropractors. He could be sure that after this she'd be on the telephone night and day to report every twinge, cramp, and bellyache to him personally.

In his pocket was the prescription for antibiotic capsules that had been given to her by someone who had staffed the Emergency Room the night before. He had taken it from Frank Jordan and was going to track down this blooper personally. Why in Hell had the idiot told her not to be examined for three days! They closed the incision as rapidly as possible.

"Blood pressure steady at 110," Goodman reported. "We've put 750 cc's into her."

"Shut it off right there, Herb," Henderson said. "Let's see how she does for the rest of the night."

"Night!" exclaimed Goodman indignantly. "Are you kidding? It's five o'clock in the morning."

"I'll be damned," said Henderson. He'd completely lost track of where the night had gone.

"Well, goodnight, anyway, Chet," he said to Ed Russell.

"Goodnight, David," Russell replied.

They stepped back from the operating table, stripping off their gloves and gowns, letting Herb Goodman and Lottie Novitska supervise the transfer of Dorothy Jordan from the table to a stretcher cart.

It was nearly two more hours before Henderson finally left the Hospital. He had talked to Frank Jordan, observed Dorothy Jordan's recovery from the anesthesia and the surgery in the Intensive Care Unit, and dictated a summary of the case and the surgery for his office and for the Hospital records. Then he had looked in on two of his post-partum patients who were due to go home with their babies in a day or two. He had no surgery scheduled and his first office appointment was not until eleven.

Driving home, he found his house in the noisy chaos that accompanied breakfast and the departures to meet the school bus. It was obvious that the whole family had slept through his encounter with the police car and Sergeant Buck. Mary was still oblivious to the communication crisis she had caused by disconnecting the telephone jack. Not now, but at some appropriate moment later in the week he would bring it up. Now all he wanted was to stretch out on the patio in his lounge chair, glance at the morning papers Mary brought him, sip his coffee, relax, and chat with the kids.

"Bacon and eggs, dear?" Mary asked cheerfully.

"Sounds just right," he replied.

The girls were scribbling away at the homework that they should have finished the night before. It seemed to him that teen-agers were ridiculously overloaded with homework but they coped with it in the damnedest ways—while watching awful television programs, listening to rock records, talking on the telephone, conversing with each other, and perhaps even while making love. He couldn't decide whether the new generation had attained new hitherto-unknown levels of concentration or were completely fragmented and buggy. A mimeographed paper was handed to him for his signature. It stated that he was giving permission for his oldest daughter to be quartered in the school gymnasium along with the rest of her high-school science class for the weekend.

"What's the experiment this time?" he inquired.

"We're doing studies on what it's like to go without sleep. We're going to take reaction tests and observe each other."

He was speechless. Stupefied. They had seen him

stumbling in and out of the house at all hours of the night for years and never questioned it.

"I can tell you what it's like," he said. "You get to be real mean and irritable. You suffer from hallucinations. I'd like to run *that* study project! I'd keep you all awake until you hated me. You'd be ready to commit murder."

Giggles.

"Oh, Daddy, you're too much!"

"Did you have another busy night, dear?" his wife asked.

"Pretty lively," he said, taking the tray of bacon and eggs and toast that she brought him.

"But everything is all right?"

"Just fine," he said. "Just great."

His domestic radar was picking up faint signals. She was just a shade too solicitous. Long experience had taught him to beware of feminine encircling movements, then the gentle inquisition once he was safely trapped. Sure enough, here it came.

"You're going to be home this morning?"

"Just for an hour or so. Then I've got to get rolling again."

"I don't suppose you'd have time to look at that fence—where the pony is getting out."

"I thought we had a man coming to put in new posts."

"He is, but he's been very busy."

The *post digger* was busy! Henderson began to glare at Mary who was now sitting opposite him, wearing her brightest smile, and contemplated blowing his top. He weighed his chances of winning an argument, considered mentioning her removal of the telephone jack and decided against it. It had been too long and strenuous a night and he had a big day ahead of him. He wasn't up to it.

Instead he intoned, "I've got no time to mess around with that fence."

"Well, I only thought that since you were right here at home and not doing anything. . . ."

He let out a roar. "Do I have to take this god damned tray out to the car to eat this breakfast in peace?"

"No!"

"All right!"

"All right!"

The screen door slammed as she retreated to the kitchen.

Silence while he ate. Then,

"I'm sorry."

"Me, too."

He stretched out in the lounge chair with the newspaper spread over his head. A soft, feminine hand slipped beneath the newspaper, tweaked his nose and massaged the all-night stubble on his jaw.

"You're grubby. You need a shave."

He pressed the fingers to his lips. "I know."

"Do you still love me?"

"Absolutely."

"As much as ever?"

"More. Honey, I'll fix that fence the first chance I get. Wake me in an hour. I've got to go to the office."

He slept.

11

The "Monster"

A huge red sun sank below the apple trees marking the end of another day in the early summer heat wave that had blanketed the Middle West for nearly a week. The evening was still warm. In his pool, Henderson submerged, exhaling bubbles, until he sat comfortably on the bottom ten feet below the surface of the cool water, enjoying the shimmering green colors emanating from the underwater lights and gentle currents stirred up by the water circulator. Rising to the surface, he reached over to the hanging bar shelf suspended from the pool's rim and sipped again from his martini. Sheer luxury! Paradise in his own backyard! A testimonial to his imagination and persistence as well as his dogged resistance to emotional pressure. The whole family had been solidly arrayed against him.

When he had concluded that he would henceforward take few or extremely limited summer vacations, he had sought estimates on the price of an excavated cement pool for his backyard. Apparently all reasonably affluent Americans could afford one. He saw the advertisement constantly in his medical journals. But the prices of the pools and estimates of the costs of their installation had appalled him.

"No, goddammit," he had announced to Mary, "we're not going to go in hock for one of those sunken cement jobs. I'm going to get one of those big round rubber or plastic things. We'll set it up right under the apple trees."

"My God, you can't be serious!" Mary had cried. "Those things aren't pools! They're monstrosities. You're not putting one in this yard, I can tell you that!"

Poor Mary had envisioned something more elegant. Leafing through *Better Homes and Gardens* and other magazines, she had envisioned herself reclining on the marble rim of some sort of pavillion-type pool, girdled with flowering shrubs and pink geraniums in Italian ceramic pots. There would be a flagstone terrace, ornamented with wrought-iron furniture, a flowered chaise-lounge, patio candles placed about here and there and stereotape music wafting across the shady lawn. An idyllic retreat for breakfast coffee, cocktails, and after-dinner conversations.

"And you'll have every teenager in the neighborhood camped out here with our girls day and night all summer!" Henderson had retorted. "No thanks! I'm not doing it. I'm going to get the worst-looking rig my money can buy."

From a mail-order discount house he had ordered "the monster." According to faded factory tags, it apparently had been intended for use by the army, either as a general's pool during field maneuvers or perhaps for decontamination from poison gas—no one could tell. It was plastic and rubber, olive drab and chemical green in color. It held one hell of a lot of water and it rose twelve feet above the backyard lawn. It looked like a circular tank for industrial use or perhaps one of those pools that high-diving daredevils at carnivals plummeted into after they set their asbestos suits on fire. It bulged and sagged and leaked. Esthetically, it was a disaster.

"A goddamned beer vat!" Mary had called it. But Henderson was proud of it. It retained most of the water (the leaks though steady were slow) and it needed no expensive fence to keep wayward toddlers and pets from falling in and drowning. It had, in fact, very definite advantages. You had to climb a ladder to get up to the rim to plunge into it and Mary soon discovered that if she hauled up the ladder after her, she could float around on an air mattress sunbathing and reading in utter privacy and beyond the reach of the young ones who wailed, clamored, and played in the mud around its leaky bottom.

The teenagers in the Henderson family were so embarrassed by its ghastly size and color that they never invited their friends around to use it and went instead to municipal pools or the luxurious private pools of other suburbanites. Spared the babble of singing guitars, rock and roll music, and mindless chatter, Henderson found that he was left in peace to enjoy his acquisition at any hour of the day or night, either by himself or with Mary. On warm evenings, returning late from the hospital, he could strip and plunge into it to slosh around, porpoising, scissor kicking, and floating languidly as the day's stresses slipped away.

By chance he had also discovered that it provided a haven of privacy for himself and his wife. Scorned by the teenagers, shielded from prying eyes by a leafy bower of branches, beyond reach of the youngest ones, once they had drawn up their ladder, he and Mary could be completely alone, save for an occasional derisive "caw" from Count Dracula, who had developed into a peeping tom as he perched in the boughs of a big apple tree nearby.

It was, most emphatically, Henderson had to admit, the most ugly pool, if you could call it a pool, that ever disgraced a homeowner's backyard. A veritable blot on the local landscape. He gloated over it and loved it.

Once again, he sipped his martini and with relish envisioned the day when the urban sprawl crept out around his farm until a bank or insurance company constructed a high-rise skyscraper on the nearby rolling Indiana farmland. High up in some executive suite a tycoon, gazing out of his eighty-second story picture window, would spot Henderson's plastic puddle.

"Gibbs," would go a sharp query to an underling, "what is that atrocity down there, fouling up our view?"

"It's some sort of old tank, sir. It belongs to a doctor, I think."

"Well, get rid of it! Offer to take the whole farm. Buy him out!"

Henderson would, of course, bleed them until they were white. He would hold out for the top price. Then with the proceeds, having disposed of his practice, he would move to New Zealand. Perhaps he would even buy a boat and with Mary sail across the Pacific, pausing at various South Sea islands to deliver the natives' babies. Later he would take Mary and any of the kids who wanted to come along and cruise to the Great Barrier Reef of Northern Australia.

"Where's my drink?"

It was Mary, clad in a brief two-piece suit, slipping into the pool.

"Right here, waiting for you," Henderson replied, scissor-kicking over to his homemade bar shelf, handing Mary her martini and placing a kiss full on her lips.

"Did you pull up the ladder?"

"I did," she said. "But I don't think I have to. They're all inside watching TV. They won't even notice we've disappeared. I brought you some more olives. Have a bite."

"I'll have more than one," Henderson said, placing his drink on the bar shelf and cradling his wife in his arms. Unsnapping the bra, he caressed both her breasts and then sank swiftly beneath the surface of the pool until he could tug down the bathing suit bottom and plant a firm, toothy kiss on the white flank of buttock below the suntan line.

He was rewarded with wild flailing of legs and a scissors-lock of thighs around his neck. When he rose to the surface, Mary was waiting with a kiss and a refill for his martini.

"Just for once," she whispered in his ear, "I hope your damn phone doesn't ring."

And for once, it didn't.

12

Cindy

"Is that a new kind of patient I see out there in the waiting room?" Henderson asked the office nurse. "That guy with the long curls?"

She giggled. "No. That's some high-school boy that came in with Cindy McDonald."

"Her afternoon date, I suppose?" He shook his head. Imagine bringing your high school boy friend along with you while you went to the doctor! And was the guy with the curls one bit fazed about being the only male in a whole room full of women most of them pregnant? Of course not! There he sat, totally unconcerned, flipping the pages of his magazine.

"Sorry to keep you waiting, Cindy," he said, as he entered the examining room. "I had a baby. Or rather, one of my patients had a baby."

His young blond patient had peeled off her slacks and sweatshirt and sat on the edge of the examining table, dangling her legs, garbed in a falsie bra and panties adorned with running lizards.

"Oh, that's all right," she said softly. The polite but vague teenager. The detachment that drove the older generation crazy.

"Where did you get that wonderful tan?"

"Up at the lake. We were there a week."

"And you wore a bikini. You see I told you there wouldn't be any visible scar to worry about."

"I know. It's just great."

"And how are you feeling?"

"Oh, just great."

He had used a pfannenstiehl incision to keep the scar well below the navel when he did her surgery six months ago. She had come in about a week before that. Or rather she had been hustled in by a frazzled mother who was in a panic about her protruding stomach. The poor woman was convinced that she had an unwed pregnant daughter.

"She says she hasn't been with anyone, Doctor," the mother had said. "But you can see for yourself something is wrong. She can't even zip up her jeans anymore!"

"Now just take it easy, Mrs. McDonald," he had said. "You sit right here in my office while I give Cindy an examination."

If there was a story to be gotten from the girl, it would come easier when he was alone with her.

"Don't worry too much about your mother," he had said when they were in the examining room.

"She's too much!" the girl had said. "I know I'm not pregnant." She sounded bored rather than indignant.

"I see what you mean," he said. His pelvic examination had quickly established that she still possessed her virginity.

"How long ago did this start?"

"I don't know for sure. I think just a few weeks ago."

There was a startlingly large mass lying somewhat toward the left anterior abdominal wall. He could easily trace its proportions by palpating the abdomen. A few days later he and Ed Russell had her on the table in surgery. They'd gone in expecting to find a tumor of the left ovary and they did—but it was no ordinary tumor. A dysgerminoma. The only other one he personally had encountered was back in his hospital residency. Now they found themselves confronted by a huge, swiftly growing tumor that had already overwhelmed one ovary and gone on to invade the other. It didn't appear to be malignant yet, but dysgerminomas almost invariably became malignant.

Across the operating table Russell stood waiting. They exchanged glances, keenly aware that the rest of the OR team was waiting for their decision.

"If we don't do it now, Ed," he had said, "we're only going to have to come back in again. I'd like to leave a piece of that other ovary but it's too much of a risk."

His partner had agreed completely. So they went ahead with a rough piece of surgery: A complete hysterectomy on a fourteen-year-old girl; uterus, ovaries, tubes, cervix. The parents who had been so upset over a possible pregnancy went into a state of numb shock. He had begun talking to Cindy while she was still in the Hospital, bracing himself for a bad time with the youngster, but it hadn't come. She accepted the outcome with no visible emotion. Apparently, the prospect of getting married and having a family was too far in the future and too vague in her mind to produce any deep anxiety or frustration, or else she was repressing it for the time being.

"I can always adopt children, can't I?" she said.

"Of course," he had answered. "You can have as large a family as you like. Space them out, too."

That was that. It was obvious there was only one thing that had really bothered her about the surgery and hospitalization—missing school and dates. She had recovered quickly and so far he had carried her successfully with nothing more than the synthetic estrogen hormones in birth control pills. In the earlier decades of the century a complete hysterectomy on a teen-age girl would have meant tragedy. She would soon have become prematurely gray, and by age twenty she would have been shriveled, physically and psychologically. Now here she was with her budding secondary sex characteristics still intact.

"Anything you want to talk to me about, Cindy?"

"No, not really."

"How's your mother?"

"Oh, she's okay."

"Well, come in or call me anytime, and I want you to stay on the same schedule. Come in every six weeks."

"Oh, sure."

She had replaced the slacks and sweatshirt and drifted dreamily out the door with her school books, joined by the fuzzy-wuzzy boy friend. Watching her go, he reflected, when you grow older, you live boxed in by the past, present, and future. When you're young, it's so uniquely the next moment!

His secretary was in the doorway. "I've got a call for you from Dr. Laden. He's on the line. You also had calls from Dr. Crawford and Dr. Harding."

"Let me take Laden first and see what he wants," Henderson said. Picking up the phone he said, "How goes it, Marvin?"

"Did you get the word on Ruth Sinclair's sterilization application yet?" Laden asked.

"Not a word yet," Henderson said. "But that Committee should be meeting this week. We're into June."

"They met," said Laden. "We got turned down."

Henderson turned to his secretary. "I'll be a couple of minutes on this," he said. "Did we get any mail from the Hospital today?"

"Yes, you did," Martha Williams answered, "but you didn't open it yet. Do you want me to find it for you?"

"Never mind," Henderson replied. "I'll find it." He began shuffling through envelopes on his desk. "I'm looking through my mail," he said to the telephone. "Tell me what happened."

"Lum Fong gave it to us. Right in the La Bonza. There were five at the meeting of the Committee. The two Catholics, Donovan and Schultz, abstained from voting. That left the three Protestants, including Gordon. He voted negative. So we were turned down, two out of five is not a majority."

"I've found the report," said Henderson.

He read the summary aloud: "The patient in Dr.

Gordon's view may continue to display an excellent response to the drug therapy that has apparently stabilized her condition." He paused. "I like that part, Marvin. It's the tranquilizers that are doing the job. Her improvement has got nothing to do with your therapy or the fact that we're promising her she'll have no more pregnancies."

"Of course not," Laden said. "Keep reading."

"At present, however," continued the summary, "Dr. Gordon believes this patient remains under such situational stress related to the pregnancy that she is not capable of making a major decision such as subjecting herself to voluntary sterilization. It is suggested that the proposal may be restudied and further evaluated in the period following the pregnancy."

"Didn't I tell you that old fox would vote against us?" Laden said. "As soon as he saw that I had a part in the case and was recommending it? I've also heard that he's piqued about being dragged in to serve on the Committee. And anyway, he's totally unconcerned about the realities of family life."

Henderson was still so stunned by the Committee's vote that he was letting Laden do the talking while he tried to take it in. His recommendations were rarely turned down—for a senior staffer like himself, it was almost a personal insult. Marvin Laden certainly hadn't been exaggerating Gordon's arrogance. No wonder Crawford and Harding had tried to call him before he got the verdict in the mail—they too must have been flabbergasted by Gordon's negative vote. He could feel the wrath beginning to simmer within him. How in God's name was he going to break the news to Ruth Sinclair? She would really flip! And she still had nearly four months to go before she would have that baby!

"I know one thing," he said grimly. "I'm not going to tell the Sinclairs about this damned nonsense. I want some time to think it over."

"I agree," Laden said. "I'm looking, however, at the calendar."

"I'm looking at the calendar, too," Henderson answered. "Those Committee appointments have been running six months."

"So Gordon will be serving until October," said Laden.

"That's too late to do us any good," Henderson added. "Sinclair's due to have that baby in September. By the time we get rid of Gordon, she'll be out of the Hospital."

"And you can't predict what shape the Committee might take," Laden said. "You might get another creep in there to take Gordon's place and we might not get a favorable vote on a sterilization for Sinclair before next Christmas."

Henderson had to admit that Laden was right. J. Arthur Gordon had completely fouled up his plans for Ruth Sinclair.

"I'd be more shook up," Laden was saying, "if it weren't that I'm glancing through a program that came in the same mail."

"What kind of a program?" demanded Henderson impatiently.

"The printed program for the Third World Congress of Psychiatric Studies," Laden said. "Sponsored by the International Federation of North American Asian Psychiatrists. To be held in Kyoto, Japan, July 10 through 21."

"Are you going?"

"Hell, no," Laden replied. "But I see by the program that among the participants will be none other than J. Arthur Gordon, M.D., Director of the Berkshire Institute. He's going to deliver a paper."

"What the hell do I care what that chuckle-headed bastard is going to be doing in Kyoto in July?" interrupted Henderson.

"Because if he's going to be in Kyoto on July 10," Laden replied, "he won't be here—and knowing Lum Fong, I'd be willing to bet that he's going on a free air ticket that will permit him to return to the United States via Bombay, Athens, Rome, and Paris, so I suggest that we plan to resubmit the application for Mrs. Sinclair's sterilization . . ."

Henderson leaned forward and flipped his calendar. "While the crumb is grandstanding around the world? I see what you mean, Marvin. If they met and approved it in July, we'd be all right."

A thought struck him. "But you forgot one point; Gordon will leave a proxy vote. With one of the other members of the Committee."

"I haven't forgotten," said Laden. "I'm already guessing that he will leave it with Donovan or Schultz. He knows he can't count on the non-Catholics to follow through with his veto."

"So where the hell are we?" asked Henderson.

"At least it will be an open-end deal," Laden said. "Even the Catholic point of view is shifting around these days."

"But not this month or next, Marvin," Henderson objected. "Come back down to reality!"

"All right then," said Laden. "Forget it. Don't resubmit the application. Just get Mrs. Sinclair's husband to have a vasectomy."

"Boy, you're really coming at me today, aren't you," Henderson said.

"It's all part of the new wave," Laden answered. "The social revolution of the Seventies is upon us. You know as well as I do that we've got to safeguard this family from growing any larger."

Henderson thought it over. It was true that the vasectomy operation was considerably cheaper and easier to obtain than the sterilization operation for women. It took less than twenty minutes to carry out and could be performed by a urologist or surgeon under local anesthesia in a private office.

The doctor simply severed the two tiny tubes that carried the male sperm from the testicles. Each tube was clamped, a small piece snipped out, and the separated ends tied off and buried in the surrounding tissue. Since the vas deferens, as the tubes were called, were enclosed within the spermatic cords, which ran close to the body as they passed over the pubic bone into the abdominal cavity, a vasectomy was really minor surgery. Once the tubes were surgically disconnected, all sperm cells produced in the testicles were reabsorbed without complications into the body. There were no effects on male virility or sexual performance.

Yet simple though this birth-control method was, many physicians didn't advocate it and few surgeons and urologists had experience in performing the operation. The widespread ignorance about the procedure was complicated by a lingering fear of legal entanglements and malpractice suits despite the American Medical Association's assertion that so long as proper consent of the man was obtained, the legal risk was no greater than for any other form of surgery.

And most of the general public knew even less and were even more confused about it. Many had vasectomy mixed up with castration. For some men it would represent too much of a threat to their virility. Bill Sinclair would probably agree if Henderson proposed it, but how would he really feel about it?

"I'm just an old fogy feeling my way with these new ideas, Marvin," he said. "What are the psychological risks in a case like this?"

"On the big boy?" Laden asked. "You mean will he be afraid his voice will change or that he won't be able to lead his fire company?"

"All of that. I'm going to have to sell him on the idea myself."

"So why don't you consider a vasectomy for yourself? That's the best way. Set a good example for your patients. You've got four kids. Now's the time to quit—before you add to the world's problems."

Henderson laughed. It wasn't the first time that Laden had made the suggestion. And it made such good sense that Henderson was hard put to find arguments against it.

"I'm considering it," he said, "just to shut you up." And then more briskly, "All right, here we go. First, we'll do as you suggest and resubmit Ruth Sinclair's application as soon as Gordon is on his way to Japan. Two, we both keep our mouth shut as far as she is concerned but I'll get him in and sound him out on whether he would consider a vasectomy."

"And three," added Laden. "You'll continue to consider the vasectomy for yourself. But you won't actually sign up for it."

Henderson was stung. "I might just go through with it, after all."

"I'll bet you chicken out."

"Not if I felt I had the right guy to do the job."

"There's plenty of them around town," Laden said. "But knowing how you surgeons like to bug out of town when you're going to be the patient, I can recommend a good man in San Francisco."

"Jesus, Marvin," said Henderson. "You mean you're actually referring people to San Francisco?"

"Every day," Laden answered. "Doctors included. From your own county medical society."

Henderson was flabbergasted. "Wait a minute," he said. He took refuge in a gulp of cold coffee from the cup on his desk and used a pen and scratch pad. "Round-trip air fare to San Francisco must run around $300.00. Plus $200.00 to the urologist. $200.00 more for expenses. That comes to about $700.00. If I go, you pay. How's that for a bet?"

"And if you don't go," Laden said. "I get the $700.00. I'm looking forward to framing your check. In fact, if you want to pay me now, I might use it to attend that psychiatric congress in Kyoto. I could sit in the audience and make faces at Gordon."

"I'm beginning to think it might be great to have you both out of the country," Henderson said. "Why don't you try to sell him on a vasectomy?"

"He doesn't need one," said Laden. "He was castrated by his mother."

13

Late Show

It was after midnight when the monthly meeting of the County Medical Society finally broke up. Henderson drove home slowly, feeling relaxed because none of his patients had gone into labor during the evening. None was due for a baby until the middle of the week and he might even be able to sleep until seven the next morning.

A full moon bathed the farmlands in shimmering silver and the whisper of a light southwesterly breeze carried the scent of ripening crops from his neighbor's corn fields. It was far too beautiful a night to go straight to bed.

The house was dark, Mary and the children presumably sound asleep. He considered reclining on the patio with a sandwich and a glass of ice tea, watching a late TV movie with an earphone plugged into the portable set. Glancing through the weekly TV program guide, he found a dazzling collection of movies. He could, for example, view:

CHINA DOLL (English. 1958.) Story Synopsis: "In 1943 in war-torn China a captain gives a beggar some money and discovers he has unknowingly purchased the man's daughter. Starring Victor Mature and Li Li Hua."

Or there was *UNDER CAPRICORN* starring Ingrid

Bergman—"A romantic drama set in Australia in 1831. Society woman degenerates into alcoholic."

Or *VIOLENT MEN*—Glenn Ford and Barbara Stanwyck. 1954. "A crippled cattle baron is encouraged by his scheming wife to drive the smaller ranchers out of 'his' valley."

Or *DEAD EYES OF LONDON* (1961)—"Scotland Yard vs. murderous band of blind men, filmed in Germany and starring Joachim Fuchsberger and Karin Baal."

Or *TENNESSEE CHAMP* (1954). "A man saved from a watery grave by a ring promoter gets into the fight game."

Sipping his ice tea Henderson strolled out to the patio and then thought of the pool. A swim would be relaxing on this hot summer night. The peace and quiet and solitude of the moonlit scene delighted him.

He stripped to his undershorts, draping his clothing over the patio furniture, scaled the ladder to the rim of the pool and lowered himself into the quiet cool water. It *was* a good idea! He felt marvelously relaxed as he swam and floated about, wiggling his toes to get the morning operating-room kinks out of his leg muscles, gazing at the moon, letting his mind wander. Water, he reflected, was really his special outdoor love. He resolved to take as little holiday and vacation time as possible until winter was at hand. Then he could set up something with the family so that they could all fly to the West Indies and swim every morning, noon, and night.

A pair of rubber frogman's flippers hung on a hook on the rim of the pool. He reached up, snagged them, and, treading water, buckled his feet into them. Back-paddling about the pool, he summoned up images of waving palm trees and coral reefs, of wearing his face mask and air bottle backpack, diving down amidst the schools of gaily colored tropical fish . . .

Suddenly the silence of the summer night was shattered by the rumble of a heavy vehicle coming up his driveway. Who the hell could that be? One of his teenage girls coming home from a late date? What in God's name was her boyfriend driving? He floated silently on his back in the pool. Perhaps they would try a moonlight "skinny dip" in the pool—as he might have done in his own teenage dating years. He would sink to the bottom and rise like King Neptune to scare the daylights out of them.

The clink of glass bottles solved the mystery. It must be the milkman. Another all-night sport like himself! He floated, waiting to hear the truck depart, but instead, the outdoor phone on the patio began to ring. At this hour it could only be for him.

"Goddammit all!" he mumbled. He heaved himself up and over the rim of the pool, dropped to the ground, and still wearing the frogman flippers, lifting his feet high to avoid tripping, dashed past the startled milkman and grabbed the phone off the hook.

"Dr. Henderson," he panted.

"I have an emergency call for you, Doctor," said the efficient voice of his answering service. "It's from Mr. Sinclair. His wife is bleeding. There's a lot of blood. He wants to know what to do." Ruth Sinclair! Already Henderson's mind was racing in high gear. It must be a hemorrhage. There goes her goddamned placenta!

"Have you still got her husband on the other line?" he asked.

"Yes, Doctor. He's on. I thought I'd better ask him to hold while I checked to see if you were home."

"Good work," Henderson said. "Plug me in. I want to talk to him."

Standing there in his dripping shorts he realized he had no pen to write with and nobody around to back him up. To the milkman who was still staring dazedly at him, holding his basket of empty bottles, he said, "Please don't go away. I may need you."

Bill Sinclair came on the line. His voice was controlled but husky with tension. "Dr. Henderson, something has gone wrong. Ruth just woke me up. She's losing a lot of blood."

He could picture it. When they hemorrhaged this way in the night, they often awoke in a pool of blood.

"How is she at this moment, Bill? Is she wide awake? Fully conscious?"

"Yes, she is."

"Okay, here's what you do. First of all, tell her that I think I know what's causing the blood and that she's going to be all right. Then you get dressed quick. Just grab a pair of slacks and shoes. Take a big bath towel and put it between her legs. Wrap a sheet or blanket around her, pick her up just as she is and carry her out to the car. Drive straight to the Emergency Entrance at the Hospital. I'll be there waiting for you."

"Our kids are still asleep," Bill Sinclair said. "I'll have to call a neighbor to stay with them."

"Don't stop for that, Bill," Henderson said. "I'll call the police and have them send a car around to your house. They can keep an eye on the kids until we work something out. What's your address?"

"Fifty-five Millwood Drive," Sinclair said.

"Okay," Henderson said. "Get rolling."

He turned to the milkman and said, "Write down 55 Millwood Drive for me. And then take this phone and dial the police. I've got to go to the Hospital."

He handed the telephone to the milkman, unbuckled the frogman feet, peeled off his wet shorts, snatched up his undershirt, and toweled himself dry.

"I'm at Dr. Henderson's house," the milkman was saying on the telephone. "He wants to speak to you."

Henderson took the telephone.

"Go ahead, doctor," said a cheerful, disciplined voice. "This is Sergeant Cavallo speaking, the night dispatcher."

"I've got an emergency case that has to be taken to the Hospital," Henderson said. "I don't want to wait for an ambulance—her husband's driving her. Can you send one of your patrol cars around to their house? There are three kids asleep there. We need sombody to watch the place until we line up a baby sitter."

"Sure thing, Doctor," the police dispatcher said. "What's the name and address?"

"Fifty-five Millwood Drive," Henderson said, reading from the order pad the milkman handed him. "The name is William Sinclair."

"We'll cover for him right away."

"Thanks a lot, Sergeant," Henderson said. "We'll call you back as soon as we can."

He handed the telephone to the milkman again and said, "Please dial me 344-6500."

During the dialing he was pulling on his trousers and shirt and shoving his feet into his loafers. He slipped into his jacket and took the phone back from the milkman, recognizing the voice of the night supervisor of the Maternity Floor nursing staff, Ellie Baker.

"Dr. Henderson, Ellie," he said. "I'm coming in with an emergency case. Her name is Ruth Sinclair. She's hemorrhaging. She's in her seventh month and I think it may be a placenta previa. Get me a lab technician. Have her stand by to draw blood samples as soon as the patient arrives. I will probably want to transfuse her so get a unit of blood ready. Middle size. No, wait. You'd better get four units ready. I don't know what shape she is in. Her husband is driving her to the Emergency Entrance. Send one of your girls down to meet her with a cart. I don't want any stalling around at the Night Admissions Desk. Tell the Emergency people to get her up to the Maternity Floor with an escort. On the double! You should have her prenatal record in your 'ready file.' Pull it out for me. I'm leaving home now. I should be there in a few minutes."

He flipped the phone back to the milkman and said, "Thanks a lot for the help."

The milkman looked at him blankly. "There's a bird on top of your car," he said.

The light from the patio illuminated a huge black bird perched on the rooftop luggage rack.

"Just a pet crow," said Henderson.

He ran for the car and jumped in. As he slammed the door and gunned the engine, Count Dracula flapped upward, squawking curses. Henderson shot down the driveway with Count Dracula flapping out in front of him like Bela Lugosi, transformed into a big bat, in the old horror movie.

The moonlit highway was deserted. Driving like a dragstrip racer, Henderson reached the Hospital in six minutes. He used his key to let himself in through the locked doors of the doctors' entrance, went up the backstairs to the Maternity Floor two at a time, paused to compose himself and then deliberately sauntered down the corridor to the nursing station next to the elevators.

"Where did you put her?" he asked, coming up behind Ellie Baker.

"She's not here yet, doctor. We're waiting for her in Emergency."

Henderson had caught his breath and now assuming a tone of calm, professional confidence, said, "Well are we all set? You've got the blood ready?"

"Ready. And here's her prenatal record," Ellie said.

"This patient," Henderson said to Ellie, her nurses, and the lab technician who was also standing by, "is a 'multip' with three normal deliveries and one spontaneous abortion in the fourth month. Her husband telephoned me to report a sudden heavy bleeding. I've been worrying about her bleeding all through this pregnancy, so this may be a previe."

The desk phone rang and Ellie took the call. "Thank you," she said. "The doctor is waiting for her."

To Henderson and the others she said, "Mrs. Sinclair is on her way up . . . she's still conscious."

Just then the elevator doors opened. In the group gathered around the stretcher cart was Bill Sinclair, a Hospital security guard, nurses.

"Thanks very much, everybody," Henderson said. "We'll take her from here."

To Bill Sinclair he said, "Good job, Bill. Have a seat out here while I examine your wife. We got a police car to check on your kinds."

"They were pulling up just as we left," Bill Sinclair

said weakly. He sank into the chair the nurses shoved under him.

Henderson followed the stretcher into Labor Room B. Ruth Sinclair was pale and moaning. "Boy, what a lot of blood," she whispered. "Where's it coming from?"

"We'll find out," Henderson said. "Don't worry."

While she was still on the cart he had his hand on her wrist. Her pulse wasn't too bad. Maybe ninety-five but strong enough to make him feel a bit better. A quick look at the bloody bath towel shoved between her legs revealed the clots. Dark red and liverish in color.

His left hand lightly palpated her abdomen. It was reassuringly soft. Not rigid. At least this wasn't the hard, boardlike, painful uterus that would signal an abruptio placenta. It might be an imminent abortion which would be marked by copious vaginal bleeding and the passage of clots. But there were no cramps.

If the placenta was partially separated, she could progress to birth—premature birth to be sure, but otherwise normal. But there was no way of ascertaining the position of the placenta at this point. For an internal examination in these cases you always had to have a patient on the operating table prepared for an immediate cesarean, because even the slightest touch of the finger introduced into the cervix might produce a torrential flow of blood. It could be so sudden and massive as to be fatal.

"Did any pain wake you up?" he asked.

"No, just being all wet."

"You've lost some blood all right, but we can put that back in you. Just relax."

With the help of the nurses he lifted her gently off the cart and into the bed.

To Baker he said, "Let's get going with that IV catheter first."

He wanted to get into a good vein before she got "shocky" and the veins collapsed, after which he would have a hell of a time getting the blood in.

"Come on, girls, let's get hooked in here," he said.

"Don't give me dextrose. Give me saline. We may want to use blood."

They handed him the intracath and he went into an antecubital vein in Ruth Sinclair's right arm near the elbow. He threaded the catheter through the needle into the vein. The intravenous stand was in place beside the bed and ready.

"All right," he said to Nurse Baker, "you can start the saline in that one."

He moved around to the other side of the bed and inserted another needle and catheter into a vein in Ruth Sinclair's left arm. This one, too, was open to a flow of saline solution. Now they could switch to the blood swiftly.

They taped her arms to IV boards and fastened them to the raised bed sides. He took another peek at the fresh pad they had thrust between her legs. It was stained with blood but nothing like the towel or sheet.

"Fetoscope, please," he said and taking the scope one of the nurses handed him listened for the baby's heart tones. There they were: flup-flup-flup in his ears. Sounded like a nice 140. Ruth Sinclair certainly still had a live baby. He went over her abdomen again gently; no sign of uterine contractions.

"I think we're doing all right," he said to Nurse Baker.

He sat down in a corner and examined the bed sheet Bill Sinclair had brought her in, then the bath towel. It looked like she had lost two pints if that was the only bleeding in progress—nothing else internally. Fortunately the sight of blood unnerved patients and their families so much that they usually overestimated how much loss had occurred.

"Give her two units," he said to Nurse Baker. "That will make up for what she's lost and keep us ahead if she starts to go again. Check her blood pressure and pulse every ten minutes. I'm going out to speak to her husband."

To the lab technician he said, "Be sure you get a complete blood count, and be sure the lab rushes in the cross match for donors' blood. You'd better get at least four more units ready."

He turned to Ruth Sinclair. "Everything is going fine," he said. "You've lost some blood but I don't think you're going into labor. Just rest and lie still. The quieter the better."

They had put Bill Sinclair in the fathers' waiting room. Henderson drew himself a paper cup of coffee and sat down beside him.

"Your wife is safe, Bill," he said. "She has hemorrhaged pretty heavily. It may mean that she's going to go into labor but I don't think so. I think the placenta—that's the afterbirth that is attached to the wall of the uterus—has partially broken down and pulled loose from the wall. It's full of tiny blood vessels and when this happens there's often a lot of bleeding. I think she has a low-lying placenta in this pregnancy—it's attached lower down than usual and when you get this situation you are liable to get this sudden bleeding. But now the bleeding has almost stopped. If it starts up again and becomes serious, now that she's at the Hospital, we can take her right into surgery."

Bill Sinclair nodded. "What about the baby?" he asked.

"We can't tell yet because we can't examine your wife right now. It might increase the bleeding. If the bleeding slows we will take X rays of her abdomen and they should show us just where that placenta is lying. If it's completely below the baby and is going to interfere with normal labor and delivery, we may have to do a cesarean to take the baby out. But of course, we would prefer to wait until she's closer to her delivery date to do that. It's better for the baby to stay inside the mother's body for as long as possible. If the placenta is only partly in the way, we may deliver it normally."

He paused to draw two more cups of coffee.

"I'm going to stay at the Hospital for the rest of the night," he continued, "but it's okay for you to go home now, get some rest, and take care of the kids. I'll call you first thing in the morning. How are you feeling?"

Bill Sinclair gulped the paper cup of coffee and stood up. "I'm okay now," he said. "It's just waking up in the middle of the night with all that blood in bed. It's funny. I work with people in big trouble all the time. Blood on the job never bothers me. But when it's your own wife, it's different."

"You did fine," Henderson said. "You got her here quickly and that's what counted. Kiss her good night and get on home."

He went back again to look at the fresh pad between Mrs. Sinclair's thighs and found only a few spots.

"Well," he told Nurse Baker, "maybe we're going to be lucky, with this one. Keep up the ten minute checks on her pulse and blood pressure and keep an eye on that pad. Call me if the bleeding starts again and wake me in one hour anyway."

He paused in the locker room to get out of his damp clothes and put on a set of fresh whites. Then he went into the doctors' bunkroom where it was dark and cool, stretched out on his back, and fell asleep.

A hand was on his shoulder. A flashlight in his face.

"Okay," he said. "I'm awake."

"Your patient, Mrs. Sinclair," Nurse Baker was saying. "Here's the latest. No more bleeding. Blood pressure good. Fetal heart tones 120-140."

"What's her pulse?" Henderson asked.

"Eighty-six—steady."

"What time is it now?"

"Four-fifteen A.M."

"Thanks very much," Henderson said. "Stay with her and call me again at 6:30 unless you see any signs of trouble. I want to be up when you girls change shifts."

When he was awakened at six-thirty he went immediately to Ruth Sinclair's room and examined the pad. It was barely spotted.

"It's the same pad we've had on her all night, Doctor," Nurse Baker said. "She's slept most of the time. No complaints of pain or cramps."

"Fine," he said. "Switch the IV's over to dextrose.

Five percent solution in water. Only clear liquids for her diet today."

The Day Supervising Floor Nurse had arrived and he went over the Sinclair case with her and Baker.

"I want blood instantly available for this patient," he said. "Right through the next twenty-four hours. Have your girls continue to keep a close watch on her. I'll be down in surgery until about eleven o'clock. Reach me there right away if there's any sign of a problem. And when she wakes up, tell her that I'm in the Hospital and she's all right. Thank you, everyone."

He descended to the cafeteria for tomato juice, eggs, and bacon, putting Mrs. Sinclair's placenta in the back of his mind for the moment and concentrating on the case he had scheduled for eight A.M. surgery.

14

A Map of the Placenta

Making the rounds at the Hospital after lunch, Henderson found Ruth Sinclair wide awake and apprehensive about losing the baby.

"It's really the same thing as a miscarriage, isn't it?" she asked. "How could I have all that bleeding and still be all right? Everything seemed to be coming loose inside me."

"This is different," Henderson said. "You were bleeding all right and thank God it stopped. You've scarcely lost any more blood since this morning. We've been listening to your baby's heart all the time. It sounds fine. It's strong and normal.

"What I want to do now is to keep that baby inside you a littler longer. As long as possible. The closer you come to your nine months, the better it will be for the baby. So today and tonight you lie right there in bed and keep still. Tomorrow, perhaps, we'll be able to do some tests to see how things are inside your uterus."

At the floor desk he dialed Radiology and got Fred Sandor, the Chief Radiologist.

"Fred, this is Bob Henderson. Can you do a localization for a possible placenta previa for me?"

"How stable is the patient?" Sandor asked.

"Okay now, I think. And if we wait until tomorrow,

there should be no problem. She hemorrhaged around midnight last night and lost about 800 cc's of blood with plenty of clots. But it quit right after we got her admitted and went to work on her. It's been holding that way since about two A.M."

"Can you send her down around nine tomorrow morning?" Sandor asked. "I'll be here myself at that time. I'll try a scintigram and see what we get."

"I'd like to look at the films myself," said Henderson.

Tomorrow was supposed to be his day off, but he would certainly want to be at the Hospital first thing in the morning to see how she was progressing and then stay with her when they did the test. Fred Sandor was a highly competent radiologist but with an emotional, unpredictable patient like Ruth Sinclair he wasn't going to take any chances. So he was there in Radiology at nine-ten the following morning when they injected a radioactive isotope into a femoral vein high up in her right thigh. Sandor had rigged up his scintiscanner, an instrument employing a scintillation counter which was used for mapping out and recording the size and location of an organ or tumor after the administration of a radioactive substance, such as the radioiodine that they were using this morning.

After about thirty seconds, the scanner began picking up radioactive counts from Ruth Sinclair's lower abdomen. Sandor would attempt to map an outline of the placenta by high and low scanner counts. The count began low: "44 . . . 36 . . . 38 . . ." Then, in the lower abdomen, it began climbing: 60 . . . 80 . . . 90 . . . 103 . . . 112. . . ." Sandor marked the spots on transparent thin paper.

This procedure was safer than an ordinary X ray. There was far less radiation to the unborn baby. Experimental work was also being done with thermography which employed infrared radiation readings from the body based on the fact that the placenta, with its large content of blood, was warmer than the abdominal skin over the rest of the uterus and therefore radiated more heat rays. This procedure avoided subjecting mother or baby to any radiation whatsoever.

When Sandor had finished the paper map tracing, he and Henderson examined it together; there was the picture of Ruth Sinclair's placenta. It was on the anterior wall of her uterus and it was low, lying close to the interior mouth of the cervix.

"Well, you've certainly got a partial displacement," said Sandor. "It may be close to total. No wonder she is starting to hemorrhage."

"She's still six weeks from term," Henderson said. "I like that baby right where it is ... if it will just hang on I'll probably go for a cesarean."

"So now what do I do?" Ruth Sinclair wanted to know when he had rejoined her in the corridor where she was lying on a stretcher cart and he had told her briefly about their findings.

"You don't do anything," Henderson answered, walking beside her as the assisting nurse and attendants rolled her back to the elevator. "Your job is simply to stay right here and lie in bed and let the time pass. I may let you out again and I may not. It's too early to tell and we've been too lucky to take any chances."

"Oh, brother!" murmured Ruth Sinclair. "What's Bill going to do at home? What about the kids?"

"I've already talked to him this morning," Henderson said. "He's going to make out. Your sister is coming over to stay at the house."

"Boy, am I a problem!" Ruth Sinclair said. "But it's better for the baby?"

"It's the best thing for the baby," Henderson responded, "and you're a true-blue mother."

He left her after they had her back in her bed and stopped at the newsstand in the lobby to gather up an armful of magazines.

"Send them up to room 506, Mrs. Sinclair," he said to the cashier.

"All of these!"

"Every one. She can take one every hour."

For the next ten days Ruth Sinclair remained completely stable. Each morning after his examination during rounds Henderson could compute the time gains they were making. He was involved with one of the major problems in modern obstetrics: the proper timing of delivery when complications threaten the life of baby and mother. He was electing to choose between premature delivery with a high risk to the baby and proceeding as far as he dared toward the completion of the full ten lunar months of pregnancy. The fetus in Ruth Sinclair's uterus now weighed about 1,700 grams (3 lb. 14 oz.), and had probably attained a length of about 42.5 cm. (16½ in.). If it were delivered in the eighth lunar month, it would be able to move its limbs quite energetically and cry feebly. But its fully developed albeit thin body, covered with wrinkled red skin and waxy vernix caseosa, really was not yet ready for the outside world. Only with swift proper care might it survive.

If they went on for another week or two into the ninth lunar month, the baby would become plumper, stronger and far more capable of resisting the shock of birth and the exposure to infections in its new environment.

The average duration of human pregnancy, counting from the first day of the last menstrual period, was reckoned at about 280 days or 10 lunar months or 40 weeks. The mean figure was close to 267 days. Counting back three months from the first day of Mrs. Sinclair's last menstrual period and adding seven days gave him an estimated spontaneous birth date that was still three weeks away.

But no such event was in store for Ruth Sinclair. As the dense network of muscle fibers of the uterus went into the contractions of labor, her placenta previa would be torn loose and the blood vessels of the inner uterus in the vicinity of the placenta would rupture. With the placenta blocking the internal os, or mouth of the cervix, there would be no way for the baby to be born normally.

As the hemorrhages increased to torrential violence,

there would be no muscular constrictions of the uterine blood vessels as take place after the normal delivery of a baby. Ruth Sinclair would bleed to death. But before this crisis was reached Henderson would use his professional knowledge and skill, plus whatever intuitive sense he might have developed over twenty years of obstetrics, to go in and get the baby out safely and save the mother.

Ruth Sinclair had been stabilized, however, and after carefully checking her record, Henderson made a visit to her room.

"We've made it into your last month," he said. "You're still three weeks from your due date but the baby is coming along nicely and so are you. Do you think if I let you go home now, you can handle things the way I want you to?"

"Yes, I do," Ruth Sinclair said emphatically. "I want to go home today. I want to see the kids and have Bill around me. I want to be in my own bed."

"All right," Henderson said. "But no kidding around. You want to be home—fine! But when you get home, you still stay in bed. I want you to get up only to go to the bathroom or to a sofa. You stay stretched out and taking it easy. Take most of your meals in bed. Absolutely no cooking or any housework or going outside the house. I'm going to check up on you. And not by phone either. I'm coming by the house without telephoning first. And when I get there, I want to find you in bed. If you're not, you'll have to come back to the Hospital. I'd better not find you in the kitchen."

"I'll do it," Ruth Sinclair promised. "Just the way you want me to, Doctor Henderson. You know I want everything to be just right. For Bill and the kids and the baby."

"That's exactly it," Henderson said. He was pleased by the note of firmness in her voice. The baby was now a reality for her. Despite the negative and rejecting attitudes she had expressed in the beginning of the pregnancy, and although she had been subjected to frightening even life-threatening episodes during the pregnancy, she was now *wanting* this baby and developing strong maternal concerns about its welfare. He knew that now he could count on her to work with him—to gain strength and trust and confidence in him until the baby was born. She would not be so easily diverted by exhausting anxieties and by destructive emotional behavior.

"Is Bill going to pick me up at the Hospital?"

"No," Henderson said. "I'm sending you home in an ambulance."

"Ambulance!"

"Certainly. You're in a delicate condition. We don't want any more jiggling or moving around than necessary. If anything does jiggle loose and you start to bleed, they can turn you around and drive you right back here. Once you get home, you're to have Bill or your sister with you at all times, day and night. Not just the kids or one of the neighbors. So home you go, and let's see if you can stay there."

15

Section

Hatless and without a raincoat, hustling to escape the gusts of driving rain, Henderson dodged between the cars, around the puddles that flooded the Hospital parking lot, and made a flying leap over a miniature lake to reach the doctors' side entrance. Awaiting an elevator, he dabbed at his dripping face and sodden shirt collar with a handkerchief, noting that the Emergency Room down the hall lacked its usual clamor. The lull that commonly settled over the Hospital in late afternoon, particularly in summer, had been intensified by an all-day deluge of rain, wind, and thunderstorms that had kept most people indoors. Now, if the weather forecast he had heard on the car radio was correct, the skies soon would be clearing. Once suppertime in suburbia got rolling, the Emergency Room would build up to its normal evening tempo as backyard barbecue and patio chefs were brought in with singed hair and eyebrows, and assorted burns and lacerations from steak knives and shishkebab skewers. Along with them would be all the tots who has swigged down charcoal lighter fluids or sprayed themselves with insect repellents while Mom was busy tossing the salad and Daddy mixing martinis.

He rode the elevator to the Maternity Floor and found the Night Floor Nurse, Esther Bates, going over patients' charts with the nurses working the four-to-midnight shift.

"Your patient, Mrs. Webster, is in Room Four," Nurse Bates said. "We just admitted her a few minutes ago."

"How is she doing?" Henderson asked.

"She seems fine so far," Bates said. "She told us that she was timing her contractions in the car and they're still about every seven minutes. We're just getting her undressed and into bed so I haven't had a chance to examine her or get a chart started on her yet."

"She's definitely in labor," Henderson said. "I examined her at my office about forty-five minutes ago. Her membranes have ruptured. Her contractions were irregular—running about eight to ten minutes. Let me get out of these wet clothes and I'll join you for another look at her."

He had loosened his necktie and was starting for the doctors' dressing room when he became aware that the group of nurses was still staring at him expectantly.

"Her 'ready file' has been flagged, Doctor," Nurse Bates said. "Do you know about this?"

Henderson returned to peer over her shoulder at the white slip attached to Mrs. Webster's file folder. On it was the notation: "Husband has participated in prenatal education classes with patient and may request permission to be present in the Delivery Room."

"Nothing doing," he snorted. "Permission denied! I don't want any husbands hanging around *my* delivery table."

He turned toward the locker room. Behind him arose mock groans of reproach and disappointment from the group of nurses. "Didn't I tell you he'd say that?" "Boy, what a poor sport!" "You never have any fun around here."

Henderson made a mental note to get even with Rosie Van Doren, the nurse who gave prenatal courses for expectant mothers and their husbands. Rosie had stuck that note there deliberately to bug him. She knew damned well, as did all the Ob nurses, that Henderson was not enthusiastic about admitting fathers to the Delivery Room during the birth of a baby. They delighted in putting him on the spot.

"Do you know Mr. Webster?" Nurse Bates inquired innocently.

"I know about him from his wife," Henderson replied haughtily. He was trying to recall from his office conversations with Mrs. Webster what she had told him about her husband. He recalled that he had some kind of an oddball job. The Websters were new in town. When she came to see him six months ago, she was already three months pregnant. This was her first baby. She was a petite and very pretty brunette, very serious about the pregnancy and a cooperative patient. But he and Mr. Webster had missed meeting each other.

"Boy, wait until you see him," said one of the junior nurses. "Like Paul Newman, only younger. He's really fantastic!"

So that was it. No wonder the girls were in a dither. The younger ones particularly always reacted when some handsome dude turned up for a delivery. Out came the makeup kits. Everybody began yanking girdles and straightening stockings and acting coolly efficient and professional.

"You can give him a smock," Henderson said, "and feed him cake and coffee and cookies, but that's as far as I go. He's not getting in."

"But Delivery Room fathers are the new big thing," one of the nurses protested. "I was reading about it in one of the magazines. It's called The Better Way."

"Their Better Way is not *my* way," Henderson retorted. "If you girls had your way, we'd have bleachers and popcorn machines up and down the hall."

Having enjoyed playing Joe Grump, he stalked off to change his clothes.

As far as Henderson was concerned, the admission of fathers into the Delivery Room was a fad and a nuisance. He heartily approved of such programs as the prenatal courses that were offered to expectant mothers and fathers. He was also strongly in favor of having husbands thoroughly indoctrinated in what pregnancy, labor, and birth was all about. And he favored husbands accompanying their wives to the hospital, donning a white smock, and lending their emotional support during labor. But after that he drew the line.

It was true that a small school of obstetricians, particularly those who were interested in natural childbirth, now encouraged the presence of the father in the Delivery Room, but Henderson knew that most of his fellow Obs didn't like it. What they wanted in the Delivery Room was total concentration between themselves and their patient, together with the complete attention and support of the Delivery-Room team. The birth of a baby was still one of the most critical of all human events. The "right" of every child to be physically, mentally, and emotionally wellborn was the greatest of human birthrights. There must be nothing that would distract the mother in these moments when she entrusted her life and the life of her child to the obstetrician's professional skill and knowledge, and certainly nothing that even for an instant might distract *him*.

The physician who became a topnotch obstetrician had reached his professional status through years of arduous training. Seasoned obstetrical nurses had achieved their skills only through years of experience and the closest work with patients and their doctors. To Henderson it seemed ridiculous, even risky, to introduce into this atmosphere a husband who was emotionally involved with the patient. A father, exposed to a situation in which internal muscular straining, copious amounts of fluid and blood, and, to a layman's eyes, an alarmingly feeble infant were the norm, was surely subjecting himself to far more stress than he might anticipate. If he keeled over or departed hastily from the Delivery Room or registered alarm or concern, he could distract his wife, the doctor, or the nurses.

Moreover, in this new "Golden Age" of lawyers and medical malpractice suits, there was a real risk of misinterpretation of the procedures of normal delivery. As

an obstetrician worked with his patient to bring about a
safe birth, there came, not uncommonly, moments
when in his judgment greater efforts on her part might
be called for and he might urge on his patient, not only
with soothing encouragements but also with a sharply
spoken command or even an ultimatum.

Seeking to communicate quickly and effectively with
a patient in the throes of a difficult delivery, deter-
minedly penetrating her haze of fatigue, tension, and
fear, Henderson sometimes had found himself getting
quite tough.

The mothers always seemed to understand your mo-
tives and indeed, later they thanked you fervently. But
what about an onlooking husband in the midst of a
crisis? How could he be expected to understand what
was going on? If, during a difficult birth, voices were
raised, a husband might later tell everybody, "Boy, you
should have heard that bum hollering at my wife!"

And it might not stop there. The next thing you
knew there might be some conniving lawyer in the
picture with accusations of cruel and inhuman treatment.

There was another reason why Henderson was opposed to nonmedical observers in the Delivery Room.
This was his deep conviction that the Delivery Room
and the Operating Room represented his last refuges.
He was inured to coping with daily office hours, streams
of patients, telephone conversations, the never-ending
need to reassure the anxious pregnant patient, the important emphasis on prenatal care with its constant
patient checkups, and all the office conversations and
examinations involved in the practice of medicine. But
finally to reach the Operating Room or the Delivery
Room was to reach a haven. There he was beyond the
reach of telephones and patient-filled waiting rooms;
furthermore he had the support of a highly trained
group of professionals; here it was possible to put aside
all distractions, whether they involved finances, family,
patients, inflation, wars, or riots, and concentrate completely on obstetrics or surgery. As far as he was con-

cerned, the Delivery Room and the Operating Room were his sanctuaries and he intended to defend them against all unnecessary intrusions.

In the doctors' dressing room he hung up his suit to drip-dry, shaved, showered, and changed into a fresh set of Ob whites. Strolling down the corridor he entered Labor Room Four where he found Nurse Bates with his patient.

Anne Webster was now in bed and still as relaxed and composed as when he had seen her at the office. She was gazing about her without apprehension, curious and interested in the nurses' preparations. The prenatal classes she had attended had worked for her. She had poise and self-control, natural or acquired during her training and experience as an airline stewardess.

"Well here I am," she greeted Henderson casually. "Doing fine, I think. But how did you get here so quickly? What did you do with all those women in your waiting room?"

"I left them all to my partner," Henderson answered. "You gave me just the excuse I needed. Now I can goof off over here with you for the whole evening. Let me hold your hand, Honey. I want to take your pulse."

"I think the nurse just took my pulse," Mrs. Webster said.

"That's all right," said Henderson. "Around here I have permission to hold hands, too."

He sat down on the chair beside the bed and glanced down at the admission chart Nurse Bates had just filled in. Pulse: 88. Blood pressure: 130 over 80. Temperature: 99. All perfectly normal, just as she herself was a perfectly normal specimen of a sportsloving young woman. You could picture her skiing, swimming, biking, or sailing. The weight-watching program he had put her on during her pregnancy had held down the extra pounds to an acceptable limit. But although you could protect the health of the mother and the baby during pregnancy to a degree undreamed of in the past, you could not control the size and weight the normal baby might reach by the time it was ready to be born. The question tonight was: could Anne Webster's baby safely negotiate the journey through the passage in her slightly narrow pelvis?

This had been an uncertainty ever since Henderson's first internal examination of Anne Webster six months previously. Measuring the width between the pelvic bones and base of the spine with his fingers, he had found the pubic arch was obtuse—near ninety degrees —and provided a good outlet for the baby but that her pelvis was of the slightly narrowed android type. In the midplane the ischial spines bilaterally were moderately prominent. The passageway between the sacrum and the pubic arch measured just slightly less than the diameter usually considered to be adequate for normal childbirth. And there was a bony hook at the end of the sacrum which might complicate the problem.

Anne Webster was only five feet one and weighed 108 pounds. Women of small stature usually had smaller babies, but there were exceptions. At the time, Henderson had noted there might be a potential problem, but was not inclined to have his patient worrying about it throughout her pregnancy.

"You know I've got such narrow hips," she had said, "that a lot of my friends have been asking me whether I've got room to have a baby. What do you think?"

"The best answer I can give you," Henderson replied, "is that we really won't know whether the passageway is large enough until we know the size of the passenger—in this case the baby. Little girls like yourself usually have small babies. I've delivered dozens through a pelvis no bigger than yours. When it's time for the baby to be born, we'll be able to tell."

The pregnancy had proceeded without complications. As could be expected, Anne Webster's baby attained its greatest growth in the last weeks before she reached her due date. Yesterday Henderson had summoned her for X-ray pelvimetry and by comparing the results of the X-ray films of the lower pelvis with the indicated size and weight of the baby, he concluded that she was still a borderline case. He had sent her home with instructions to stay quiet and await developments and, as he anticipated, she had been on the phone this afternoon with the news that she felt as if she were going into labor. He had her come by his office for an examination which confirmed it and directed her to have her husband drive her to the Hospital.

Now her contractions were spaced about eight minutes apart but they were still so mild that it was impossible to tell what the outcome was going to be. He was surprised on vaginal examination to find that she was five cm. dilated but still high.

"I'm still not hurting as much as I expected," Anne Webster said.

"Who needs a lot of pain?" Henderson replied. "I'm going to give you some medication to relax you and a touch of local anesthesia in the cervix."

He took the Kobak needle that Nurse Bates had prepared and injected a small amount of lidocaine in each of four places in the tissues adjacent to the cervix and vaginal walls.

"Now put your hand here beside mine," he continued, resting her hand lightly on the mounded abdomen so that she could feel the next muscular contraction of the uterus.

"There it is," exclaimed Anne Webster. "But now I don't feel anything, not even a cramp."

"Great!" replied Henderson. "That ought to keep you comfortable for more than an hour."

He went over the explanation of how paracervical anesthesia relieved the pain and discomfort of labor. "The main thing now is to keep track of how your labor progresses. Mrs. Bates and her nurses will be checking you and the baby, but you can help by timing and gauging those contractions by putting your hand on the muscles, even though the pain won't be getting to you. Where's your husband? Didn't he bring you in?"

"Mike?" said Mrs. Webster. "Yes, I wonder what's happened to him. He forgot his pills. He went out to the car to see if he might have some in the glove compartment. Oh, here he is now. Mike, this is Dr. Henderson."

Henderson had to admit the nurses were right. Mr. Webster did bear a strong resemblance to Paul Newman. He was lean and tanned and had the same intensely blue eyes. But as he gripped Henderson's hand he seemed oddly taut and preoccupied.

"Hi," he said. "We're here for the night, eh?"

Henderson was bemused. Was this the eager tiger who wanted to assist with the delivery of the baby? Already so tensed up that he was popping pills?

"Could be," he responded amiably, "but you've got the best room in the house. Twin beds and your own TV and private shower. The baby is definitely on its way and we're all set to take good care of your wife, so all you've got to do is relax while you keep her company."

"Relax!" exclaimed Webster glumly. "That's my problem."

"That damn job has Mike all wound up," Mrs. Webster said. "He was working the Tower all day today."

Now Henderson remembered. Mike Webster was an air-traffic controller. He worked at the city's international airport with radar scopes at an air-traffic-control center and in the Tower. Anne Webster had told him that the pressure on her husband and the other controllers was awful.

To Mike Webster he said, "You must have had some hangup out there with this weather."

"Murder!" was the response. "My stomach is still in knots."

He paced the room restlessly and peered out the window. "The rain is letting up," he said. "If Annie's going to be okay for a while, I could drive down to a drugstore and refill my prescription."

"Sit down," Henderson said. "We've got our own pharmacy right down the hall. What are you taking?"

Webster found a slip of paper in his wallet and handed it to Henderson. It was their family physician's prescription for a tranquilizer. A low-strength maintenance dosage.

"I'm supposed to take one after work and before I go to bed, but just as I got home Annie asked me to drive her to your office, and I forgot the bottle."

"No problem," Henderson said. "We have the same thing right on our shelf. I'll get you enough pills for tonight. Then we can let the nurses look after your wife. We've got a good cafeteria downstairs. How about joining me for some supper?"

"I couldn't eat," said Webster.

"Well come along and keep me company anyway," Henderson persisted. He knew Nurse Bates wanted to get on with her patient's preparation procedures and he wanted to get a line on what Mike Webster was really like. If you were going to consider admitting a husband to the Delivery Room—or maneuver to keep him out— it was better not to be dealing with a total stranger.

He escorted Webster past the admiring gazes of the nurses at the floor desk, picked up the tranquilizer pills at the dispensary, and then took him down to the cafeteria. They went through the line—still light because of the weather and early evening hour—and took their trays to a table. Henderson had helped himself to a generous portion of cold cuts, salad, strawberry ice cream, and coffee. Mike Webster had selected only a tall glass of iced tea. He gulped down his pill, sipped tea through the straw and then, fixing Henderson with a piercing eagle-eyed look, demanded, "How is everything going with my wife?"

"Good," Henderson replied confidently. "She's doing fine and so far as we can tell, so is the baby."

"What about those X rays you took yesterday?" Webster said. "What did you find out exactly?"

"Just what I had expected," Henderson said. "We've known all along that she's got a small pelvis. The baby is a bit large for her. This makes her borderline for a normal delivery."

"Nothing you could have done about it any sooner?"

"Not a thing. Babies customarily gain weight and

reach their full size in the last weeks of pregnancy. You just have to wait until you see what their proportions are when it's time for them to be born. And even then you can't always be sure until the mother has been in labor for several hours. That's what I'm here for. If there's a problem, I know how to handle it."

"With an operation?"

"Just a standard procedure. We call it a cesarean. You probably know all about it."

Webster nodded. "They covered it during the courses we took. I went to all of them with Annie. I even did the exercises with her at home. We had a lot of fun with the nurse who gave those classes. She was always telling my wife, 'If your husband can talk an airliner down to the ground, he certainly ought to be able to help you a lot when the time comes for you to have your baby.' "

A bid for an invitation to the Delivery Room? Henderson hastily changed the subject.

"A lot of pressure in that job you've got?" he asked.

Webster grimaced. "It's loaded," he said. "You know it's not just me that's taking pills. There's not a guy at the Tower or the traffic-control center who hasn't got something wrong with him. Stomach trouble. Ulcers. High blood pressure. Migraine headaches. Insomnia. You name it. We've got it. There's just too many planes and not enough manpower. We're working extra-duty shifts with unreliable equipment."

He paused for a sip of iced tea and pressed on. "You should have been out there today. We had that weather front move through. Thunderstorms and crosswinds on the runways gusting up to eighty miles an hour! And then our radar starts acting up. We had to close the airport. No flights in or out. For forty minutes we had planes full of people stacked up for fifty miles around, flopping and bouncing all over the sky. But when we talk to the pilots, we have to play it cool, right? You don't want to shake up a guy who's flying blind through turbulence with 150 passengers behind him. So you take it out on yourself. The strain gets to be too much."

Henderson was fascinated. Here was a young fellow, still in his twenties, handling a complex job that had hardly existed when he was born, and already he was working under such stress that it was driving him buggy. Anne Webster, preoccupied with her pregnancy—as was particularly the rule with women having their first babies—didn't even realize yet how disturbed he was becoming. Nevertheless, it was important that Mike Webster should feel that she did. Otherwise he might feel even more alone with his problems.

"Your wife is very much concerned about you. I guess you know that."

Webster shrugged. "I don't like to load her up with it too much. Particularly now when she's having the baby. It's just gotten worse since I was tranferred back here."

"Where were you?" Henderson asked.

"The Pacific," Webster said. "I did three years in the Air Force as a radar man. Then I was assigned to Air Force bomber bases. That's when I got my training as an air-traffic controller. Then in Hawaii I met Anne. She was flying for United. When we got married, I took my discharge out there and went right into one of the FAA air-traffic-control centers in the islands."

"What's it like to live in Hawaii?" Henderson asked.

"Good and bad," Webster said. "They shaft you with high prices. But there's the climate and all that swimming and surfing and sailing. I was taking courses in oceanography at the university and Anne and I had a ball being married. Just the way it's supposed to be. When we traveled on our vacations, we went the other way. To Japan and Australia. Never came back here to the States. Then last winter, they transferred me. They told me they needed top men back here because of the manpower crisis. What a shock! You stay away from the States five years right now, and when you come back, you can't believe it. They're going out of their minds in this country! You try to do your job and you can't."

Henderson reflected. It reminded him of the plight of Bill Sinclair. Why was it that so many guys who were in the business of helping keep the country running—trying to save somebody else's neck—were in such a bind? Why was it there was money, money, money for so goddamned much military nonsense and so little where it really counted? So you had a crisis in medical care, a crisis in the cities, and here was a crisis in the skies. The grinding pressures were chewing people up.

"You know what I think," he said to Webster. "After your wife has had the baby and everything is all right, six months from now, you ought to quit that job."

"You mean it?"

"Sure I mean it. You're probably one of the best but they don't deserve you. They'll wreck your health and kiss you goodbye."

"We've got guys who are already burned out at forty," Webster said.

"That's what I mean," Henderson said. "Five years from now when you're bogged down with a bigger family it may be too late. If I were you—still young and with a wife like you've got, I'd get the hell out. Go somewhere you can enjoy life. You had a taste of what it can be like. No wonder this looks so bad back here."

Webster, benefitting from his tranquilizer and Henderson's sympathy and the unexpected pep talk, brightened considerably.

"I think you're right," he said. "I'm going to start making plans. I've had a feeling I was trapped."

"Damn right," Henderson said. Conversational therapy paid off. Over the speaker system came the page, "Dr. Henderson. Dr. Robert Henderson . . ."

"I'll take that call back up in Maternity," he said.

He and Webster walked back to the elevator and got in the car with a group of nurses from Maternity.

"You've met my staff," Henderson said to Webster. "The nursing shortage is so bad we have to grab everybody we can get. These girls are on parole from women's prisons—sex-starved, hostile, aggressive . . ."

From behind him arose chortles and gasps of protest. Mike Webster responded with a wide if slightly crooked grin. He was coming along nicely but Henderson already had concluded that tonight was not his night to be admitted to the Delivery Room. He left it to the nurses to escort Webster back to his wife while he paused at the Maternity Floor desk to answer his page.

"Mrs. Henderson is calling you, I think," the desk nurse said. Henderson noted there was suddenly loitering and lots of business with patients' charts around the desk. The nurses enjoyed his domestic phone calls. Mary Henderson had no inhibitions about involving him in open-end conversation and he had long ago lost any about responding. For years the latest crises in the domestic dramas that unfolded in the Henderson household, whether they concerned the children's report cards, bouncing checks, the unpaid telephone bill, or unexpected holiday visits from in-laws, were freely discussed, debated, and argued over the Maternity Floor desk phones with the nurses providing an appreciative audience. They tuned him in as if he were the Dick Van Dyke show.

Henderson sometimes felt as if the nursing staff knew more about his family life than he did. However, since he, in turn, had delivered many of their babies, treated their gynecological problems, and counseled them about their marital woes, the score was about even.

And as hot and heavy as the telephone disputes became, there was always a happy ending sooner or later because he and Mary still cherished each other.

"The thing that amazes me about you and your wife," one young nurse had told him, "is that you're still talking to each other. You've been married how long? Eighteen years? And you're still talking to each other *all* the time!"

"Well, only over this telephone," Henderson had replied. "When I'm home, it's just sex, sex, sex. That's why some nights I sleep at the hospital."

He picked up the telephone and heard the most recent news bulletin.

"Henry is loose," Mary said. "He went out through that broken fence."

"Where is he now?" Henderson asked, settling down into a chair beside the desk nurse, stretching out and crossing his legs.

"He's running through the neighbors' yards down toward the Wilcoxes' house."

"Did you send the kids after him?"

"Yes, but they can't catch him. The ground is all wet and muddy from the rain and it's a horrible, slippery mess!"

"Where are you calling from?" Henderson asked.

"Me? I'm right here at home. Where do you think I am?"

"Why aren't you out helping them round him up?" he asked.

"Because I'm sick of that job, that's why! I told you that he was going to get out through that fence!"

"And I told you to get the fence fixed."

"Well, I'm not running after him tonight. If you think I'm going to make a spectacle of myself out there in that mud, you're crazy. I've had it! He's running through peoples' yards and gardens—he may be doing thousands of dollars' worth of damage, trampling everything to pieces."

"Why are you calling me here at the hospital?"

"Because I want you to take a few minutes to come over here and catch him."

"I'm with a patient."

"You've only got one delivery tonight so far," Mary snapped. "I talked with the girls at the office and they said she'd only been admitted to the hospital an hour or so ago so she's probably not going to have that baby for hours. You've got plenty of time if you come right now."

Henderson was astonished. Godalmighty! Now his wife was prying information out of his own office staff.

"I am also about to make evening rounds," he replied with great professional dignity, "and I'm not leaving here to play cowboy."

"Well, neither am I!"

Pause. Silence on both ends of the wire.

"All right then," Henderson said loudly and firmly. "There's only one thing to do. Sell the pony."

"What!"

"That's right. Don't try to get him back. Just have anybody—a neighbor—the police—it doesn't matter—tie him to a tree. Call the newspaper. Place an ad. 'Pony for sale. Ten Dollars.' We'll get rid of him once and for all."

"But the children . . ."

"If you and the children can't take care of him, we can't keep him," Henderson said, and then, raising his voice again another notch, "I want that goddamned pony off the property by the time I come home!"

He hung up and announced casually to all the enchanted eavesdroppers, "I'm going to make rounds."

There were only three patients to see and all were doing well. Twenty minutes later he was back at the Maternity Desk.

"How is Mrs. Webster?" he asked Nurse Bates.

"Her contractions are regular—about every six minutes—but they're not very strong. The baby's heart tones are 140. She's been resting comfortably."

"I'll have a look at her in a moment," Henderson said. He got out the local phone book, found the number of his neighbor, Donald Wilcox, and dialed it.

"Dr. Henderson calling," he said. "I'm at the Hospital. I heard from my wife that our pony was loose tonight. Have you seen him?"

"He was here," Wilcox replied rather bleakly. "But he's gone now. Your wife and kids have got him."

"Oh, I'm glad to hear that," Henderson said. "I hope he didn't damage your garden."

"He wasn't in my garden," Wilcox replied. "He was in my garage."

"Oh?"

"My wife couldn't get out of the car. The pony didn't get into the garden but that damned dog with him was all over the place."

"The black one?"

"That's the one. He's yours, isn't he?"

"He's mine, all right," Henderson said. Bingo! A perfect obscenity of a dog! The pony's friend! Tonight he had no doubt accompanied Henry on his rambles, gamboling exuberantly through the Wilcoxes' flower beds, barking, chasing prized cats, leaping about with muddy feet, adding to the festivities.

"Say," Wilcox said. "Was that pony ever in a show?"

"Horse show?" Henderson replied. "No, I'm afraid not. He's just a family pet. The children ride him around."

"Not a horse show," Wilcox said. "I mean like a circus or carnival. The way he rears up and walks on his hind legs made me wonder. His front feet are higher than your head."

"Oh, that's just a trick the kids taught him," Henderson said.

"Pretty scary," said Wilcox. "When my wife got out of the car, he reared right up at her. He scared the wits out of her."

"What happened?"

"She got back in the car and slammed the door. But she had to sit there in the car until your wife came and got him. The police got here first. Sergeant Buck helped your wife get a rope on the pony. Everything seems to be all right now."

Henderson breathed a sigh of relief. Thank God, Bucky had been on duty. He could be counted on to keep everybody cool.

"Well, I certainly am sorry, he said. "The pony is supposed to be fenced in. We'll try not to let it happen again. I'll send someone around to repair those flower beds. Did you say my wife has left?"

"They've gone up the street with the police car. Your wife and children and the dog. The pony's still walking on his hind legs."

"Headed toward home, eh?"

"I imagine so," Wilcox said.

"Well, thanks and good night," Henderson said. He

hung up and sat for a moment. He could picture the homeward-bound procession: The police car in the lead. The gallant little band trudging along behind up the muddy, puddly road into the setting sun. Mary tugging grimly on Henry's halter. The pony prancing along on his hindlegs. The children, from the two teen-age girls laden with ropes down to little Casey, probably in his pajamas and toddling along with a nosebag full of oats. The clownish Bingo, bringing up the rear, tail waving triumphantly, reveling in the adventure and watering all the neighbors' shrubs. The entire Henderson clan, ill-housed, ill-fed, and abandoned, carrying on bravely while the loutish Dr. Robert Henderson was missing, no doubt off consorting shamelessly with one of his patients. A pretty sight to set before the neighbors.

In defiance of his ultimatum to sell the pony, Henry would be returned to the barn. No one save Charlie would speak to him when he got home and he would be provided with no information about Henry's roundup. However, since he had craftily found out the whole story by telephoning Wilcox, he could relax.

A ten-dollar bill was being offered to him on a plastic serving tray.

"What's that for?"

"The girls want to buy your pony," Nurse Bates said.

"Too late. Mary and the kids have taken him home again. But don't you dare let her know that I found out."

Leaning back in the chair, he grinned and stretched expansively. "How do you suppose we baby doctors could ever practice if it weren't for an understanding wife?"

"You're a monster," Nurse Bates said.

Henderson chuckled. "Do you realize what that pony's bust-out is going to cost me?" he retorted amiably. "First, if I ever get home tonight, I'm going to have to watch my step because my girls will have probably put Fred in my bed."

"Don't tell me you've still got that damned snake," Nurse Bates said.

"We sure have," said Henderson. "He's three years old and enormous and until you've slid your bare feet into a bed holding five feet of boa constrictor, you haven't lived."

"Damned crazy family," Nurse Bates muttered.

"Furthermore," Henderson continued, "to pacify Mary, I'll probably have to take her to the trotting track. All that betting and yelling is good for her but we'll probably come home broke. The girls will get some great new rock records. The boys will be taken out for hamburgers and super-sodas. The fence man will show up to fix the fence. The landscape man will probably swindle me when he replaces a couple of neighbors' shrubs. By the time it's all over, it will cost me more than I'm going to make from this delivery and I may still wind up back there in the doctor's lounge sleeping in 'the tin box.' I'm telling you, it's a dog's life. Let's go see Mrs. Webster. Bring along another paracervical pack."

In Room Four he found Mike Webster placidly leafing through a magazine. Anne Webster lay quietly with her eyes shut but she was wide-awake and Henderson knew that as the local anesthetic wore off, she would soon be tossing and restless.

"How are you feeling?" he asked.

"All right, but a little tired. And I think the pain is coming back."

"We can take care of that," Henderson said. He took the needle that Nurse Bates had ready and repeated the injections of the lidocaine to prolong the paracervical block. Sitting down beside the bed he listened to the baby's heart tones and noted a steady 140. The contractions, he noted, were lasting longer but not building much in their intensity. It was after nine o'clock, but Mrs. Webster soon was once again free of pain and Henderson was content to let her drift along for another hour at least. It was nearly 10:30 when another pelvic examination stirred her to wakefulness.

"Is the baby okay?"

"The baby is fine," he said. "We're getting good strong heart tones. Let me check again on how you're progressing."

Between contractions, he palpated her abdomen, gently outlining the shape and position of the baby with the pressure of his palms. In Mrs. Webster's athletic and muscular abdomen it was easy to distinguish the position of the baby and its arms and legs. Just above the pubic bone, between thumb and fingers of his right hand, he could feel a moveable object. Encouraging participating, he took Mike Webster's hand and placed it at this point on his wife's abdomen. "Do you feel that? Right there?"

Webster nodded. By now they were getting along like buddies.

"That's the baby's head," Henderson said.

"Let me feel it," Anne Webster said. She let Henderson guide her hand and then exclaimed, "Gosh, that's low enough to be born, isn't it?"

"Not quite," Henderson answered. "If the baby had descended into the passageway between the pelvic bones, you wouldn't be able to feel it like that. What's happening is that your labor is progressing. The contractions of the uterus are closer together, but only a little stronger. And we don't have what we call an engagement. That happens when the baby descends into the pelvic passage. We've got several factors to consider. There is the size and shape of your particular pelvis. There is the size of the baby and its position. And there is the strength of the uterine contractions. That's why I told you yesterday that we would have to wait until you had gone into labor to see how everything worked out. If we had an engagement, we would have a clear indication that the pelvic inlet is adequate for this baby's birth."

"Well, damn!" exclaimed Mrs. Webster. "That's all I can say. I feel like it's all my fault."

"Don't be silly," Henderson said. "You're a perfect patient. And you probably got your pelvic bones from your great-grandmother anyway. You can't do anything about that."

He glanced at Mike Webster who had returned to his chair. "How are you feeling?"

"All okay," Webster replied. "I'm just sitting here. Anne's doing all the work."

"Aren't you supposed to have another pill tonight?" Henderson asked.

"Well, if I were home I would. I usually take it when I go to bed around eleven o'clock."

"Stick with your schedule," Henderson said. "Take it just as if you were at home."

He poured a glass of water for Mike Webster and watched while he took his tranquilizer. So did Nurse Bates who never missed much of what was going on.

Once again Henderson checked the baby's heart tones and closely observed another contraction.

"Any better?" asked Anne Webster, resting with eyes shut again.

"Not bad," Henderson said. "I want you to just lie there quietly. If you want me, I'll be just down the hall."

He went out to the Floor Desk and once more went through Mrs. Webster's folder, studying the X-ray pictures from the pelvimetry they had done the day before. With these X-ray measurements and with what he knew about the size and position of the baby, he had the results of nearly six hours of labor. The cervix was not proceeding to dilate past five centimeters. The contractions remained unimpressive. This had been his hunch about the way this delivery would develop. That was why he had preferred to linger at the Hospital where he could observe Anne Webster's progress and note any signs of impending difficulty. To Mary, it might seem that he was just hanging around, but as the evening advanced he was evaluating this patient in order to reach a decision. It was really a matter of patience. Or perhaps patience redefined as another way of measuring time.

In obstetrics, particularly, you learned not to hurry.

To act impulsively was to take needless risks or court disaster. In a case such as this one you did not administer drugs to hasten or force the labor process. Nor did you prematurely summon the Operating-Room team if there was still a chance for a safe and nontraumatic normal delivery.

He locked his hands behind his head, eyed the clock and the ceiling overhead and stretched.

"What's it going to be?" Nurse Bates asked.

"Section," he said. "I'll be with you in a moment."

He went down the hall to Room Four and pulled up a chair to talk to Anne and Mike Webster.

"You've been a good girl about this labor," he said to her, "but it's not progressing. I'm satisfied that we've tried it long enough. You know that we've talked about the possibility of you having this baby by a cesarean operation. I've concluded that's the answer."

"How much longer will it take to arrange for that?" Anne Webster asked.

"No time at all," Henderson replied. "Probably less than half an hour."

He turned to Mike Webster. "You've done a great job supporting your wife," he said. "I know that you were ready to stay right with her through the delivery, but we'll be doing this in the Operating Room. I'd like you to wait right here while we deliver the baby."

Mike Webster nodded docilely. Fatigue, the tranquilizer, and the rapport that Henderson had managed to establish had done the trick. "Sure thing," he said.

"Make yourself comfortable," Henderson suggested cheerfully. "After we take your wife down to surgery you can take off your shoes and stretch out on that empty bed. I'll let you know how we're doing."

He returned to the Floor Desk to talk with Nurse Bates.

"Who's on in the OR tonight?"

"Betty Dickson came on at midnight."

"Good. Tell her to round up her crew. I'm going to be ready in thirty minutes. I'll call the anesthesiologist." Henderson dialed the hospital laboratory. "I'm doing a section as soon as possible. I'd like you to cross-match 1,000 cc's of blood. Also a complete blood count and a urine specimen."

Running his finger down the call list he found that Herb Goodman had the night duty for the anesthesiologists. He grinned, dialed him at home and got a sleepy voice.

"Herbie," he said. "Good morning. Bob Henderson calling. I've got a primary section to do. Any time you're ready."

"Let's do it tomorrow after breakfast," Goodman said sleepily.

"I told the OR we'd be ready in 30 minutes."

"The fire chief!" exclaimed Goodman. He was awake now. "Why don't you get yourself a siren and wake the whole town up?" He sighed heavily. "Okay, I'll struggle over."

Henderson hung up and said to Bates, "Is Dr. Wilson still around?"

"He's just finished a delivery. He's in the doctors' lounge."

In the lounge he found Dr. Robert Wilson, fellow obstetrician, completing a chart summary of a case.

"What's up, Bob?"

"I've got to do a 'section.' I was about to call my partner to scrub with me but I know he's got early surgery."

"Would you like me to give you a hand?" Wilson asked.

"I sure would appreciate it. We're setting up for her right now."

"Just call me when you're ready," Wilson said.

"I'm going down to stir up the OR crew. I'll give you a ring up here," said Henderson. He took the backstaircase down to surgery. When he opened the door to the first-floor corridor it was dark save for dim night lights. He blinked as a flashlight was thrust in his face.

"Oh, sorry, Doctor!"

It was one of the security guards.

"We're looking for a patient. He's from the medical ward. A diabetic."

"When did you lose him?"

"Just a little while ago. He was in the solarium watching the TV Late Show. He couldn't sleep, he told the nurses. Now he's gone and his clothes are missing. We think he may. . . ."

Henderson interrupted the guard with a grip on his elbow.

"Maybe that's him," he whispered. A dim figure had let himself in through the door from the doctors' parking lot and was approaching them.

"Shine the light on him when he passes us."

They flattened themselves against the wall and waited. Then the light went on in the stranger's face.

"Stop right there, Buddy!" snapped the guard.

The flashlight illuminated the startled countenance of Dr. Herbert Goodman.

Henderson had known it was Goodman when he saw the door open but the opportunity was too good to pass up.

"It's all right, officer," he said to the guard. "I know this man. He's an out-patient."

To Goodman he said, "Come with me to the Operating Room, son. We're all set up to transplant your ovaries."

"I have to get up in the middle of the night for your gags," Goodman said plaintively as they sat in the dressing room next to surgery, getting into green cotton pants and jumpers. "How's this patient? Any special problems?"

"She's young and healthy but she's got the pelvis of a twelve-year-old. I just want to get the baby out of her."

"I'm planning on a spinal anesthetic."

"She's had 20 milligrams of lidocaine as a paracervical block in the last three hours. Atarax 20 milligrams. That's all. Let's go in and meet her."

The OR nurses had Mrs. Webster on the table. She was more curious than frightened. The decision to have the cesarean section obviously had been a relief to her.

"This is Dr. Goodman, Mrs. Webster," he said. "He's the greatest anesthesiologist in the United States."

"I'm the only one Henderson can get to work for him," Goodman said. "They took away my license two years ago. That's why I work only at night."

He took over skillfully to administer the spinal anesthetic and Henderson went back to the surgery lounge to wait. He drew a paper cup of coffee from the urn, sipped it while he looked over the laboratory technician's report and then called Dr. Wilson down to scrub.

"She wants to know where you're going to cut," Goodman said when he and Wilson went into the operating room. "I told her you usually just drew a big circle and lifted up on the lid like you would on a pot."

"Does it have to be a big scar? That's what I want to know," Mrs. Webster said. She was now totally without feeling from the waist down but very wide-awake.

"We do nothing but 'Bikini' incisions," Henderson responded. "You'll be able to go to the beach in one of your Hawaiian hula skirts without this one showing. It won't be much of a scar, anyway."

The incision that he was making was well below the navel but wide enough so that he and Wilson, who was across the table from him, had plenty of room to work. There was only a thin layer of fat in this patient and the muscles of her abdomen were well developed. Under spinal anesthesia, however, the muscles were totally relaxed and loose, so that they were easy to manipulate. There were only a few "bleeders" of any consequence and they clamped them and freed the fascia from the muscles. Then they thrust their fingers beneath the muscles to expose the peritoneum. Another interior incision and there was the uterus without any signs of rupture. The nurses had the baby cart ready. When Henderson got the uterus open, Wilson cleared the fluids away so that Henderson could reach in and put his hand under the head of the baby.

"Is it a boy or a girl?" Mrs. Webster asked.

"So far, all I know is that it's a baby," he answered.

He was maneuvering to guide the baby out through the incision as Wilson gently but firmly exerted pressure at the top of the uterus to force the baby out. Henderson delivered the baby's head and then, grasping its shoulders, drew it slowly forth and picked it up by the feet. Wilson clamped the umbilical cord and cut it and Henderson held up the infant.

"It's a girl, honey," he said to Mrs. Webster, "and I think she's okay."

The baby was gray and discolored but making good initial gasping efforts at breathing and in a few moments all was well. Henderson was glad that he hadn't waited any longer. If he had let her stay up there in Maternity and try to push the baby out, it wouldn't have done either the baby or her any good.

"I'm so happy," Anne Webster was saying. "I want Mike to know. Will someone please tell my husband?"

"I will, honey," Henderson said. "Right away."

In a few minutes he was back up on Maternity and, entering Room Four, found Mike Webster stretched out on the second bed, sound asleep. Henderson sat down beside him and roused him with a hand on the shoulder.

"Mike," he said. "It's Dr. Henderson. I just wanted to let you know your flight has landed. You've got a little girl."

"Oh, wow!" Mike Webster murmured. "That's great! How is my wife?"

"Just fine," Henderson said. "She'll be in the Recovery Room for a while so don't bother to get up and don't try driving home. We'll leave an early call for you. Go back to sleep."

16

House Call

"Hi, Doctor Henderson!"

The Sinclair children, gathered around a washtub on the front lawn, recognized him immediately when he pulled into their driveway.

"Hey, there," he said to the two blonde girls and the little red-haired boy. "How's everybody today?"

"We're all right," the little boy replied. "We're playing with our frog. But Mommy is sick. She took Daddy's car keys."

Car keys? This was news. Just as Henderson was leaving the hospital there had been a message from his answering service—some sort of trouble at the Sinclair house. Ruth Sinclair's sister was calling. When he tried to return the telephone call, the line was busy and rather than waste any time he had driven right over to the house.

"Well how about that," he replied to the little redhead. "I guess I'll go inside and see your mother. Take it easy with that frog."

"We will. We're going to give him a swim."

Henderson took his medical bag and hastened up the front steps. He was admitted by Ruth Sinclair's sister and immediately sensed domestic tension. Ordinarily Bill Sinclair would have been on his feet to greet him warmly, but instead Henderson glimpsed him sitting on the screen porch, his face dark and brooding. He was

221

downing a glass of beer and staring at a baseball game on the television. Ruth Sinclair's sister bore the look of the in-law who was keeping her lip buttoned in the midst of marital strife.

"Is she bleeding?" Henderson asked the sister.

She shook her head and tilted it in the direction of the screen porch.

"How goes it, Bill," Henderson inquired amiably, ignoring all storm warnings.

Bill Sinclair shrugged. "Not too good."

"I heard about the rescue job you pulled off last night."

"Yeah, me too," Bill Sinclair replied shortly. "That's *all* I've been hearing."

From the downstairs bedroom there came an outburst of sobbing. Ruth Sinclair had noted his arrival and didn't want to be left out. Her husband reached forward and deliberately turned up the volume of the TV.

"Nuts!" he said. "That's what she is. Nuts!"

"What's going on?"

Sinclair gulped down some beer. "She's got the car keys in there under her pillow or somewhere, that's all. Trying to keep me from going to work. I've got to leave here in twenty minutes to catch a train to the city and she's playing games!"

"I'll give you a lift to the train," Henderson said. "What's it all about?"

"Big deal about that thing in the city last night. She claims I don't care about the baby."

So that was it. Bill Sinclair, Henderson knew, had figured in another daring rescue with his fire company. Lowering himself on a rope from the roof of a burning building, Sinclair had rescued a firefighter who was dangling five stories above the street with a child in his arms. The fireman had been trapped when a fire escape had suddenly collapsed. Bill Sinclair had buckled on a life belt and dropped down from the roof of the building to where the fireman was hanging. He had locked his legs around him and helped him hold the child until all three of them were hauled up to safety. Roving TV news camera crews had filmed the rescue and it was also plastered all over the front pages of the city's newspapers. It would mean another medal of honor for Bill Sinclair—but now apparently all hell was breaking loose at home.

Henderson walked into the back bedroom. Ruth Sinclair, her face already swollen from crying, dissolved in a new flood of tears. Strewn around the bed were boxes of Kleenex, a tray of uneaten sandwiches, newspapers featuring Bill Sinclair on his rope: a human fly focused in the glare of searchlights against a background of smoke, aerial rescue ladders, and spouting fire hoses.

"I thought you promised me you were going to take it easy," Henderson said. He had shut the door behind him, flung back the covers, and was conducting a quick external pelvic examination. There was, he was immediately relieved to note, no sign of any impending crisis. She wasn't spotting. Her high-mounded abdomen was firm but not crampy. He got the stethoscope and sphygmomanometer out of his bag and found her pulse was eighty and blood pressure close to her normal readings. The baby's heart tones were a strong 140.

She was perspiring profusely but not more than might be expected from a lot of thrashing around on a warm summer afternoon. The car keys, he noted, were clutched in her left hand but he ignored them.

"He doesn't care about the baby!"

"Of course he cares," Henderson replied. He had already decided on his course of treatment.

"He doesn't! He doesn't! He doesn't! Or else he would never do such a thing!"

She raised herself off the bed and shouted through the closed door in the direction of the screen porch, "Big damn fool! Boob! Movie Star! Show-Off! Rotten Cook!" and then collapsed again in a sobbing heap.

Henderson took a thermometer from his bag, shook it down and stuck it in her mouth to shut her up.

"Don't touch that," he said. "Keep your mouth closed."

He left her temporarily silenced, breathing heavily through her nose, and went out to the kitchen.

"Don't worry," he said to Ruth Sinclair's sister. "Everything is going to be all right."

"I didn't want to bother you, Doctor, but she was getting *so excited*. It's been building up all day."

"I'm glad you did," Henderson said. "What does your sister drink besides beer?"

"Drink? Oh, she likes highballs. Rye and ginger ale."

"That's just what I want," Henderson said. "Can you bring it out to me on a tray with a bowl of cracked ice and a wash cloth? I'll be on the porch with Bill."

He went out to the screen porch and took a seat next to Bill Sinclair.

"She's telling you I don't care about the baby, eh?"

"She sure is," Henderson said. "But don't worry about it. Or about her. She's going to be all right."

"I'm quitting the Fire Department," Bill Sinclair said. "It's too much for me. Not the job. But all her raving around about it."

"To hell with that idea, Bill," Henderson said. "You can ride this out. After she's had the baby, we'll work on her. I'm going to talk to the psychiatrist about it. I've got some ideas about helping her out."

"Where do we stand with that sterilization thing? Did they approve it over at the Hospital?"

"Not yet," Henderson said. He wasn't going to try to explain in one minute what had been going on with "Chinese Gordon."

Sinclair shook his head gloomily. "No matter what happens," he said, "this has to be the last one." He lowered his voice.

"You remember you told me about that operation I could have? To be sure there would be no more kids?"

Henderson nodded. "I remember. It's called a vasectomy. It's minor surgery."

He was glad Bill Sinclair had brought it up. It was exactly what he had been intending to propose in their talks after the baby was born if he didn't get the committee's approval to sterilize Ruth Sinclair.

"And it won't affect your sex life a bit," he added.

"My sex life! With that maniac in there?" Bill Sinclair shook his head.

"You might get around to it," Henderson said, and then to Ruth Sinclair's sister who had appeared with the tray, "Fine, put it right here on the table. This will sedate her as much as any pill I can give her and it's easy on the baby."

Both of them watched with fascination as Henderson mixed a moderately strong highball, swizzled it and then walked back to the bedroom with the drink, the bowl of ice, and the wash cloth. He plucked the thermometer out of Ruth Sinclair's mouth, found her temperature was ninety-nine, and before she could get started again, handed her the drink.

"Sip this slowly, please," he said.

Taken by surprise, she swallowed a mouthful, paused and sniffed the glass.

"It's whiskey!"

"Sure is," said Henderson cheerfully. He dropped the wash cloth into the bowl of ice and swished it around to soak up the cold water.

"Why are you giving it to me now?"

"Because I want you and your uterus to relax. Take some more of it."

She dutifully took another swallow and then, as the pleasant, familiar taste of ice cold ginger ale and rye whiskey began to reach her, settled back on the pillows.

"I'm exhausted," she announced feebly.

"Sure you are," Henderson said. "You've been exhausting yourself. I want you to quit it. It's not good for you or the baby."

He had rung out the ice cold wash cloth and now began to bathe her face with it.

"But look what he's been doing!" She gestured at the newspaper photos.

"I know all about it," Henderson replied while continuing to bathe her face. He began talking slowly in a low earnest voice, "That's just my point. Bill knows what he's doing. He's practiced that rope trick a hundred times. He knows how to do it the right way or he wouldn't have tried it. Do you understand that?"

She nodded, sipping the highball and letting him dab her swollen eyes with the cold cloth.

"That's what you've got to get through your head, Honey," Henderson continued. "He knows his job. He's good at it. Tops. He knows how to take care of himself and it just happens he saved two lives. So let him do the worrying. Quit bugging him and getting yourself so shook up."

"But he's a father . . . a husband . . ."

"Don't you think he knows that? Let him make the decisions. Do you want to get him so jumpy and distracted that he makes a big mistake?"

"No."

"Well, then you do your job. Take care of the kids. Have this baby. Let Bill watch out for himself. And be proud of him. All he wants is for you and the kids to be happy. Don't you really know that?"

"I guess so." She sank back on the pillows, blowing into more wads of Kleenex. "I'm sorry."

Henderson took the half-empty highball from her hand, reached under the pillow and recovered the car keys.

"Now take a nap," he said. "I'll drop by to see you tomorrow."

He walked out of the room and handed the keys to Bill Sinclair.

"She'll sleep for a while now," he said. "Can you still make your train?"

"Easy," Bill Sinclair said. "Doc, thanks a lot for coming by. We appreciate it."

"We sure do, Doctor," Ruth Sinclair's sister said. "Ruth gets excited but she can't help it. She doesn't mean it the way it sounds."

"Of course not," Henderson said. "When she wakes up, she'll probably be ready to eat. Give her another highball, a light one, with her supper. Then a cup of tea. And I think she'll sleep most of the night. But look in on her once in a while. Make sure she's not bleeding. Call me right away if there's any problem."

He went out and walked Bill Sinclair over to his car.

"You sure were on the ball last night, Bill," he said. "That was a great job you did up there."

Sinclair shrugged. "They make a lot out of those things these days," he said. "Suddenly there was a problem. One of my men was in trouble. I went to help him out. That's all there was to it."

"That's the way it ought to be," Henderson said. Bill Sinclair had reacted automatically. In such men there was no collapse of the human spirit under the stress of danger. As Mark Twain had said, "Courage is the recognition of fear, mastery of fear—not the absence of fear."

"Oh, by the way, Bill, just one more question. Back inside just now, you probably heard your wife. Why did she call you a rotten cook?"

Bill Sinclair broke into a grin. "That's because I like to dish up the meals for the boys at the firehouse. It started out as a way of passing the time and became a kind of hobby for me. But Ruth can only get me to cook at home when I'm in the mood. It burns her up."

"Well I'll be damned," Henderson said. "Sometimes it seems like it's the silly little things that bug them, right?"

"Damn right," Bill Sinclair said.

"What's the chef's specialty of the firehouse?" Henderson asked.

"Barbecued spareribs," Sinclair replied. "With my own sauce. But we try all kinds of stuff—French, Italian, German. Why don't you stop by the firehouse some night when you're in town and try some?"

"I'm going to do just that," said Henderson.

He was suddenly struck by a vision of burly Bill Sinclair scaling an aerial ladder and bashing his way into a burning building with a copy of *The Joy of Cooking* stuffed in his hip pocket. He waved goodbye, got into his car, and drove off laughing.

17

Saving Lives Before Birth

"I can feel your baby's little rear end, Kathleen. It's right here under my hand, just above the pelvic bone."

Henderson's brown-rubber-gloved hand rested lightly on the lower abdomen of Kathleen Burns. She lay motionless on her back on an X-ray table in the center of a high-ceilinged Operating Room in the Medical Center. Her body was draped in sterile white sheets from feet to waist and from bust to neckline. Only her abdomen, rounded and stretched by an unborn baby, painted pumpkin-yellow with an antiseptic, was in view of the members of the Operating Room team.

Here was something, he reflected, that would never seem like a routine medical procedure to doctors of his generation. Popping needles into invisible babies was too far removed from their brand of medical education. He had to admit that it still spooked him, even though he had put in a good deal of time in the last year learning intrauterine techniques at the Medical Center.

Kathleen Burns was an Rh-negative mother. Her blood differed from her husband, who was Rh positive. This combination occurs in about eleven percent of all marriages, yet only less than one percent of all babies show any effect from the Rh factor. Many of those affected have only a mild form of the condition, requiring no treatment at all. But in the Burns family, the difference in blood groups created a medical problem that became increasingly serious with each pregnancy.

The Burnses' first two children were normal, healthy babies. Then the Rh-negative antibodies created within Kathleen Burns' bloodstream during her pregnancies became strong enough to attack the red cells of the next baby, causing a severe anemia. As a result, it was born dead. Her fourth and fifth babies, similarly damaged, lived only a few hours after birth. Now, her sixth child, entering its seventh month of growth within her body, was threatened.

When Kathleen Burns had come to him as a new patient six months earlier, he had told her about this radically new technique for saving human lives before birth. Only a year before it had been new to him.

"We'll want to follow the course of your pregnancy very carefully," he had told her. "From the sixteenth to the twenty-second weeks of pregnancy, we'll want to have you come to the Out-Patient Department at the Hospital so we can tap the uterus with a hollow needle and draw out a few drops of the fluid that the baby is floating in. Then we'll check the fluid for signs of a buildup of the antibodies that frequently occurs in mothers with Rh incompatibility during the seventh and eighth months of pregnancy."

"Can you be sure you'll save the baby?" she had asked.

"Truthfully, no. If the blood damage caused by the Rh factor occurs very early in pregnancy, the damage to the baby may be too severe for an intrauterine transfusion to save it."

But this apparently had not happened. They had checked the uterine fluid samples regularly beginning with the twenty-second week with no evidence of danger. Then, just forty-eight hours ago, the laboratory reported the first evidence that her antibodies had suddenly soared. Damage to the baby's red blood cells, which would lead to anemia and death, was imminent.

Only a few years ago, he would have felt powerless to aid the baby unless it was far enough along in pregnancy to take it safely by a cesarean section and immediately give it a blood transfusion. How had one pediatrician described such frustration? "We are quite capable of recording the pulse, blood pressure and temperature of astronauts as they travel at incredible speeds hundreds of miles above the earth. Why, therefore, have we been allowing unborn babies to die from anemia when they are only inches away from a blood transfusion?"

Now, to deliver such a transfusion, they were about to enter the heretofore untouchable sanctuary—the uterus of the pregnant mother.

As soon as he got the lab report about the rising antibody count he had called John Barker, the obstetrician at the City Medical Center who was directing a research program with intrauterine techniques. For nearly a year now, ever since he had heard Barker deliver a paper on his program, Henderson had been making a point of getting better acquainted. He had been passing along all his Rh-negative mothers to Barker's Medical-Center team (Barker had first seen Kathleen Burns two months ago) and whenever his schedule permitted he went down to the Center with the patient himself when Barker was going to do an intrauterine transfusion for him.

Now on this summer morning he had driven down to the Center and stationed himself with his patient, stepping out of the way as Barker returned to the table after one more look at the X rays. There was a growing attendance at these intrauterine procedures—the amphitheater above them was filled with medical students.

Placing his left hand on the rump of the invisible baby, Dr. Barker pressed gently upward along Mrs. Burns' right side.

"This baby," he reported to the team around him, "is lying on its left side with its back well over against the wall of the uterus. I now have definitely located the head . . ." He cupped his hand over a bump within the abdomen.

"So, I conclude that it is safe for us to go in over here . . ."

He took a long hairlike hollow needle handed to him by a blue-gowned nurse, positioned it carefully and then thrust it downward, feeling it penetrate the abdominal muscles and then the uterine wall.

"Did you feel that much, Kathleen?" he asked.

Her eyes shut against the glare of the cluster of overhead lights, Kathleen Burns shook her head.

"Not much," she murmured. "It was like a pin prick."

Well, Henderson felt, watching with some relief, Barker was in all right with the first needle. No doubt about that. And the baby hadn't stirred. He was into nothing but the uterine fluid. He was completely sure of it.

"Fine," Barker said. "Now just hold still so we can take the baby's picture."

With a syringe that the nurse handed him he injected an X-ray dye through the hollow needle, watching as it disappeared into the uterus.

Attendants had quickly rolled a portable X-ray machine into position directly over the table on which his patient lay. With the rest of the medical team he withdrew behind a screen. There were a series of hums and clicks. A technician kneeled to withdraw the exposed X-ray plate and hurried it to a film developing room just down the corridor.

With arms folded, Barker, Henderson, and the other doctors stood watching the long hollow needle still embedded in Mrs. Burns' uterus. As it protruded from the abdomen, it suddenly wig-wagged back and forth in a series of jerky movements. Beside him Henderson heard the intake of breath of one of the residents.

"Well, look at him in there," said Barker cheerfully. "He's wriggling a bit but not enough to bother us. Now let's see what he looks like."

"How do you know it's a boy, Doctor?" asked Mrs. Burns.

"I don't. But it sure is a lively baby."

The technicians were back with a large X-ray film negative, still dripping wet. As soon as they had snapped it into place on a wall lightboard, he could see clearly the outline of the head and spine of the unborn infant. The hollow needle appeared as a thin line slanting down into the uterus. Safe with number one!

"Our next step," Barker said, "is to provide an avenue into the fetus for the blood transfusion."

He took another hollow needle, poised it near the first and thrust it downward, first into the uterus and then, with a firm decisive push, into what he estimated to be the abdominal cavity of the baby.

"X rays, please," he said. His voice carried a slight edge of urgency. If you misjudged your position you certainly wouldn't do the baby any good!

Again the medical team stood with folded arms, staring in fascination at the two needles which quivered slightly as Kathleen Burns breathed. Once again the dripping X-ray film was hurried back to the Operating Room and he stepped forward with the others to examine it closely under the bright light.

"Well, there we are!" Barber said. He obviously felt both pleased and enormously relieved as soon as he saw how the second needle showed up. His aim had been all right.

"We're okay," he said. "Right where we wanted to be."

With his gloved hand he traced the outline of the needle on the shadowy film. It was easy to see the contour of the baby's skull, spinal column, and body contours and he wanted the nurses and medical students who had come into the Operating Room gallery to see it. They were observing what comparatively few doctors had ever witnessed. Not until a New Zealand obstetrician named A. William Liley first performed this feat in an Auckland hospital a few years earlier had anyone been privileged to witness intrauterine transfusions in a human being.

"The second needle is inside the baby's abdominal cavity," Barker said. "And now we're ready to do the transfusion."

From the nurse he took the slender plastic tube and threaded it down through the hollow core of the needle.

"Okay, let's have it," he said. "Slow and easy."

The nurse reached up to open the gate on the transfusion bag and the tube turned dark red as a capsule of warmed blood, heavily packed with red cells, obtained from an Rh-negative donor, flowed into the baby. Since these new red cells were the same as Kathleen Burns', they would not be harmed by the antibodies in her circulatory system. If all went well, the unborn infant would absorb the new cells into its bloodstream and be protected from any damage until birth.

Rh incompatibility is estimated to affect one of every 200 babies born in the United States. Each year it causes about 10,000 infant deaths. Until something better came along these intrauterine transfusions could save the lives of about 3,000 of these babies. As Dr. Liley had put it, "The unborn baby is just as much of a patient to us as if he were lying in an incubator or crib. It just so happens that he's got his mother wrapped around him instead of a blanket."

Henderson's interest in intrauterine procedures—both diagnostic and therapeutic—had grown steadily. In a short span of years he had seen the first intrauterine work develop steadily into an entire new aspect of obstetrics and gynecology. The transfusions to save the lives of babies of Rh-negative mothers was only the beginning. If fact, this treatment, radical though it was, was being overtaken by newer procedures and would soon seldom be necessary.

Several men in the early 1960's were developing a vaccine against Rh-negative antibodies. Earlier research had indicated that blood fractions containing antibodies might provide the kind of immunity that vaccines, built up with slight doses of a disease-bearing bacteria or virus, provide to repel the disease. It was speculated that it might be possible to produce antibodies in an Rh-negative woman by injecting her with a serum containing anti-Rh antibodies. This would prevent her body from manufacturing more antibodies during a pregnancy, thereby eliminating the cause of the Rh condition in her future babies.

A vaccine had been produced that was proving ninety-nine percent effective when administered within seventy-two hours *after* the birth of the first baby. The vaccine's protective effects were only strong enough, however, for a single pregnancy, so that the mother would have to receive another vaccination after the birth of each child, in order to protect subsequent babies. And it did not work on those Rh-negative mothers who had acquired permanent antibodies from having given birth to an Rh-positive baby. For those women the intrauterine transfusion was still the only avenue of treatment.

But having taken the giant step of entering the uterus of a pregnant woman, medical science was progressing rapidly to another field: genetics.

Each year 200,000 American children (out of some three and a half million annual live births) were being born with disabling, crippling defects. Some twenty percent of these disabilities were caused by environmental factors during pregnancy—drugs, diseases such as German measles, and radiation from X rays. And many of these conditions could be determined by examining samples of cells taken from the fluid in which the developing fetus floated.

By the same procedure that Henderson had participated in this morning—amniocentesis—a sample of fluid could be withdrawn through the abdomen and analyzed for specific deficiencies. In that small amount of fluid might live important clues to birth defects. Already, analysis of the chromosomes in the cells of the fluid made it possible to predict if a child would be born with Downs syndrome—a mongoloid.

Amniocentesis could also be used to detect hemophilia or other sex-linked diseases in the fetus of a woman who was known to be carrying the harmful sex-linked gene.

Analysis of the fluid could remove—or confirm—the fear that a defective child was developing. But then what did you do? Did you allow the abnormal fetus to go on to become a baby with perhaps a lifetime of emotional and financial burdens that could shatter a family? Or did you decide to end the pregnancy?

Already abortions based on intrauterine diagnoses were being performed in hospitals in various parts of the United States. In the case of a child whose mother had been exposed to German measles the question was even more crucial. Abortion was now authorized by many hospital committees, but there were still strong objections on the grounds that some such babies would be born with no defects. If by withdrawing fluid from the womb of a woman whose pregnancy had been threatened by German measles the doctor could determine whether the fetus was affected by the disease, the risk to the baby could be accurately predicted. Or perhaps eventually you could correct the defect at that point, as they had done with Kathleen Burns' baby this morning.

As he drove back home musing on such matters, Henderson turned his thoughts again to his patient Ruth Sinclair. What was happening within *her* uterus? At least she didn't have an Rh problem, but something was certainly troubling her placenta. Was something causing its blood vessels to rupture or causing it to rupture blood vessels in the uterine wall? Was the placenta, seeking a firmer grip on the uterine wall, sending out fingers toward the cervical os or internal mouth of the cervix? If so, and if it got in the way of the fetus, there might yet be trouble.

He thought of the application for voluntary sterilization that he and Laden had resubmitted after Gordon had left for Japan. If the Committee voted it down, how would he break the news to Ruth Sinclair? Certainly he would have to wait until after she had had her baby. Another thought struck him. Suppose the Committee had not yet met? Marvin Laden had called him the previous day to say that according to rumor, Gordon was cutting short his stay in foreign parts and was on his way home.

"A rich patient," Laden had said wearily, "so much so that Lum Fong wants to take the case himself. He's afraid that otherwise one of his staff might make off with what he considers as *his* pigeon. Knowing what I do about that den of thieves, I suspect he's right."

Still, Henderson thought, the worst that could happen would be that they would be turned down again. Even without Gordon, the old fox had certainly left his proxy with one of the two Catholic physicians, Schultz or Donovan, just to make sure that it would be defeated if brought up again. And Henderson did not share Laden's hope for a switch in anyone's vote. If he had a shred of hope, it was due to the arguments that he and Laden had put down on the resubmitted application justifying their request that the case be considered anew. He had also hoped to find a way to bring his case to the members of the Committee even more forcibly and in person, but time had worked against him and he had not had the opportunity.

At the Hospital he spied Dr. Donovan scrubbing for a delivery and joined him at the scrub sink. The subject of the Committee meeting came up and to Henderson's dismay the Committee apparently had already met.

"That was a most interesting case review that you provided us with," Donovan said.

"I'm glad you thought so," Henderson responded tactfully. Donovan apparently had decided to let him down gently.

"Ordinarily, as you know," Donovan continued, "I'm against a lot of these cases because beyond my own personal convictions, they seem to be a matter of convenience."

"I suppose that's true for some of them," Henderson admitted.

"But, occasionally," said Donovan, "I must admit

that I see enough evidence to justify a case on the grounds of mental health."

He finished the scrub. "At least that's the way I felt this morning," he added. "Another morning I suppose I might change my mind. It depends on the individual presentation. That was a very thorough job. Indeed, most impressive."

Henderson was taken by surprise. So Donovan was letting him know that he had approved Ruth Sinclair's voluntary sterilization! Perhaps Laden was right and there really was a new liberal element in Catholic opinion making itself felt.

"That's very gratifying," he answered. "We're touch and go with a placenta previa development in that case but . . ."

The Delivery Room Nurse stuck her head out of the double doors of the Delivery Room.

"Excuse me," she said. "Dr. Donovan, could you examine the patient . . . ?"

"Excuse me," Donovan said hurriedly to Henderson and he followed the nurse into Delivery.

Henderson was satisfied to let him go. It was a surprise but a good one. Now no matter what happened, he had a choice on Mrs. Sinclair's sterilization. A memorandum confirming the Committee's approval of the tubal ligation would immediately be typed up by medical records and a pink slip attached to the prenatal record on Ruth Sinclair already on file up on the Maternity Floor, ready for instant referral when she went into labor. The file would accompany her, whether she had the baby by normal delivery on the Maternity Floor or by a cesarean section in the Operating Room. It would be up to him to decide what to do when the baby was born.

Marvin Laden would certainly be elated, but Henderson chuckled to himself as he thought about the reaction of "Chinese Gordon." The old faker could return from his trip any time now. And what a fit he would have when he found that he had been bypassed and overruled during his absence!

18

The Ninth Month

He was just finishing his shrimp cocktail when Pete, the night manager of the restaurant, appeared at his elbow.

"Phone call for you, Dr. Henderson. Where do you want to take it—in the lobby, in my office, or in the kitchen?"

"In the kitchen, Pete. With the tomato juice," Henderson said.

He disliked taking his medical calls at the lobby desk—too many people who were waiting for tables suddenly got interested in what you were asking a patient—and although they always offered him the privacy of the manager's office, he actually preferred the phone at the table in the corner of the restaurant kitchen. The waiters and kitchen help never paid any attention and he could continue eating right there if he was tied up on the telephone for any length of time. They always gave him a large glass of tomato juice to start with. That was enough to fortify him if he had to depart for the Hospital. He got up and headed out through the swinging doors. His answering service was on the line, holding a call from Bill Sinclair.

"Doctor, Ruth is bleeding again. Just like that night last month. Her robe is soaked."

"When did it start?"

"It must have been just a little while ago. Maybe five

238

minutes. She was lying here on the couch watching TV."

"Carry her out to the car, Bill," Henderson said. "Do it just the way you did last time. I'll have a stretcher waiting for you at the Hospital Emergency Entrance. I'll be there myself in ten minutes."

He hung up the phone, took a swig of the tomato juice they had brought him, and quickly began dialing telephone numbers.

First the Hospital Operating Room Supervisor.

"This is Dr. Henderson calling. I'm admitting a maternity patient for immediate surgery. I'm going to do a section. I'll need a local anesthetic to start with. One-half percent carbocaine. Please grab whoever is in anesthesiology and pediatrics to back me up. I'll be needing all the help you can give me."

Then he called his office where he knew his partner was seeing patients.

"Ed, my placenta previa patient is hemorrhaging again. Can you help me do a section on her right away? Like now?"

"Be right over," Ed said and clicked off. Henderson knew he could depend on him to be out to the door before the patients in the waiting room had even had time to turn another page in their magazines. He called over to the restaurant manager who was talking to the head waiter, "Pete, I'm going to need my car. Will you tell them out front?"

"Right away," the manager said. They always parked his car close to the entrance so no time was lost running around the parking lot. He finished his tomato juice in a gulp and went back out to the table to break the news to Mary.

She sighed. "What about your steak?"

"Have them put it in a doggy bag. We'll grill it up at home when I get there. Get Pete to call you a taxi."

He gave her a quick kiss, hurried out to the front entrance, and tipped the parking lot kid who had his car waiting for him. To avoid the Friday evening traffic, he cut across the back streets of town, setting himself up for the operation he was about to perform and anticipating what he was going to do when he saw his patient.

If Bill Sinclair's estimation of when the hemorrhage had started was correct, he might make out fine with both mother and baby. It was becoming increasingly rare today for a woman to bleed to death from a placenta-previa hemorrhage if you confirmed the diagnosis in the operating room by gentle vaginal examination and were set for an immediate cesarean section.

As for the baby, the major cause of infant loss in placenta previa was premature birth, and he was well past the danger point here. This baby must be within two weeks of term. He would estimate that it would weigh about 2500 grams, or just about six pounds, and could come out with a section in good shape. Getting the baby out should slow or stop the hemorrhage because the uterus would automatically contract and the pressure of its muscles on the ruptured blood vessels would squeeze off the bleeding like a tourniquet.

It was unfortunate that this placenta was on the anterior wall of the uterus. That meant that they were going to have to go through it or under it to get at the baby. There was always the added hazard of severing a uterine artery.

At the Hospital he found the Operating Room deserted except for the team of OR nurses who were waiting for him, and Herb Goodman, who happened to be on duty. There was no word on Ruth Sinclair from the Emergency Room yet, but if Henderson knew Bill Sinclair he could count on him to come barreling up to the door at any moment.

"How are we on blood?" he called through the half-open door of the doctors' dressing room as he slid his trousers off and pulled on green cotton operating-room pants and jumper.

"We've got six units ready," the Chief OR Nurse said. "Did you want a double set-up?"

This would make it possible for him to examine and

deliver Ruth Sinclair vaginally on the operating table if he changed his mind at the last minute.

"No thanks," he replied. "I've made up my mind for a section. This is a total previe."

The phone rang; the Desk Nurse took the call.

"Emergency has your patient on the cart, Dr. Henderson," she said. "They're sending her right in."

"Open those doors and let them in," said Henderson.

He was dressed in his greens now, bare feet in a pair of white operating-room shoes. As the OR doors were swung open, he saw the procession coming down the corridor, nurses and orderlies trotting alongside the stretcher cart, Bill Sinclair right behind them, looking like an ambulatory auto-accident case. His shirt was soaked in blood. So was the sheet in which he had wrapped his wife when he had carried her out to the car.

"Just drop that sheet right here with us, Bill," Henderson said. "The girls will give you a clean shirt. Get yourself a coke, and a seat in the cafeteria. We'll take care of your wife. I'm going to deliver the baby."

He could see instantly that this was a massive hemorrhage, probably triggered by Ruth Sinclair going into labor. Her belly was hard as a drum. Her face was pale and contorted with fear.

"Blood!" she gasped. "Blood all over the car! I was holding myself but the blood kept coming! Doctor Henderson, am I all right? Am I going to die? Can you help me?"

"You're going to be all right. I'm going to get the baby out. Just take it easy, Honey."

The nurses had stripped off her blood-soaked housecoat and lifted her from the stretcher cart to the operating table. While Herb Goodman was getting a blood pressure cuff on her left arm the chief OR nurse helped Henderson get an IV catheter into a vein in her right arm and started the first unit of blood into her.

"Pulse 120," Herb Goodman reported quickly. "Blood pressure 70 over 40. Pretty shocky."

She certainly was going into shock this time. Not good for her and very bad for the baby.

"Give her oxygen, Herb," Henderson said coolly. "And, girls, go easy with the 'prepping.'"

They were swabbing her mounded abdomen with antiseptic solution a bit too vigorously to suit him. Any additional pressure on that placenta might cause it to hemorrhage even more violently.

He bent over her on the table and with a fetascope picked up the beat of the baby's heart, plus a lot of gurgling within the uterus.

"Heart tones, 120," he said. "Is Dr. Russell here yet?"

"Yes, he's here," one of the nurses said. "He's in the dressing room."

"Then we'll move right along," said Henderson. "Drape her for a midline incision."

While he was at the sink, scrubbing, his partner joined him. They knew what they were going to do and wasted no time in conversation. They completed their scrubs and turned to the nurses who were holding out the green operating gowns. They shoved their arms into the long sleeves, held out their hands, and let the nurses snap on the rubber gloves.

Herb Goodman had a mask on Ruth Sinclair and was administering oxygen. The instrument tray had been swung into position over her knees and drapes arranged across her breast, leaving exposed the abdomen.

Usually Henderson's procedure for a cesarean section operation was a neat transverse incision, but with a placenta situated so low on the forward wall of the uterus as this one he couldn't go in that way. He started putting in a local anesthetic with a series of pricks of the hypodermic needle filled with carbocaine. Just enough to numb the outer layers of skin.

Ruth Sinclair was sinking into such a state of shock that she didn't know what they were doing anyway. Her skin was cold and clammy and her face was dripping with perspiration. His partner joined him, standing on the opposite side of the operating table. Henderson took the scalpel from the nurse and made an abdominal incision from the pubic bone to just below the navel. Immediately the swollen uterus thrust upward through the incision and they packed warm moist towels around its exposed portion to keep as much amniotic fluid, blood, and placental debris as possible from spilling into the peritoneal cavity, where it might start peritonitis.

With a pair of scissors Henderson extended the incision a bit. They put in retractors, applied some pressure, and the uterus bulged out a bit further. With Russell holding a suction tube ready, Henderson took another scalpel from the scrub nurse and nicked open the wall of the uterus. There was a strong gush of blood which Russell caught with the suction tube.

Henderson used his fingers to open the uterus a bit further and then snipped open the membrane around the baby. He thrust his gloved hand into the pool of blood, gently thrusting around and under the mass which must be the placenta, searching, feeling, while the rest of the OR team waited silently.

"I've got the feet," he announced. "I'm coming out as a breech."

He slowly drew forth the legs, rump, chest and head of a very bloody but apparently intact baby. Russell clamped the umbilical cord. Henderson snipped it with scissors. Holding the limp baby in the crook of his left arm, he aspirated its mouth and nose and sponged off its tiny face.

Silence gripped the operating table for a long moment. Then there was a weak movement of the tiny chest, a feeble gasping effort at respiration. Ruth Sinclair's dropping blood pressure had put her baby into shock.

Suddenly everything was going to worms. The condition of both mother and child was critical.

"Is the pediatrician here yet?" Henderson asked, still working to free the air passages of the baby.

"Right here," said a voice at his elbow. He recognized it as Dr. Lewis Caplan.

"We have a breathing difficulty with this one, Lew," Henderson said, very calmly. "Would you resuscitate it?"

The pediatrician took the infant from him and placed it on the newborn intensive-care resuscitation cart. A second anesthesiologist adjusted a miniature oxygen mask to the baby's face and got a Bennett respirator working. Henderson wanted to turn around and work with them to save the baby but Ruth Sinclair was still in critical shape—still hemorrhaging at a rate that threatened her life. Blood gurgled up from the open uterus and the bottle connected to the suction tube beneath the OR table was filling rapidly.

"I'm going to see what's going on in that uterus," Henderson said.

With Russell assisting him, he gently lifted the uterus upward and out through the abdominal incision. They swiftly packed more moist warm gauze towels around the exposed uterus and clamped the bleeders. Henderson could see that the bleeding was along the anterior wall of the uterus. It was originating at the point where the placenta had clung to the wall. If he had waited for natural contractions to stem the hemorrhage, he would have been betting with Ruth Sinclair's life. Already he wasn't sure which way it was going to go with the baby.

Carefully he used his gloved fingers to free the placenta, peeling it off the wall, taking care to avoid leaving behind any fragments of membrane.

"Now the ergotrate and pitocin, Herb," he said to Goodman, "we'll need both for the uterus, too," he added to the nurses.

Goodman administered the drug intravenously. In a moment they could see its impact as the uterus suddenly contracted, squeezing down in a muscular lump. When the contraction eased, there appeared to be slightly less blood, and Henderson sponged the anterior wall and waited through another contraction.

"Her blood pressure is holding," Herb Goodman said. "But the pulse is still 120."

Behind him Henderson heard a faint squawling.

"Baby breathing now," the pediatrician said. "The color is better. Pinking up. Respiration stabilizing. No immediately discernible defects."

Out of nowhere came Ruth Sinclair's voice, "Is my baby a boy or a girl?"

Henderson was startled out of his concentration. He had thought she was so low she couldn't hear them.

"You've got a boy," he said. "He's all right and so are you. Take it easy."

He asked Herb Goodman, "Can you sedate her now? I think we're shaping up a bit."

He looked across the table to Ed Russell. "Let's put it back in but leave the incision open for a little more observation."

Together they swiftly began suturing the uterus. They packed all but the incision line with moist towels.

"Save me that placenta," Henderson said. "Keep it right there on the tray. I want to look it over when I finish here."

He stared down at Ruth Sinclair's uterus. It now had been through five pregnancies. The placenta in this pregnancy could have caused either a baby's death or a maternal fatality and he now suspected another poorly emplanted placenta had had a lot to do with the fragile pregnancy that had resulted in her miscarriage, with or without the automobile accident.

As she lay there on the operating table, she was ready for some preventive medicine. And thanks to Laden and Donovan he could proceed with her sterilization.

"Now I want to do that tubal ligation," he said to Ed Russell.

They concentrated on the fallopian tubes. As Russell lifted up the left tube with a Babcock clamp, Henderson prepared to clamp, cut, suture, and ligate the ends. Suddenly, Lottie Novitska, the Operating Room Nurse Supervisor, was peering over his shoulder.

"What's going on?" she asked.

"What's it look like?" said Henderson. "I'm doing a subtotal salpingectomy so this lady won't have any more babies."

"There's no Hospital approval for it," Lottie said.

"Of course, there is," Henderson answered shortly. "We have an approval from the Abortion-Sterilization Committee. It's right on the prenatal record.

"No it isn't, Doctor," Lottie said. Her voice was a bit tight.

Henderson came out of his concentration on the surgery. What the hell was going on? There was no doubt that Lottie suspected that he and Ed Russell were pulling off a fast sterilization by themselves and she had just happened to overhear it. Ordinarily, he would have discussed it with her before the surgery but events had occurred too swiftly in this case tonight. He had forgotten that she didn't know anything about Ruth Sinclair as a patient or about Henderson's plans to sterilize her. As Operating Room Supervisor, she was supposed to keep track of what surgery was performed and be sure that Hospital rules and regulations were adhered to.

"Godamnit, Lottie," Henderson said. "We've been all through this before. Believe me. We're cleared to do this sterilization."

"Not according to the records," Lottie said stubbornly. "There's absolutely nothing in the file to show it."

No wonder she was worried. The whole voluntary sterilization situation was still a touchy problem, even in this hospital. If she permitted him to proceed without any evidence of approval, she'd be liable for all sorts of hell. Wrathfully, Henderson wondered what had gone wrong and what he ought to do about it. He considered his alternatives. He could take out the whole uterus and justify it on the grounds of the placental hemorrhage that had occurred tonight and earlier. Oddly enough, this move would probably be completely acceptable to Lottie because it was a matter of professional choice. It would also be completely acceptable to any committee. But it would also mean at least twenty more minutes of crucial surgery on a patient who was already in shock with her belly wide open. Suppose it all proved to be too much for Ruth Sinclair and he lost her? It was a grim possibility.

Of course, he could simply defer to Lottie and delay the surgery until a later date. But here again he would have to return Ruth Sinclair to surgery after she was recovering from the cesarean section. Abruptly it occurred to him that perhaps he didn't have the Committee approval after all, in which case he would not be able to sterilize Ruth Sinclair in this hospital. Was it possible that he had misunderstood Donovan? He had been absolutely positive that Donovan had meant to tell him the Committee had voted approval on her case. Was there any room for a possible misunderstanding? Was it possible that the goddamned Gordon had somehow done something to delay the approval? It was no time for emotion, but Henderson felt rage surging through him. He was inclined to bull ahead. He moved a bit closer to the operating table to let Nurse Bates wheel out the new Sinclair baby in the warming cart.

"I can't find any approval," Lottie repeated.

"Well, you damned well better find it," Henderson snapped. "Because we'll be completing here in about four minutes."

Lottie Novitska was frozen, not quite sure of what to do next. In theory, she could order him to stop. At the least, she would have to note in her official reports that he had sterilized a patient without permission and had refused to heed her warning.

"Where are you trying to put both of us?" she asked tensely. "Up in that board room—on the carpet?" They were old and good friends but she was ragged as everybody was from the stress they'd been under tonight.

"Take another look, Lottie," Henderson said. "Will you please take another look for that pink slip?"

Nurse Essie Bates, wheeling the baby out, paused and said in a low voice, "I know where it went."

"Where?" Henderson asked.

"Into Dr. Gordon's pocket."

Henderson took a very deep breath.

"When?"

"Just the other night. He was up on the floor and asked to see this patient's prenatal file."

Swiftly Henderson put it all together. Gordon must have been wild with fury when he found out that Laden and Henderson had run the ball around him while he was out of the country. But to fiddle with patient records! If Marvin Laden hadn't told Henderson a good deal about Gordon, he might not have believed it. But Henderson, too, had been around long enough to know that there were men like this in the practice of medicine. Too arrogant to accept defeat. Petty enough to go to any lengths.

So Gordon had seen the approval in the prenatal file and he couldn't help himself. In a fit of anger he must have ripped it out and stuck it in his pocket. And Essie Bates, who missed nothing, had seen him do it.

"Why the hell didn't you tell me?" he said softly through his mask to Essie Bates.

"Because I was off-duty until tonight."

Henderson understood. It was not the kind of thing a nurse would put down on paper. She would wait until she could tell Henderson alone. And she had assumed there would be time enough, that they wouldn't be here in this operating room with this patient tonight.

Suddenly Henderson felt a tremendous buoyancy. Raising his voice, he said, "Proceeding with this ligation. Let's go, Ed."

"Wait a minute, Doctor," Lottie said. She didn't know what was going on but he couldn't tell her.

"Never mind, Lottie," Henderson said. "Forget about that file. It's all right."

"It goes down in the report," Lottie said.

"Of course it does, Lottie, of course it does," he answered jubilantly. "Put it down. Call it just as you see it."

It had flashed through his mind that there was another copy of that approval: a carbon on file in medical records. If there were to be some sort of board of inquiry, not only was Lottie in the clear, he need not involve Nurse Bates, either.

There would also have been a copy in his office mail which as usual he was a day behind in reading. Marvin Laden probably had received and read his copy and gone off for the weekend in his Ford camper to celebrate with a free-loving female. But, engrossed with his mental crossword puzzles, Marvin would be busy for a long time analyzing the Hospital Committee's motivations. Did Dr. Donovan's vote really indicate that there was a new liberal element in Catholicism or was the Committee approval of Henderson's request merely a move to support a colleague and long-time fellow practitioner? Had they felt that Henderson had been embarrassed by the first negative vote and so moved to make amends? Or did Donovan's vote merely reflect a distaste for a conceited interloper like Gordon who was used to getting his own way at his Institute and now had thrown a tantrum when he didn't? In any case, it wouldn't be difficult to establish that a copy of the approval had been attached to the file, that Gordon had been up on the Maternity Floor, and had had access to patients' records. When Gordon realized this he would know that the best thing for him to do with that piece of paper was paste it in his hat. He would have to shut up but he would know that Henderson knew and that he would tell Marvin Laden about it.

So, Ruth Sinclair was getting her sterilization.

"It's your funeral," Lottie said, but she seemed to sense that he knew what he was doing and that it was going to turn out all right. They were bringing in another case for emergency surgery and she left to direct her nurses.

Working with Ed Russell, Henderson swiftly snipped both fallopian tubes, ligated them with sutures, and using the Irving sterilization procedure, buried them in the musculature of the posterior wall of the uterus. Satisfied that the hemorrhage was stopped, they closed the uterine incision and then sutured the fascia and skin in separate layers.

"What was the Apgar on the baby?" Henderson asked. (This useful evaluation system scored the new-born's heart rate, respiratory effort, muscle tone, reflex irritability, and skin color.)

"Eight," said the pediatrician.

"Lucky Joey!" Henderson said. "His father's a fire-man. A strong kid."

"So is your patient," said Herb Goodman. "She had lost about 1600 cc's of blood when she was asking how was the baby."

"She's a beaut, isn't she?" Henderson said. "She's stronger than all of us. I'm glad we got her ligated. She'd have killed us all with another pregnancy."

"You'd better keep the IVs in her but I think she's okay. I don't think that hemorrhage is coming back to her."

He and Russell helped the nurses transfer the sedated form of Ruth Sinclair to a stretcher cart so that they could wheel her off to the Recovery Room. Then he stripped off his OR gown and sat down on a stool to stare at the placenta. He had lived with it for nearly nine months, sustained it with his professional skill and patience and managed to check it when it threatened the life of his patient and her baby. Now it would be tossed in a deep freezer and shipped to a drug concern for distillation of its hormones.

He glanced up at the clock on the wall of the oper-ating room. It was nine-fifteen. He and his medical team had worked with such furious speed and total concentration that only an hour had elapsed since he entered the Hospital, yet he felt completely bushed, as if he had been on his feet for hours. You couldn't explain this kind of medicine to any other professional person or to a layman. You worked hard because you enjoyed the work and earned money, but when you got going on a case like this one you were working flat-out to win it.

Later in the evening when he was absolutely sure

that his patient was stabilized, and his partner took over he would head for home to a very cold, strong martini. He would exhume Pete's cold sirloin steak from its doggy bag, sizzle it on his charcoal grill and then flop into his leaky swimming pool where he could float in further reveries about his triumph over this particular placenta. Perhaps he would be able to lure Mary into the pool for some splashing and lovemaking. The nurses were rolling Ruth Sinclair off to the Recovery Room.

"Good night, Dr. Henderson," one of them said. "Congratulations."

"Thank you," Henderson said. "Good night, everybody. Thanks a lot."

He was happy about the way everything was working out. It was proper, he felt, to have respect for anyone who did something extremely well. He reserved his greatest admiration for those who performed such work in conjunction with a genuine feeling for people, individually, and as they existed in groups, large and small, on this earth.

Tonight he had had the support of a team of highly trained and disciplined men and women, performing with the intellectual precision and willingness to work together professionally that was so basic to the accomplishments of modern men in the realms of science, medicine, and social progress. Whether it was Bill Sinclair's firefighters or the astronauts and space engineers reaching for the moon and the universe beyond, human judgment and human relationships still dominated all technology. Human behavior would still be the essential key in man's ability to cope with his accomplishments in his own or any other universe. Despite medicine's wondrous achievements, it was still basic that you had to care about the patient as a fellow human being. His triumph tonight would have been limited indeed if he had not felt that he knew Ruth Sinclair and her family as individuals.

He stripped off his rubber gloves, shed his operating-room gown and walked out to find Bill Sinclair. He was pacing the corridor, wearing a white hospital coat that one of the orderlies had given him to replace his blood-soaked shirt.

"Everything is just fine, Bill," Henderson said. "Your wife is safe and so is the new baby."

Bill Sinclair stared at him is dazed disbelief. It was obvious that the shock of his wife's second hemorrhage had nearly flattened him, too.

"Both okay?" he asked.

"Both doing fine. We'll keep a close watch on them. Your wife will be in the Intensive Care Recovery Room. The baby is in an incubator. Bill, you've got another boy—another little redhead. Let's take a look at him."

The baby was in an incubator which would maintain a balance of body temperature, humidity, and proper concentration of oxygen.

"He'll stay in there for a couple of days," Henderson said. "He got out a little early so we want to be sure that he's well protected against infection and drafts but he's going to make it all right. I don't think he'll have any problems."

Bill Sinclair stared at his new offspring. He shook his head. "It's still hard for me to believe they both came through it," he said. "I'm glad it's over. You know while she was in there with you—having the baby, I've been thinking. She can't go through anything like this again. I want that operation we talked about. I'll be ready any time you can set it up."

Henderson suddenly remembered. "Hey," he said, "I wanted to tell you. We've taken care of that. The Hospital Committee finally approved your wife's sterilization. After the baby was born, Dr. Russell and I went ahead with the surgery. It only took a few minutes, but from now on neither of you will be able to worry about her having more babies. You're all set."

Bill Sinclair was dumbstruck. Too much was happening all at once. He sat down heavily on the nearest corridor bench.

"Does she know it?"

"No. Not yet," Henderson said. "I'll explain it to her tomorrow after she's rested up. I want her to understand all about it."

He found himself waxing enthusiastic. "You know, Bill, this will give you all a big lift. She's going to be crazy about that little redheaded baby. She won't have to suffer any more anxiety about getting pregnant. You may find her a lot easier to get along with."

"There's still the way she feels about the job," Bill Sinclair said dubiously.

"Well that's true," Henderson said. "But we can work on that. You know my wife doesn't always like my line of work either."

"She doesn't?"

"Hell no," he added. "She complains about it all the time. The way I hang around here at the Hospital is as bad as you sleeping at the Firehouse. Women don't want their men away at night. It bugs them."

"Doc," Bill Sinclair said. "You're a wonder." He began to laugh as the stress of the last hour drained away from him. "You've really fixed us up."

Henderson chuckled and then began to laugh with him.

"Remember your invitation?" he said. "Some night soon when I'm in town, let's celebrate. I'll drop around at the Firehouse for some of your homecooking."

Bill Sinclair beamed. "Make that a promise and I'll have those barbecued spareribs waiting for you. I'd like you to meet the men in my company. Maybe you'll roll with us to a couple of alarms."

"Do I get to wear the helmet and boots?" Henderson asked.

"You sure do," Sinclair responded. "I'll lend you a set of 'turn-out' clothes myself."

He lowered his voice to a conspiratorial whisper. "But don't wait too long to come in. I haven't told Ruth yet but I'm going to lose my own hook-and-ladder rig."

Henderson was startled. "How come?"

"They're giving me the 'white hat,'" Bill Sinclair

said. "I'm being promoted to Battalion Chief. I'll be in command of two hook-and-ladder companies and four pumpers but I'll have to ride in a chief's red car."

"Well, congratulations, Bill," Henderson exclaimed. "That's great news!"

He paused, suddenly considering the impact of this development on his patient. No wonder Bill hadn't told his wife. Ruth Sinclair would be riding another emotional pendulum, swinging high with pride in her husband but gripped with new anxieties about his safety. Garbed in his Battalion Chief's white helmet and coat, Bill Sinclair would be a large and highly visible target for the bottles, beer cans, and stones so enthusiastically rained down on city firefighters in some of the ghetto districts.

"But for God's sake, Bill," he said, "don't tell your wife until we get her out of here and back home."

In the corridor, the Hospital's public address system had begun intoning a message: "Code 94," an operator was saying. "Code 94 . . . Room 509. . . ."

Henderson shook Bill Sinclair's hand. "See you later," he said. "I've got to go."

"Code 94" was the Hospital's confidential emergency signal notifying the staff that a patient was in the midst of life-or-death crisis. The patient in Room 509 must have stopped breathing, suffered a sudden hemorrhage, heart attack, or other internal or external injury. Any staff physician or nurse who was free was expected to respond to "Code 94" as one would to a cry for help.

Hastening down the corridor, Henderson noted there was a cluster of people awaiting the elevators. He yanked open a side door and raced up the back staircase for the fifth floor, putting the Sinclair case out of his mind, setting himself up for the patient in Room 509.

Somebody needed a doctor.

Have You Read These Current Bestsellers from SIGNET?

☐ **THE FRENCH LIEUTENANT'S WOMAN by John Fowles.** By the author of **The Collector** and **The Magus**, a haunting love story of the Victorian era. Over one year on the N.Y. Times' Bestseller List and an international best seller. "Filled with enchanting mysteries, charged with erotic possibilities . . ."—Christopher Lehmann-Haupt, N.Y. Times (#W4479—$1.50)

☐ **LOVE STORY by Erich Segal.** The story of love fought for, love won, and love lost. It is America's Romeo and Juliet. And it is one of the most touching, poignant stories ever written. A major motion picture starring Ali MacGraw and Ryan O'Neal. (#Q4414—95¢)

☐ **JENNIE, The Life of Lady Randolph Churchill by Ralph G. Martin.** In JENNIE, Ralph G. Martin creates a vivid picture of an exciting woman. Lady Randolph Churchill who was the mother of perhaps the greatest statesman of this century, Winston Churchill, and in her own right, one of the most colorful and fascinating women of the Victorian era. (#W4213—$1.50)

☐ **CHOCOLATE DAYS, POPSICLE WEEKS, by Edward Hannibal.** A story about today, about making it, about disaffection and anguish. Here is a modern love story told from the inside and told with an honesty that is sometimes beguiling, sometimes shattering but never doubted. "Sensitive . . . fresh . . . Mr. Hannibal works close to the bone—and he works very well."—New York Times Book Review (#Y4650—$1.25)

THE NEW AMERICAN LIBRARY, INC.,
P.O. Box 999, Bergenfield, New Jersey 07621

Please send me the SIGNET BOOKS I have checked above. I am enclosing $_____(check or money order—no currency or C.O.D.'s). Please include the list price plus 15¢ a copy to cover mailing costs.

Name_____

Address_____

City_____State_____Zip Code_____

Allow at least 3 weeks for delivery

Recent Bestsellers Now in SIGNET Editions

☐ **LISTEN TO THE SILENCE by David W. Elliott.** A total and unique experience—gripping, poignant, most often, shattering. A fourteen-year-old boy narrates the chronicle of events that lead him into, through, and out of an insane asylum. "Each page has the ring of unmistakable truth . . . a well written tour de force, another **Snake Pit** . . ."—The New York Times Book Review
(#Q4513—95¢)

☐ **THE SUMMIT by Stephen Marlowe.** Intrigue, blackmail, treachery and romance, THE SUMMIT is a wire-taut novel as devious as LeCarre, as fast moving as Ambler or Greene—chosen by **The New York Times Book Review** as one of The Year's Best Criminals at Large, 1970 . . . "A shining example of the political extrapolation that pumped new lifeblood into the espionage novel in 1970."
(#Y4632—$1.25)

☐ **SANCTUARY V by Budd Schulberg.** A gripping study of men and women under the most extreme kinds of pressure in a Cuban political haven. Writing with power, compassion, and with a rare gift for characterization, Budd Schulberg reconfirms with SANCTUARY V his position as one of America's master storytellers.
(#Y4511—$1.25)

☐ **THE STUD by Jackie Collins.** A novel about the ambitious, fast living—and loving—people among the swinging "in-crowd" of London's discotheque scene . . . and Tony Burg, ex-waiter, ex-nothing—now elevated to the rank of superstud.
(#Q4609—95¢)